My Life
in the
Trenches

By
Sam Ross

PublishAmerica
Baltimore

First printing

ISBN: 1-4137-4409-5
PUBLISHED BY PUBLISHAMERICA, LLLP
www.publishamerica.com
Baltimore

Printed in the United States of America

The education of our children, who are our greatest natural resource, must be one of the primary concerns of the leaders of this great nation. If we continue to fail in this endeavor and do nothing to reverse the tide of the numerous social epidemics that are now rampant in our schools, communities, and our nation at large, all of the unique qualities that helped make the United States a beacon of hope, freedom, and enlightenment for so many people in this world, may eventually be lost, never to be rekindled again.

DEDICATION

This book is dedicated to those teachers who have given so much of themselves in order that our children reach their fullest potential.

Special thanks must be given to my daughter for her unwavering support when this oft times unforgiving endeavor became almost unbearable. She would never let me surrender to the brutal pain I experienced from the eleven operations I underwent while writing this tome. I will forever be grateful for her tenacity and the many sacrifices she made helping with my rehabilitations and giving me the encouragement to continue with this autobiography.

Finally, it is with a deep sense of sadness that FM, my best friend, missed seeing a published copy of My Life in the Trenches come to fruition. His unfortunate and shocking passing has left a void in my heart that will never be replaced. Rest in peace, my brother, until we meet again.

TABLE OF CONTENTS

PROLOGUE

The year 1969 could best be described as both tumultuous and dramatic, as far as the life of Sam Ross, the author of this book, was concerned. Having graduated Brooklyn College that January, I was about to embark upon my lifelong ambition: At the ripe old age of 20, I would finally be known as Sam Ross - Teacher.

Being a byproduct of the New York City School System, I remember being educated by teachers who were either spectacular or a downright disgrace not only to their profession, but also to the way they treated their students. My dislike of the latter, plus an innate love of history, inevitably guided me toward a career in the field of education.

Having met all of the qualifications mandated by both the city and state of New York, it was with great pride that I now possessed a license to teach either junior or high school social studies. Of equal significance was the fact that I was the first member of my family to have gone to college and graduated with a degree. No son could have made his parents prouder than I had.

Finally, the long-anticipated day arrived when I received notification from the New York City Board of Education of my first teaching assignment: Sam Ross—Social Studies Teacher, I.S.24. Talk about being on cloud nine! I was literally unconscious with both enthusiasm and pride. Never did I realize that, inherent in this "cheap quality letter of notification," would be the following reality: The next 12 years of my life would be demanding, disheartening, gut-wrenching, and yet at times as rewarding an experience any individual could possibly encounter in their chosen profession.

For the reader to truly understand what, at times, will seem totally incomprehensible, it is extremely important that they are privy to what my life was like before becoming a Junior High School teacher in the city of New York. Having roots in both the South Bronx and the East New York section of Brooklyn, I was never shielded from the "Real World." Hand-me-down clothes, few toys, sharing a 10-cent bottle of Coke with three people, and enduring my youth with an alcoholic parent, regrettably, left a lasting impression on me at a fairly young age.

The expansion of my horizons in regards to this "Real World" would continue during my teenage years with my chance encounters with three individuals who would die of violent rather than natural causes. There would be a male in his 20s who would be shot to death on the stairs leading into a magnificent-looking church. I would observe an elderly drunk male die, as the result of stab wounds inflicted on him by an irate female who was kind enough to allow me to witness her vicious fit of rage. Finally, I would barely miss a middle-aged woman commit suicide by jumping off the clock tower above the YMCA on Atlantic Avenue and splatter on the concrete. I would witness this gore as I exited the train station, moments after her ill-fated flight. I fervently believed that nothing in my future, except the possible horrors of war, could shock me after my exposure to these events.

Adding to my ever-growing, callous attitude was the fact that during one of my summer vacations, while working in the sporting goods department of Times Square Stores, an individual from a gang called The New Lots Boys came in to purchase a rifle. Having known this individual for many years, I inquired quite innocently:

"Going hunting, Stan?" I asked, just making conversation.

After laughing for a while, his face lost all features of enjoyment and took on a stoic, almost catatonic look:

"Yeah, Sam, I'm going hunting. Hunting for niggers!" he said without giving what he'd just said a second thought.

The fact that approximately five years later, we would "bang" into each other in downtown Brooklyn, and he'd have on the uniform of a police officer, left an indelible impression on me.

So here I was, a 20-year-old, having seen and experienced so much at such a young age, thinking that nothing could shock me as far as the children who would be my students or the neighborhood I would teach in was concerned. Well, I must tell you, in no uncertain terms, nothing, and I mean nothing, in my wildest imagination could have prepared me for the insanity that would transpire over the next 12 years!

Since my retirement in 1981, I've bantered around the notion of putting my teaching experience and its repercussions on paper. What finally gave me the impetus to start this dissertation, I honestly have no idea. For those of you that believe in "psycho-babble," do not misinterpret this journey as a catharsis of my soul. If anything, just accept this book as my ultimate desire to share with the public, an experience which few people will ever have a chance to be a part of.

I cannot overemphasize that what is revealed in this book is what happened during my tenure as a teacher in two special service schools in Brooklyn, New York. Not one fact has been fabricated in order to add some spice to this adventure. What you see is what you get, and what you get in this book is the truth!

On many occasions, I reflect back to the unique world that I found myself a part of, and wonder if other schools had, and still have, the same problems we faced at I.S.24 and to a lesser degree, I.S.302. Twenty-two years later I can, with utmost confidence, say: YES! The social ills found in today's educational system, such as drug use, violence, sexual promiscuity, illiteracy, etc., are nothing but the failures of so many of our predecessors, who never effectively dealt with these issues. Not only are these problems still present, but they also are far more rampant and geographically dispersed than ever before.

When reading this book, I implore you to recognize the fact that although I bring forward ideas on how to handle certain situations that exist both in our schools and society, in no way am I "The Great Innovator," a Joe Clark, or even a Jim Beluchi, who starred in the movie, *The Principal*. There is no way that I have the almost mystical intellect needed to revamp and rectify the inordinate problems found in today's educational environment. Although I will present ideas which warrant serious consideration, only an Educational Revolution, which I advocate, can undo the failures that so many have contributed to. Until this time ultimately arrives, we must not succumb to feelings of educational impotency when solutions to these problems are difficult to formulate, no less implement. "One step at a time" would be an acceptable approach to follow. Real people solving real problems must be at the forefront of this long, arduous journey. Hands-on experience must finally replace lip service, which was so common in the past.

Finally, for those of you that are skeptical about the events I present to you in this autobiography, I'm quite willing to take a polygraph test, which will attest to their authenticity. Admittedly, I have changed the names of all of the individuals involved in this educational foray, mainly due to legal issues and in no uncertain terms, the threat of bodily harm. Even with these changes, there is no doubt in my mind that those I write about will unequivocally recognize their role in this oft times unforgiving drama.

I honestly hope that everyone can accept that my ultimate goal in writing this book was not just to castigate the primary school system in this country or those who are part of its, at times, merciless environment. I just wanted to present to the reader a biographical review about a period of my life which, upon reflection, often leaves me wondering how I was able to maintain some sort of dignity as well as my sanity. In essence, I just wanted to give the reader an unimpeded view into *My Life in the Trenches.*

CHAPTER ONE

Welcome to My World

Walking up Van Sicklen Avenue to catch the New Lots Avenue bus to my teaching assignment in the Bedford Styvesant section of Brooklyn was nothing out of the ordinary. East New York was considered a tough neighborhood in its own right, and having survived there, I believed "Bed-Sty" would be no great shakes. Sure, I couldn't deny the fact that a previous "scouting expedition" had instinctively left me with some trepidations, yet with my South Bronx and East New York background, I knew I'd survive anything that could be thrown at me, either verbal or material.

The bus ride in itself was quite uneventful. Only the urban decay found in most inner cities progressed as I got closer to my destination. Of course I had been a participant in this type of environment during my entire life, so I wasn't overly apprehensive. Having been a super athlete, before knee injuries took their toll, I had played ball in every possible neighborhood in Brooklyn, so the ride down Bushwick Avenue posed no real threat.

Street smarts and natural instinct kicked in as soon as I departed from my deplorably hot mode of transportation. Knowing I looked out of place due to my attire and color, I walked at a brisk pace and finally reached what would be my new home for the next ten years.

I punched my first time card at approximately 7:30 and was informed that my first teacher's conference would be held at 8:30. This and other meetings would transcend the entire day, in order to indoctrinate the 25 new teachers who had been appointed to I.S.24. This being a Wednesday, the next three days of orientation would entail numerous meetings, administrative paper shuffling, etc. The "regulars" would report on Monday with the student population. Within minutes of my arrival, other recruits (my future colleagues) began to show up.

Before attending my first conference and getting the 5-cent tour, I decided to go outside and smoke a cigarette. As I stood inhaling one of my Kools, I took in as much of my new surroundings as possible. Directly across the street were the Hopkins houses, otherwise known as the "projects." On the block next to the school were a number of small businesses, including a "bodega," (i.e. grocery store) where I'd purchase many lunches over the forthcoming years and where many of our students would purchase their daily supply of marijuana. One other fact could not be overlooked: The heat and humidity were oppressive and here I was, dressed to kill, in a school that had no air conditioning.

It hadn't been but a few minutes when a youngster walked up to me.

"Hey, man, are you a teacher?"

"Of course," I responded.

"Are you a new teacher?"

"No," I adamantly replied.

The look on his face gave away the fact that he knew I was full of shit, and I had learned my first important lesson: Never try to bullshit these kids. The old expression of "honesty is the best policy" would become my 11th commandment. This aside, it was his next question that would set the tone for the next 12 years of my professional career:

"Hey, man, you want to buy a knife?"

As he proceeded to pull a miniature machete from under his windbreaker, all I was able to say in my toughest voice was, "Nope, don't think so, man!"

"Well, I'll be back next week, and by then you'll need it."

Little did I realize at that moment in time how prophetic this youngster was. How could I possibly know that I was having a conversation with a reincarnation of Nostradamus? This youngster was all-knowing and all-seeing. I, on the other hand, was beginning to feel like a sacrificial lamb.

In retrospect, I've come to the conclusion that this was a fine young man. Just think, he definitely was a proper host, since he was so kind as to welcome me to the neighborhood. To tell you the truth, I was more impressed with him than punching my first-ever time card. There was no doubt he had gotten my undivided attention and had left a lasting impression on me! Upon reentering the building, a question arose in my mind that I would ask myself innumerable times during my teaching career: *Is this what I went to college for?*

CHAPTER TWO

Day 1—Oh, My G-d!

Monday, or "Judgement Day" if you like, finally arrived. I was psyched and ready to go. I was equipped with all of the materials the Board of Education deemed necessary to be an effective teacher. I had purchased a Delaney book with cards, and was given two erasers, a box of chalk, two rulers, lined paper, five pencils, and two pointers. Wow, was I lucky! When they presented me with my class rosters, as well as my homeroom class's program, it was now official. Sam Ross was a teacher. My only regret was that they hadn't issued me an MI6 rifle, tear-gas canisters and other armaments. These items would have been more applicable during the many chaotic times that would occur during the school year.

Looking at my schedule, I noticed that I had six science classes, a homeroom class, as well as hall patrols. By now I'm sure you're asking yourself:

"How is he teaching science if he has a Social Studies license?"

Well, the answer is quite simple. Although I had been appointed to I.S.24 as a Social Studies teacher, there were no openings available in this department. As a matter of fact, almost every new teacher had a Social Studies license, except for two individuals who had accreditation in home economics and physical education.

When we were informed that there was an opening in the Science Department, I immediately volunteered. I had taken numerous science classes in college and figured my students would enjoy the experiments and other visual aids that I could offer teaching this subject. Little did I know at that moment in time, that this would be one of the smartest decisions I'd ever make in my entire life.

In preparation for Monday, I spent Sunday night finalizing some lesson plans, formulating my "welcome speech," and getting ready with whatever I felt would make the next day successful. As prepared as I was, I still spent a sleepless Sunday night. I wasn't cognizant of the fact that this would be my routine before the start of the first day of school for the rest of my career. The only change from my first September to my last would be the onset of diarrhea, which would commence about a week before the start of the new school year. You must realize, as I would eventually learn, that the teachers were just as apprehensive about the new school year as were the students. Just knowing that we were in "their world" and were trying to have them adjust to ours, with its rules and regulations, was a difficult task. Just the thought of this entire process with all of its inherent pitfalls, was enough to give anyone "the runs."

Having set my alarm clock for 6:30 a.m., I had no problem getting up since I hadn't slept anyway. Weighing 125 pounds soaking wet, I decided to "bulk up" for my first day on the job. Sweat pants and a cut down sweatshirt worn under my sports jacket, shirt, and slacks made me look like I lifted weights. I was definitely impressed with the new me and hopefully my new students would share in my enthusiasm. In retrospect, my kids must have thought I was scared to death due to my profuse sweating that entire day. What an idiot! Here I was dying from the oppressive heat. The temperature in the building had to be at least 100 degrees, since the temp outside was in the upper 90s. To suffer like this, just to look like Hercules? Did I say I was an idiot? How about a total moron!

Getting to work that morning was quite uneventful. After punching the soon-to-be-infamous time clock, all of the staff proceeded to the auditorium where our students were being assembled. What seemed like utter chaos was nothing more than a first-day entrance into the school building. You could immediately see how nervous some of the students were, especially the new 7th graders. Just a look in their direction by any teacher and they would shut up immediately. Of course, as the year progressed, and they became more comfortable with their surroundings, "the look" meant nothing at all.

It didn't take more than five minutes for the first fight of the school year to break out. Having been told to expect this, I wasn't a bit alarmed. During the altercation, I heard some magical words, and they would leave a lasting impression on me:

"Fuck you, Nigger! Get your fucking hands off of me!" This came from a black student to a black teacher.

Two thoughts came into my mind at the same time: *Where is that kid who wanted to sell me the machete? I really hope he comes back.* Of greater significance was the fact that here was a black student who apparently hated this black teacher, who was breaking up the fight, with as much vehemence as any black kid could hate a white teacher. This was so important because it began my desensitization to such words as Whitey, Honkie, Cracker, and so many other racial slurs.

As the day progressed, things seemed to be going pretty well. Some of my female students flirted with me and told me how cute I was. One Spanish girl, in particular, told her friends how she would love to fuck my brains out. Although flattered, I was somewhat taken aback by her unabashed feelings. I thought, *Better this than wanting to stab me!* I found it so amusing listening to girls 12-16 years of age expressing such intense sexual desires. Of course, since I was an "Anglo," all of these romantic notions were expressed in Spanish. Little did they know that I had taken six years of Spanish in high school and college, as well as played ball on an all-Spanish team, thereby making me near fluent in "their" language. When I finally spoke to them in Spanish, there were quite a few embarrassed senoritas, especially the young lady that was interested in my "brains."

All in all, it had been quite an exciting day. I had met most of my students and gave on five separate occasions what would be my annual "welcome speech." I must admit that each year this speech would greatly improve, especially as I added more adjectives to it. My students, for their part, were able to complete the necessary school and district office paperwork. Class and school regulations were explained to them, amongst other first-day requirements. Finally, dismissal from my homeroom went off without a hitch.

The walk back to my bus stop was interrupted with calls of:

"Hey, Teach!" from numerous students.

"Yo, Whitey!" and other epithets not worth mentioning came from some neighborhood clowns.

With the bus's arrival, I was soon seated and ready to relax. Just as I was beginning to unwind, this individual in front of me took out a joint, lit it, and started blasting his boom box. I must admit that I was impressed with his arrogance since it was against the law in New York City to smoke a cigarette on a bus, no less a joint. Of course, the bus driver did nothing, and basically, I didn't blame him. Why get into an altercation with this twenty-year-old youth and possibly suffer an injury over a loud radio and a joint? I'm positive that this was not part of his job description. Although I felt a bit uneasy, no one else seemed too upset, so who was I to complain?

I fervently believe that if nothing else had occurred during my ride home, I would have rated day one a total success. Unfortunately, this thought completely evaporated when this youngster across from me took out what looked like a 38-caliber hand gun and began twirling it around like he was Jesse James. In the blink of an eye, I knew there was a possibility that I could die my first official day on the job. Remaining as cool and composed as possible, I silently prayed that I would be able to get home alive. Where nobody on the bus cared about the pot-smoking radio blaster, this Wild West impersonator managed to get my fellow passengers' attention. How ironic that only five days earlier I had been welcomed to the neighborhood. Now, I didn't know if I'd live to get out of it.

Various notions began to infiltrate my brain's thought-processing center.

Should I try to forcibly take the gun from this idiot? Where the hell is that damn kid who wanted to sell me a machete? Why is it that he's never around when I need him?

By now, I was soaking wet from those damn sweats I had on, from the non-air-conditioned bus, and from Jesse himself. Finally, when the bus stopped near some intersection, Jesse got off. All of us breathed a sigh of relief. I swore at that moment that I would never again take the bus to or from work. Thankfully, a colleague in the Science department lived near me and gave me rides until I purchased my first automobile. What a day it had been after all!

CHAPTER THREE

Discipline in the Classroom

"Let's get something straight right off the bat. I will be the best teacher you've ever had. I will get you out of trouble with other teachers, your parents, the police, and other students. But, if you try to fuck me one time, you will wish you never walked into my classroom! I promise you that I will make your life a living hell. If by chance you decide to 'go with me,' you will learn that you made one of the biggest mistakes of your life!"

What an incredible, hard-hitting, attention-getting speech that was! You could hear a pin drop. Once the shock of what I had just said had worn off, I would hear:

"Ooh, the teacher cursed!" from one of my young female students or:

"I'm going to tell my mother!" from another.

"Let's cut the bullshit!" I'd say in a stern tone of voice.

"I'm sure I'll hear some real gems coming out of your mouths that will make what I just said sound like a Sunday sermon. Do me a favor and save your bullshit for someone else and let's get down to work!" I'd reply in an angry tone.

Excuse me if I'm not at all shocked by your abhorrence to the content of my opening-day speech. I can just imagine the thoughts that are swirling around in your minds about my using the word "fuck," as well as my possible incompetence as a teacher. Before you condemn me as a foul-mouthed bully and a despicable individual, all I ask of you is not to lose sight of my major goal. I wanted my kids to learn! As expediently as possible, I wanted my new students to know I cared, and despite the brutality of my oration, many immediately recognized this fact.

To fully comprehend what was going on at I.S.24, it is imperative that the reader never lose sight of the fact that my students were from one of the most dangerous neighborhoods in New York City, no less the United States. In far too many instances, they were the by-products of the mean streets they lived on. Some were gang members, numerous had juvenile records, and many more were well known by the local authorities.

Caught in the middle of this quagmire of troublesome youth were many wonderful kids who just wanted to go to school, get an education, and ultimately better themselves. Irrespective of which of these categories a student found himself a part, mostly all shared in one conviction. They were distrustful of anyone in a position of authority or, in this case, their new teacher, Sam Ross.

Although I was just a raw recruit myself, I innately knew that I could not be perceived as Mr. Nice Guy or Mr. Joe College, or these teenagers would have eaten me alive. Unfortunately for many of my colleagues, this is exactly what would be in store for them.

Discipline, in its most basic state, is nothing more than the following of rules and regulations and the methods used to obtain compliance. Becoming a better disciplinarian is an arduous process. It ultimately entails earning the trust and respect of your students and treating them in the same dignified manner that you would like to be accorded. I would use this brutal, unforgiving, opening-day speech as a stepping stone toward achieving this goal.

This speech conveyed to my students, in no uncertain terms, that they would suffer consequences if they betrayed my trust. They would immediately realize that all of the help I promised them hinged on the fact that they had better not double-cross me. It was time they learned that, just as on the streets, you had to give me something in order to get something in return. What they would soon comprehend was the fact that they had to give me their best effort and I, in turn, would be there for them in all aspects of their lives. They would learn that I would curse with them, fight with them, and make their lives as miserable as possible if they broke our special covenant. Finally, for the first time in many of their lives, they would have someone who would never give up on them!

You, the reader, be you a parent, grandparent, guardian, or just an inquisitive spectator, must never lose sight of the fact that any number of my students could and would slit your throat in a heartbeat. This was still their "real world" in which I was teaching. It was a world of drugs, assaults, rapes, and unimaginable hurt. Never delude yourself with the notion that upon entering the school building, the outside world, with all of its pressures, problems, and ailments, ceased to exist. I.S.24 was a microcosm of this world and failure to realize this could be disastrous.

Before any of my students had an inkling of what they would learn during the year, it was imperative that they understood that an educated person (a.k.a. Sam Ross, their teacher) could know the streets, curse, act or be nuts, yet still be there for them when the situation arose. They would learn that what you saw was what you got, which in this case was a crazy, yet caring, lunatic who knew that he could never change the world but just maybe help some of its inhabitants.

Yes, you could definitely be upset with my language and lack of professionalism, but not the results I eventually brought to the table. What you have to ask yourselves is: Did the parents of my students want a teacher with proper etiquette and the acceptable teaching practices that had failed their children so miserably in the past? Or did they want someone with honesty, vulgarity, and a street smart, wise ass named Sam Ross, who could reach and teach their children?

The fact that in 12 years, I never had a single parent complain about my classroom persona, should lend some credence to the methods I embraced to fashion an atmosphere that I felt was conducive to learning. I made sure that there was never a doubt in my students' minds that I would employ any method necessary to gain their trust and respect. Once this was accomplished, I knew I would then have the environment necessary to make learning a reality for every student in my classroom. Anything less would have meant failure on my part, and this was totally unacceptable!

Throughout my years as both a student and a teacher, I always found it amusing to pass a classroom and listen to a teacher screaming at the top of his or her lungs, hoping to get their students quieted down and ready for work. Unfortunately for many of my future co-workers, all that their screaming accomplished was the conditioning of the students to this type of behavior and its overall ineffectiveness.

Thankfully, I was a quick learner. Of greater importance was my belief, that I was born to be a teacher, and with this came an innate sense of knowing how and when to adjust to situations. At times, I felt like I as an actor taking on new roles, or a chameleon changing my personality rather than my color. These attributes made my survival eminent and a positive learning environment an achievable goal.

Believing that constant screaming would only lead to laryngitis, I looked for less vocal ways to secure an atmosphere conducive to learning. Eventually, I would formulate a three-part method that showed great promise and, in most instances, never lost its effectiveness in dealing with this problem. As will be seen throughout this book, I tried to use what I considered a simple approach to solve a difficult problem. The old adage that "the answer is right in front of your nose" was right on the money in formulating my non-violent approach toward classroom discipline. To this day, I'm still amazed at this simple, yet effective method:

A. The sound of a door slamming is both dramatic and an attention getter. Most students will stop what they're doing to find out the source of such a loud noise. With at least one-half to three-quarters of your class now paying attention, you can now focus on the rest of the non-attentive culprits.

B. Slamming a heavy textbook down on your desk has its attributes, as well. Done correctly with a properly weighted book, it almost sounds like a shotgun blast or at the least an M-80 exploding. This definitely will get the attention of the majority of those students that slamming the door had no effect on.

C. Finally, just sitting at my desk and staring at the class with a look of impending death would ultimately lead one of my more intimidating students to scream:

"Shut up. Mr. Ross is waiting, and he's getting pissed off." Before you knew it, a couple of other students would be yelling for everyone to shut up. Meanwhile, I would slowly stand up, walk over to the black board and write "Punishment Assignment" in bold capital letters, and before I turned around, there would be complete silence.

I would continually be amazed at the effectiveness of this process, which in its totality consumed maybe three minutes. No need for cough drops or lozenges. I had not said one word during this entire time period. The only sounds emanating from my direction were a door slamming, a book smashing on the desk, and the sound of chalk meeting the blackboard. This entire procedure was so simple, it could be taught to a ten-year-old in a matter of minutes.

In contrast to this semi-sedate formula, far too many of my colleagues, although gifted with tremendous intellect, were screaming and wasting so much energy, yet never exploring an alternate method to quiet down their students.

As my career progressed, I constantly deleted, revised, and honed the ingredients and skills that I felt were necessary to achieve the classroom discipline mandatory to be an effective and successful teacher. I was fortunate to realize that both rigidity and flexibility were essential components of this overall process, and when properly employed, greatly enhanced the classroom atmosphere for which I was striving. Eventually, I would compile a list of five rules, which, when adhered to, would make me a more effective disciplinarian and make my job much easier.

A. Never bullshit your students. Such simple advice, and yet far too many of my colleagues never accepted this as fact.

B. Always back up a threat. Once you make a threat, you must carry it out. Failure to do so shows a lack of conviction and overall weakness.

C. Never, unless under extreme duress, send a student to the office of a principal, assistant principal, or dean. Once you do this, you exhibit weakness, and your students will not only recognize this, but seize on any opportunity to further erode your authority.

D. Never berate a student in front of his or her classmates, since this will only inflame the existing situation due to their need to "save face" and keep their respect.

E. If you are wrong, apologize! Your students will respect you more since they'll realize that you are big enough to admit when you are wrong. Once they see and hear that you are willing to say you're sorry, they too will react in the same manner when a situation arises and their apology is warranted.

Through dogged determination and a multitude of other contributing factors, it was finally possible for Sam Ross to implement a methodology that helped attain the classroom discipline I was desirous of. Yet, what must never be overlooked is the reality that no matter how successful I was in my quest for a positive educational environment, there were various times during my career that events would unfold that would defy the disciplinary techniques that worked so well under normal circumstances. The following incidents should give you an idea as to what I'm referring to.

One day, while in the middle of a lesson, a student burst into my classroom. "Fuck!" he screamed.

He then proceeded to turn over chairs and a few desks, and run out the back door. Both my students and I were stunned, yet amused by this event. The following day, when this same scenario was repeated, I was no longer amused at all.

Assuming this fool would continue this pattern of behavior, the next day I was prepared to explain proper classroom etiquette to him. Without disappointing anyone, my intruder, as if on cue, arrived. After his typical verbal outburst and rearrangement of some classroom furniture, being both unprofessional and immature, I chased after and caught up with "the room wrecker" in one of our major staircases. Before I knew it, confrontation time had arrived.

While trying to get this brazen young intruder to go with me to the Assistant Principal's office, which in itself was a major mistake, a barrage of expletives, highlighted with, "You white mother fucker," were directed at me.

Then, without warning, out of the corner of my eye I saw a punch heading towards my face. As I blocked his punch I instinctively slapped him extremely hard in his face. With tears rolling down his cheeks and after threatening to kill my car, my family, and of course yours truly, this youngster came at me with the fury of a raging bull.

Now, we were engaged in an all-out street fight. With an ever-increasing number of onlookers, I began kicking his butt down one flight of stairs after another. Nothing, and I seriously mean nothing, would stop this out-of-control teenager from constantly charging me. I ultimately realized that unless I knocked him out, there was no positive way of ending this confrontation. I begrudgingly accepted the fact that I had placed myself in a no-win situation and would have to accept the consequences.

My error in judgement was never more apparent, since I had failed to take into consideration that my entire class would follow me when I gave chase. I had also failed to realize that my adversary would rather die than lose face in front of an ever-growing crowd. Once these realizations penetrated my thick skull, I broke off our engagement by turning around and heading back up to my classroom. From behind, I could hear the cheers for my rival emanating from the students that had borne witness to this fiasco. My own class's cheering didn't make me feel any better about the stupidity I had just exhibited. In essence, I had achieved nothing. Donald conversely was the "man of the hour."

Later that day, I tracked down Donald and removed him from his music class. In the hallway, we verbally went at it one on one. Now, there was no audience, no peers to impress, nothing—just the two of us. Within minutes, I had this former out-of-control raging maniac crying like a baby, and I had not laid one finger on him. What I did was tell him how disappointed I was in him:

"What's your problem?" I asked him. "We don't even know each other," I said, enraged.

"How embarrassed would your family be if I phoned your mother and let her know that you were being suspended for fighting and calling me a white motherfucker?" I inquired.

Before ending my lecture, I made sure to let Donald know that I hoped that there weren't any other children at home, since in all likelihood, I'd probably be one of their teachers when they came to I.S.24.

Whatever it was, something I said must have hit a raw nerve because Donald began to cry uncontrollably. This tough street kid was now bawling like a baby. Later I would learn that his mother was very sick, and when I said he had embarrassed his entire family, this raw nerve was exposed.

I must inform you that this individual who had threatened to kill my car, family, and of course, me, gave Sam Ross the utmost respect from that day until he finally graduated. I, in turn, showed him the same courtesy, and I never had another problem with him. I would be remiss if I failed to mention the fact that Donald became my most trusted monitor, as well as my protector, and would get into it with anyone who had something negative to say about me.

In regards to Donald's mother's illness, I know she was sick for a long time. Unfortunately, I never found out if she recovered, but from what I was told, optimism was not in the cards.

The ramifications of my encounter with Donald were numerous to say the least. Although I initially felt that I had achieved nothing from this confrontation, I soon realized that nothing could be further from the truth. The immediate effect of this encounter was the fact that my students saw firsthand how well I could handle myself should I become involved in a physical altercation. They also bore witness to the fact that I could make a complete ass of myself. This, too, became a positive because my students realized that I was human and therefore capable of making mistakes.

As important as these revelations were to my kids, undoubtedly, the most important outcome of this entire episode was a daily visit to my room by Donald. Each day he would knock at my door.

"Mr. Ross, could I come in to say hello?" he'd inquire.

"Sure, Donald. How's it going?" I'd reply.

After our usual exchange of pleasantries, he would leave. My class would continually ask me what I had done to Donald to achieve such a change in his behavior. I told them nothing special had occurred, and if it had, it was none of their business. I would never ruin the respect that Donald had worked so hard for, both in the school building and out on the streets. To tell everyone that I had made him cry would have accomplished many things, none of which were positive. Donald still had his respect, and I gained further esteem from my students just by Donald's now-conciliatory actions. They knew something had happened but had no idea what. "Keep them guessing" became one of my favorite mottos.

The Donald incident served me quite well for the remainder of my teaching career. It taught me to be ready for the unexpected and to make sure that if a confrontation arose, it would be at a time and place that I chose, if at all possible.

The 1979-80 school year would show how important being non-confrontational in front of a class of students could be. It was in the middle of the school year that Principal Leonard Pell informed me that a new student would be admitted to my self-contained class. Leonard Pell knew that I never wanted to know the background of a new student, thereby insuring that a fresh start was in order for this youngster. Part of my success with the kids in my self-contained class was the fact that they learned from their predecessors that what they had done in the past was of no concern of mine.

When Pell summoned me to his office to tell me about William Tony, he knew he was breaking a promise I had made to my students, and myself, to never seek out their past history. For Leonard Pell to even consider such an action meant that my new student was major trouble. Upon learning that this youngster had broken the arm of a teacher and then had thrown her down a flight of stairs, I understood Pell's apprehension and concern for my safety. The fact that this juvenile was not incarcerated led me to believe that the teacher, fearing further injury, had not pressed charges. As I thought about my "good fortune," good old Donald began to jump into focus. No matter what, there would be no way Mr. Tony would lure me into a confrontation in front of my class. If anything, I would pick the time, date, where, and how this drama would play out, and my rules would apply. One fact was almost a certainty: slamming a door, a book on the desk, or giving the stare of death would not cut it with my new transferee.

The day Tony showed up at I.S.24, I had already secured his transfer papers along with his school record, compliments of Leonard Pell. When I had looked at his official record, I understood Pell's trepidations. I wasn't sure if I was looking at a student's school record or a police rap sheet. This kid had been in all sorts of trouble. Besides being disrespectful to everyone, he had numerous suspensions for fighting, perpetuating assaults, using strong-arm tactics to get money, and a host of other infractions. Due to the fact that he was a juvenile, I was not allowed to get a look at his police record, but I was told at a later date that it was something to behold!

Feigning no knowledge of his past history, when William came to my classroom, I took the papers he had been given in the Main Office, assigned him a seat, and continued the lesson I was in the middle of upon his arrival. Once seated, it didn't take but a moment until Tony proceeded to put on his hat and sunglasses. When he refused to remove these items, rather than create a scene that could only add fuel to a potentially explosive situation, I calmly asked him to step out into the hallway. Undoubtedly, staring or slamming the door at this moment in time would not help me in averting this seemingly inevitable confrontation.

"Listen, man. I'm only going to tell you this one time. Nobody wears a hat or shades in my room. Either you take them off, or you can spend the rest of the school year standing in the hallway, by my front door!" I said in a pissed-off tone of voice.

"I ain't taking them off!" said a defiant William Tony.

"Fine! You stay the hell out of my room and make sure you don't walk away from this front door!" I replied.

Although I was seething, thanks to the Donald incident and my ability to adjust to a situation, not one student had knowledge of what had just transpired.

To his credit, tenacity, or whatever was driving him, William came to school each day and, rather than remove the items in question, just stood outside my front door, except to go to lunch and gym. This continued for an entire week until an assistant principal informed me that this type of discipline was unacceptable and that William must be allowed into my classroom.

"There's no way this kid is coming into my classroom donning or later putting on a hat and sunglasses! I worked too damn hard to achieve the discipline I want from this class of so-called incorrigibles, and no one student is going to ruin it!" I told an unhappy-looking Clarkson.

"I'm going down to Mr. Pell's office to report this!" Clarkson responded in an irritable tone of voice.

"Have a ball," was my response to this threat.

Within a matter of minutes, a monitor came up from the main office with a memo, summoning me to Principal Pell's office. Warning my kids not to give the teacher who was to cover the class any bullshit, I began my trek down to the main office. As soon as I stepped into Pell's sanctuary, I immediately went on the offensive. Basically throwing down the gauntlet, I told Pell, " If you don't like the way I'm handling this situation you can have back your class of thirty-five crazies!" as they were often referred to.

I made it clear to Pell. "I'll gladly return to teaching a regular program with 'normal' students."

With this subtle, yet unmistakable threat, Pell backed me 100% by informing Clarkson that if I felt this hallway action was necessary, I could continue with this practice for as long as it took to achieve what I was aiming for. Needless to say, Clarkson was not happy with this rebuke. I remember thinking, *What's he all upset about? He stinks at his job! Why should Pell back this loser when I'm teaching 35 proven or potential juvenile delinquents*? The bottom line was, I was of greater value to Pell, taking care of these so-called incorrigibles, than this inept assistant principal, whose job performance was mediocre at best.

After three weeks of this battle of wills, William Tony finally asked if he could enter my classroom. Knowing what the deal was, with his hat and shades in hand, William proceeded to his seat and sat down. A standing ovation by my class helped ease the tension and overall embarrassment that William must have felt by acceding to my demands. I made sure to compliment him on the heart he had shown by standing outside my room for three long weeks. I did this to help restore some of the dignity he had lost, and to hopefully avert a future confrontation.

Now, was this form of discipline found in any teacher's manual or *The Guide to Better Classroom Management*? Of course not! It's as ridiculous as the aforementioned title which I just made up. When William finally entered my classroom, every one of my students knew he had acquiesced to my demands. I had basically issued a threat, and there was no way I was going to back down. If this test of wills had continued, William would have ultimately been suspended and later transferred to still another school.

Instead, here I was, quite satisfied that I had bested a formidable opponent, "the Arm Breaker." How could I possibly foresee that this victory would be a prelude to an event that would forever change my life? Yes, it would be this same William Tony who approximately three months after gaining entrance into my classroom would get into an altercation with a colleague of mine, eventually leading to my intervention, and culminating in my undergoing two major arm operations, retirement, and enduring a lifetime of excruciating pain. As I will state on many an occasion, you never knew when something dangerous could happen in this profession, and unfortunately, it did happen—to me. So much for the ABCs of discipline!

28

The fact that I had won the William Tony confrontation by outmaneuvering a second-rate assistant principal and circumventing proper procedure by forcing a student to remain in the hallway for three weeks shows to what lengths I had to go to gain control of a situation that could have easily eroded the discipline I had fought so hard to attain. I always realized that, as good a disciplinarian you thought you were, events could unfold that would test your ability to adjust and improvise, two critical ingredients necessary to be an excellent disciplinarian. Failure to be able to do so could easily lead to the loss of control over your class, and the results could be outright rebellion. Thankfully, this didn't occur during this test of wills.

Although I'm not proud of my actions during the following incident, please understand that the path I ultimately took was to defuse a situation, which if left unchecked, could have resulted in serious bodily injury to a number of my students. Without a doubt, not even individuals with the most fertile of minds could possibly have conjured up my solution to the problem that confronted me on that occasion. Only a riot years later posed a similar threat, although on a much grander scale. I guarantee the reader that there has never been an essay or book written on discipline that recommends the action I took that day.

During the spring of 1975, I had one of my classes enter my room totally off the walls. The period before, as I would later find out, they had a substitute teacher and had given this individual the royal treatment reserved exclusively for subs. Somewhere along the route from his room to mine, events unfolded, which, if I hadn't acted as quickly as I did, could have resulted in a tragic outcome.

Despite the respect this class had always bestowed on me, it wasn't more than a couple of seconds after their entrance into my room that a melee broke out. Neither slamming the door nor my book on the table, nor just staring at them deterred this free for all from spreading. As I previously stated, although quite effective, my disciplinary technique was not 100% foolproof! Eventually succumbing to screaming like an insane lunatic, I managed to get the attention of a couple of noncombatants. As I expressed earlier, I had always believed that screaming was a worthless venture, and this was reinforced with the breakout of two new fights during my verbal outburst. Yet it was my ability to be flexible that did allow me to get the attention of some of my kids, and in this instance, the trade-off was worth it.

Adding significantly to the mayhem that was at hand was the fact that four of my girls were among the combatants, and their intent was to gouge their opponent's eyes out or inflict as much destruction as possible. Never forget that when girls fought, unlike the posturing that preceded a fight amongst boys, they went right at it! Not only were they vicious, but they also had incredible heart.

To this day, I have no clue what gave me this insane idea. Before running next door into the science lab, I asked two of my noncombatants to close all of the windows and get those who weren't fighting out of the room. In the lab, I quickly secured some sulfur, a petrie dish, and an alcohol lamp. I then returned to my classroom and lit the lamp under this stand that held the dish of sulfur. Meanwhile, twelve students, who had never caused me any grief, were only focused on one goal—to destroy each other. Concentrating intently on this objective, not one had noticed that their classmates had left the room and that something was burning in the sink. When I finally departed my room, I had two of my strongest boys grab onto the door knobs and hold on for dear life.

In a matter of minutes, my gladiators began to smell the sulfur fumes that were now spreading throughout the classroom. Finally realizing what was happening, they began screaming to be let out of the room. I was amazed that not a single student, from my smartest class, could gather their thoughts and realize that all they had to do was blow out the alcohol lamp and open up a window. It appeared that their rage had completely disrupted their abilities to think. This entire fiasco was nothing short of being pathetic!

With the cessation of fisticuffs at hand, I told my kids to release the doorknobs, and my rioters, bitching and cursing, came streaming out into the hallway. In the process of their exiting my classroom, I had two of my boys go back in to open the windows as well as put out the alcohol lamp.

When I finally entered my classroom, I was shocked to see that in the span of a couple of minutes, my room looked like a bomb had detonated in the middle of it. Desks, chairs, books, and everything imaginable were strewn all over the place. Further inspection led to the discovery of two knives, a couple of nicely rolled joints, a syringe, some nondescript pills, and other paraphernalia.

After a massive cleanup effort, my room resembled what it looked like before it had been trashed. My students eventually took their seats and waited for my inevitable tirade. Although I rarely ever yelled, they were sure they were going to get an earful in a couple of minutes.

I must have walked back and forth across the front of my room at least ten times. Each time my kids grew more apprehensive, knowing that there would be a price to pay for their despicable behavior. Never raising my voice above an audible whisper, I told my students how disappointed I was in them. I made sure that they knew all they had accomplished from the first day of the school year had now been destroyed. Just as they learned how to trust me, I made it known that I had lost all faith and trust in them. No one uttered a sound.

I never brought up the knives, joints, and other articles that were found since this room was used by other classes. Any number of students could have been the owner of these items. Besides, I'm sure no one would have volunteered the information that the knife or one of the joints belonged to them. By the time the bell rang, signifying the end of the period, no more than a few students dared look at me as they exited to go to their next class.

The only positive to come out of this potentially dangerous situation was the fact that this class, out of all of my classes, would be the most well-behaved group of students I'd have for the remainder of the school year. Except for a couple of bruises, scratches, and a minimal loss of blood, I was thankful that no one was seriously injured. I really hoped that the two knives belonged to other students because, if they were the property of any of my combatants, who knows how much damage could have been inflicted during this free for all.

Although my actions may be difficult for you to understand, I can assure you that under no circumstances was I trying to harm or kill any of my students. I can just imagine what is going through your minds: *This guy was out his mind! He must have been crazy! He tried to kill those kids!* Although I know that this may be an impossibility on my part, let me assure you that this was not my goal. First of all, I had used sulfur in a number of experiments prior to this incident, and none of my students became sick, nauseous, or vomited. Not one child had an allergic reaction. Their only response was to hold their noses from the terrible smell of rotten eggs, or as they stated, "farts." You may castigate me for the method I employed to stop a riot. That's your prerogative. When you calm down and think about the action I took, you'll realize that although definitely out of the norm, the use of sulfur ultimately could have saved a number of students from being seriously injured or possibly killed.

The options that I had available to resolve this situation that day were slim at best. With the exception of one other class, every room on the floor was empty due to the seventh grade lunch period, and the teacher of this class was a total incompetent and would only have inflamed an already precarious situation. Adding further misery to the chaos at hand was the fact that the phone hookup to the main office was out of order despite a repair request months earlier.

As I stated earlier, I'm not particularly proud of the fact that I had to use sulfur fumes to defuse a dangerous situation. Yet, what if one of the confiscated knives belonged to one of the combatants? Would he or she have used it? Could one of my kids have been stabbed to death? What about the other knife? Who owned that one? These are just some of the questions that have haunted me over the years. Can you possibly imagine what would have occurred if one of my students had smashed a metal chair over the head of a classmate? The damage could have been catastrophic. There were so many possibilities for a tragedy to occur, yet so few options available to avert one.

I realize that no matter what I say, many of you will never accept the method I used to prevent a possible catastrophe. I'm sure you're smarter than I am and therefore have all of the correct answers. Maybe in the middle of this mayhem, I should have taken out *The Teachers Guide to Discipline* and checked out page 23. I bet that this page would have told me what to do. Better yet, what would you have done?

All I know is that every student that entered my classroom that day was healthy enough to leave. Nobody was stabbed, no one suffered any broken bones, and of the utmost importance, nobody died! Every parent, relative, or guardian that sent their child to school that day had that child return home that afternoon. Not one parent or student wrote a letter to my principal condemning my actions. Not a single charge was brought against me by any branch of law enforcement. None of my students asked me if I was trying to kill them because they all knew how much I cared about each and every one of them.

I cannot count the number of times I've thought about every aspect of this incident since my retirement. I've always tried to figure out an alternative solution and have failed miserably. In retrospect, the most acceptable option would have been to send a couple of students down to the main office to secure some help. Realistically, the time that would have elapsed before help arrived could have been disastrous. My monitors would have had to go down three flights of stairs, run to the other end of the building, tell someone in a position of authority what was occurring, wait until he/she assembled a group of individuals who could help break up this mini-riot, run back up the stairs, across the entire length of the school building, and finally enter my room. What would your guess be as to their time of arrival? Three minutes, five minutes? To tell the truth, even five minutes is an overly generous calculation. What I cannot be generous with is the number of my students that could have possibly been injured waiting for adequate assistance to arrive. Also, how many adults could have been injured separating the combatants?

Hey, remember William Tony? You will soon learn about the devastating effect breaking up the fight between him and a friend of mine had on my life. Guess what? Maybe there just isn't a right or wrong answer. Undoubtedly, I could have opted for the safe and sure way out of this mess, by sending two students to the main office to get help. Could the parents or guardian of one of these children have accepted this decision if their child was maimed or possibly killed? I don't think so! By the way, could any of you have lived with yourself if one of these students was severely injured or killed while you waited for help to arrive? I couldn't! Sometimes it's best to go with your instincts and the hell with protocol! This is exactly what I did.

Being a realist, I'm positive that, as you read further about my exploits in teaching, you will probably want to have me jailed for some of the methods I employed to get students to conform to what I felt was acceptable behavior. Yet no matter how much you vilify my methods, you will never be able to deny the successes I achieved. Nothing you can say will change the fact that Yolanda Blackman's mother continuously came up to school to thank me for what I had done for her daughter. Being hugged and kissed by this wonderful mother easily outweighs your ill-conceived sanctions.

When Yolanda was transferred into my self-contained class, her reputation was that of a troublemaker. Yolanda was constantly being sent to the Dean or Assistant Principal's Office for numerous infractions of the code of conduct expected of our students. When not on suspension, she was constantly cutting classes and causing all types of mayhem.

The moment I met Yolanda, I knew that there was something very special about her. I told her that I didn't care about what she had done in the past and that I would not look at her school record. I let her know that she now had a fresh start, which, most probably, was the last she'd ever get. I also warned her of the consequences she would face if she double-crossed me. From our initial meeting until I watched her graduate, she was the ideal student as far as behavior was concerned. Whether it was due to the fact that I carried out any threat I made, or the realization that I truly cared about her, something triggered an evolution and what emerged was the "new Yolanda."

I was amazed by the transformation in Yolanda's overall attitude. This young lady, dreaded by many of her former teachers, now came to school on a regular basis and never cut class. She constantly worked her butt off and showed me the respect that I accorded her. The improvement in her behavior, grades, and self-esteem was remarkable. Her perpetual smile and newfound confidence made us both feel special. This amazing young lady, who in our first meeting had been warned that if she didn't follow my rules, a number of my students would beat the living crap out of her, made her mother and me the proudest parent-teacher combo on the day of her graduation.

I made sure from the outset that Yolanda, just like all of my students, knew what was expected of her and the consequences she faced if she failed to conform to what I considered acceptable behavior. My form of discipline, in Yolanda's case, was to have her answer to her classmates if she failed to act properly, thus causing unnecessary tension in our "little world." You may not agree with the path I chose, but I never promised anyone that life in my classroom would be easy. Ultimately, like those who preceded her, once Yolanda learned that she was part of a family, "my family," she excelled. Watching her mother cry when she received her diploma was as much gratitude as I could ever have hoped for. The fact that over 95% of her fellow "incorrigibles" joined her made all of my hard work worthwhile.

Discipline has been written about, dissected, bisected, and placed under an educational microscope for so many years. There have been papers, seminars, panels, and a host of other avenues of exploration. The final results of this entire mega-million-dollar odyssey have been nothing to write home about. To this day, there are so many ways discipline can be used and abused, and I'm the first to admit that I used, abused, and confused it. My gratification came from watching "my kids" getting that fake piece of parchment placed in their outstretched hands, knowing it would be replaced by the Real McCoy after the graduation ceremony. This made me feel awful good about myself, and what I had been able to accomplish. Some of you can loathe me for the methods I embraced or for my disciplinary techniques. One fact is certain, you will never be able to take away my successes or the love I had for "my kids"!

CHAPTER FOUR

Does Anyone Want My Job?

I awoke at approximately 2:30 a.m. in excruciating pain. My left arm, which had been surgically repaired on two separate occasions, felt as if a burning knife was slicing through it. Twenty-two years later and I'm still in unimaginable pain—morphine, double Vicodin, and so many other meds, and nothing helps!

As previously alluded to, I had suffered severe ulna nerve damage in 1979 while breaking up a fight between William Tony and a fellow co-worker. To reiterate, Tony had been transferred to our "educational paradise" after assaulting a female teacher in another school. We had traded one of our dysfunctional students for one of theirs, hoping a change in scenery would be beneficial to both the students and their former schools. No one could have imagined the ramification of this administrative trade off. When William Tony became a student in my self-contained class, I never envisioned that three months after this transfer, an altercation would ensue which would reconcile a life of broken dreams, unfulfilled promise, and unfathomable pain and misery for an individual who loved his students and just wanted to help them be successful.

What would originally be diagnosed as a strained left ulna nerve, i.e. "funny bone," would in fact be an injury of such magnitude that the simplest of tasks, such as putting on a pair of socks, would at times seem insurmountable. The severity of this injury caused by the unconscionable stupidity of a colleague who threw hot coffee in William Tony's face, would eventually lead to retirement, disability, and a life sentence of unabated hell.

Violence in and around our schools as exemplified by such modern disasters as Columbine, Seth Trickey, and Westside Middle School in

Arkansas, has become a major source of conversation, analysis, and psychiatric evaluation. As unfortunate as these events were, history shows us that before our "great awakening," the threat of violence in and around our schools was never a national concern as long as it was confined to our inner-city or low-class neighborhood schools. These poor unfortunates who were enrolled in these educational facilities were of less importance than your average middle-class white students, and considered a total writeoff by those in positions of power. As long as the children of the "movers and shakers" were in predominately white public or private schools, who cared? As violence, drug use, and the breakdown in our social values permeated "civilized" arenas, they now became an American cancer, rather than just a ghetto problem. This incubus had infiltrated Main Street America, and we as society had no idea how to deal with it.

Where were all of those know-it-alls, with their fancy degrees in education and related fields, when we teachers needed their help? Unfortunately, during my twelve years in the trenches, I suffered numerous injuries. Never being one to turn my back on an altercation, I suffered five hand fractures, wrist damage, a major knee injury requiring three months on crutches, and of course the major "killer" left ulna nerve damage. This was okay since Sam Ross taught in "the ghetto," and nobody cared. I was expendable, and to tell you the truth, none of this phased me.

Let it be known to one and all that Sam Ross didn't care that no one gave a damn about him. I loved the action! It definitely wasn't boring. You never knew what could happen at any given moment. What an adrenaline rush! All this would change with the birth of my first child. The commonality of violence that I experienced on a daily basis took on new significance: I realized that I could get severely injured or even killed (how prophetic). Where were my saviors then? Oh, how stupid of me. This violence wasn't going on in their white suburban middle-class schools. Their kids and teachers were safe. The bottom line was, "Tough shit, Sam Ross! Your problems are not ours." Well, people, the wake-up call has arrived, and now they're your problems, too!

How many professionals report to their job, never knowing whether this may be the day he/she is either injured or possibly killed while performing their duty? The tragedy and horror of 9-11-2001 unfortunately showed us what could happen to police, firefighters, and emergency service personnel when they respond to the unknown. The same holds true for those in our armed services. I knew from growing up in tough neighborhoods and attending their schools how dangerous the teaching profession could be, but never did I expect to encounter the "insanity" I would come face to face with!

Teachers at I.S.24 never knew when a brawl or a riot would break out or in what location. It could occur in the lunchroom, hallway, outside in the yard, or in the confines of a classroom. Fistfights, fires, and so many other forms of violence were all part of the normal school year. As cynical as it sounds, for 180-190+ days in a school year, we were cops, firemen, soldiers, and what have you! The only difference between us and, say, the police or members of our armed services was the fact that we weren't allowed to carry weapons to defend ourselves, whereby many of our wards could and did!

It is quite unfortunate that in many of today's schools the teaching environment is so dangerous that many caring, loving, and intelligent individuals are doomed to failure, since they cannot adjust to the brutal environment they find themselves thrust into! Fortunately for me, and quite unfortunately for an unnamed student, an event occurred during my first year as a teacher that set the tone for my entire career at I.S.24.

Good Friday has more than a religious connotation for many in the business world. For most workers, it signifies the end of an arduous workweek. For myself, my "Good Friday" took on a special significance. My adventure began that Friday after our students had been dismissed and I had punched my time card signaling the end of my workweek. To say my limited teaching experience had been a cakewalk would be absurd. It had been a learning process as well as a time for me to reevaluate my priorities as far as this job was concerned. As I approached my car, which I had parked about three blocks from the school, I noticed a student approximately six feet, two inches, 175 pounds, standing in front of my just-purchased T-Bird. He and a number of his friends, who had congregated on the sidewalk, had been spouting racial epithets at any white person who crossed their path. Even an imbecile would realize that there was going to be a problem with my arrival at my car.

As I proceeded to open the door to my car, I asked the lanky individual if he could move so I could be on my way. His response was simple.

"Fuck you, Whitey! I ain't movin'!"

Not having a cell phone and realizing this imbecile and his friends would jump me long before I got back to the school building, my East New York smarts kicked in:

"Listen, man, I'm going to get into my car and start it up. I'm going to count to five and if you don't get out of my way, I'm going to knock you on your fucking ass!"I said in a no-nonsense tone.

In retrospect, I guess he thought I was kidding since he didn't budge an inch. In reality, what were my choices? No phone, no police, not a colleague in sight. Instinctively, I knew we weren't going to sit on the ground and begin negotiations. If anything, I was beginning to feel like George Armstrong Custer at the Little BigHorn, surrounded and ready to be annihilated!

Even as I started up my car, I gave the intimidator another warning:

"Hey, man. I'm not kidding around! You better get the hell out of my way!" This time I used the meanest tone of voice I could conjure up.

"Fuck you, Whitey! You ain't gonna do shit!" he replied.

As I barked out each number, there was no movement on his part. Having learned the first week that you never make idle threats, I decided to carry out my role in this mini-drama. When my count reached five, I put my car in drive, hit the accelerator, and knocked him right on his ass.

With his friends howling in laughter, he arose with a look of astonishment on his face. I knew I had "explained it" to him!

"You're fucking crazy, man!" were the first words out of his mouth.

"You're fucking right!" I responded.

"Make sure you tell all of your friends that Mr. Ross is one crazy mother-fucker!" I screamed, although I was shaking like a leaf.

My reputation was made at that moment. By the time Monday arrived, news of my insane exploit had spread throughout the school population. When I entered the building to punch in, everyone kept his or her distance. The word was out; Ross is crazy! From that moment, I can honestly state that only two other students said "Fuck you" to me during the rest of my entire career. I know you "Monday Night Quarterbacks" have figured out a million other ways I could have handled this situation—bullshit! By the way, do any of you want my old job?

I believe it's time to get down to the world of reality in regards to my job and the people who coveted it due to my summer vacations, paid holidays, and other "great benefits." First of all many new teachers were, and still are, totally unprepared for the environment they may find themselves residing in during their teaching careers. Taking the education courses mandated to be a teacher does not mean the future educator has been given the necessary tools to be effective. In most instances, what is taught in these programs would be great if schools existed in an artificially controlled environment. Sorry, people, there's a cruel world out there and this educational *Garden of Eden*, for the most part, does not exist!

Not to be an *Educational Grinch,* I'm willing to concede that certain education courses, which deal primarily with the early elementary school grades, have many redeeming features. They definitely help the future teacher as far as learning the basics of classroom management, the mechanics necessary to assist in student socialization, and numerous other processes that these youngsters should acquire in the early years of their public or private education. As successful as these classes are in dealing with the early stages of education, they are pathetic and fail miserably when trying to prepare the future educator for the junior and high school experience. Their application is further diminished when applied to schools in high crime areas where violence abounds, and the unimaginable can occur at any given moment. How can these sterile courses prepare a new teacher for the following occurrence?

While teaching one of my classes during the 1975 school year, I heard a spine-curdling scream from the hallway. Although noise was common by normal school standards, both experience and an innate feeling, which I never acquired by taking education classes, led me to believe that something was terribly amiss. Since every classroom on the floor was vacant due to the seventh grade lunch period, I sent a student to the main office to get help, making sure he used the side staircase. As the screams grew louder, I cautiously went outside, all the while hoping an assistant principal might be patrolling the hall and could come to my assistance. All this time, there was no doubt in my mind that it was going to be me against who or whatever was out there.

Before I knew what was happening, I had grabbed this kid by his neck, lifted him up, and proceeded to beat the ever-loving shit out of him. I hit him in the face with such force that he flew through a pair of heavy metal doors and landed on his back. Had it not been for the cries of a hysterical female student, who knows how much damage I would have inflicted on this kid; that's how infuriated I was. The fact that this "thing" had been a student of mine a few years earlier made no difference to me. What I now saw was a doped up piece of shit trying to rape one of my girls.

As I went to her aid, although bleeding and somewhat disoriented, my former student ran down the stairs and out of the building. Although quickly nabbed by the police, Christopher was back out on the streets by the next day. Failure on the part of my student to press assault and attempted rape charges for fear of retaliation left this low-life rapist free to strike again. Thankfully, this "white piece of trash" moved with his family to another neighborhood: So much for Education 101.

All of a sudden, I'm beginning to get the feeling that you might be getting a handle on the atmosphere I dealt with during a major portion of my teaching career. Truthfully, you're not there yet, but you're gaining some insight into a world quite different than what you expected. Just remember: off all summer, holidays, every weekend, decent medical benefits. Still pretty good, but the downside seems to be gathering increased momentum.

By the way, do any of you start your work day with, "Good morning, everybody. Anyone with a knife or gun, please bring it up here, now! If you give it to me, you'll get it back at 3:00. If you don't and I find out about it, it's mine!" Fortunately, I never did have to take a gun away from any of my students. On the flip side of the coin, I did manage to acquire a tremendous knife collection, which came in quite handy since I was an avid fisherman.

The fact that I would give a knife back to a student must have you talking to yourselves. Remember, people, a cruel world existed outside those school doors and nearly every kid carried a knife for protection. Better to get suspended for carrying a knife than to be dead because you couldn't defend yourself on your way home!

"Alright, everybody line up, shut your mouths, and let's get the hell out of here!" was all I had to say to my class.

As unbelievable as it may sound, during one year at I.S.24, we had over 100 fires. It became so bad at one point, the fire alarms were going off 4-5 times a day. It almost seemed like the fire department had their personnel punching their time cards at our school. Granted, most of the fires were of a waste paper basket variety, but due to the frequency of these occurrences, many members of our staff were becoming cynical when they heard the fire alarms go off. Some teachers were almost impervious to the sound, and the results could have been catastrophic!

I remember it being spring and with the onset of warmer weather, many of our students were beginning to feel "antsy." While a large number of our pupils were engaged in various sports activities, and other forms of entertainment, there were a few who decided to reach a new plateau as far as fires were concerned. Better known as "arsonists," these youths brought into school cans of gasoline and stored them in the ceilings of a few classrooms. How they had gotten these cans into the building in the first place, nobody knew for sure. One day, with our fourth floor vacant due to the eighth grade lunch period, these "wonderful citizens" took some of these cans and emptied their contents into two classrooms, as well as down a significant portion of the hallway. With the simple flick of a match, the hallway and classrooms soon became engulfed in fire and smoke.

Due to the quick response of the fire department, as well as a couple of firemen "wannabe's" on staff, the fires only caused moderate damage. Thankfully, nobody was injured. Furthermore, as luck would have it, a teacher had witnessed the entire episode, ultimately leading to the arrest of one of our students. I'm not sure if it was our judicial system, or the fact that this young man was a nephew of a prominent member of a noted subversive group, which struck fear into the hearts of many New Yorkers during the 60s and early 70s, but the following dialogue took place in a courtroom in downtown Brooklyn and ultimately blew the minds of most members of the I.S.24 staff. To be honest, I'm not sure if this was a preliminary hearing or what, but the result was still shocking.

After disposing of all the basic nonsense that was the norm for such a case, my colleague was eventually sworn in before the court to testify what she had witnessed. She was asked the normal array of questions symbolic of such a case:

"Do you know the defendant?" she was asked.

"Do you have anything against him?" asked his attorney.

"Are you sure he started the fire?" he continued.

When asked this question, our witness basically stated that she had seen him throw the match. She also stated that when he was apprehended, his eyebrows were singed, some of his clothing was burned, and that he smelled from gasoline. Sounds like an airtight case, right? Wrong! When our arsonist's attorney asked our witness:

"Did you see him light the match that he supposedly threw?"

"No," replied our whiteness.

Case dismissed was the sound that echoed throughout courtroom. Although this isn't the actual transcript of the case, it basically gives an overview of what occurred downtown. To say that the majority of our staff was outraged with this outcome would be an understatement. It was inconceivable to some that such a decision had been reached. Unfortunately, if you lived in our little corner of the world and were not the consummate optimist, this should not have surprised you at all. Adding insult to injury was the fact that when "our little arsonist" returned to I.S.24, he was accorded the accolades of a hero. The ultimate insult was his winning the election for

Mayor of I.S.24 and being the representative of the student body at monthly meetings with the school administration. By the way, are you sure you still want my old job?

I'm really starting to get the impression that many of those individuals that were jealous of the so-called benefits my job offered are, at this point, having some serious trepidations. I fervently believe this next incident will not only exorcise your jealousy, but quite possibly elicit your support for higher teacher pay, increased dental and medical benefits, lower class size, reevaluation of the courses mandated for those entering the field of education, and so many other necessary changes.

Part of our contract with the city of New York and the board of education required that every two years teachers were assigned hall patrols or lunchroom duty. It just so happens that one day, I was on patrol and was making sure that all of the rooms that were empty were locked. I eventually found myself by an assistant principal's office testing the doorknob. As I turned the knob, I did a double take. With my mind beginning to race a mile a minute, I couldn't believe what my eyes were trying to show me. There was no way this could be happening. A final glance reinforced my original observation and still I didn't want to accept what was now an undeniable fact. There in the office was a colleague, and might I add a close personal friend, standing with his hands raised to the ceiling and a gun pointed at his head.

I remember thinking, *Holy shit! What do I do now? Run for help? Call 911?* With all I had experienced in both my private life and in my career, I had always hoped never to be involved in this type of situation. I had learned to expect anything, but when this happened, I definitely was not prepared for it. If there was one saving grace, it was the fact that I knew who this gun toting "cowboy" was.

Standing in my line of vision was a parent that I had known for a number of years and who I respected very much. He had always cared about his son's well-being and showed it by being involved in many aspects of his child's life. To me, he epitomized what a parental role model should be.

Later, when everything calmed down, I realized that the correct course of action would have been to call 911 and then inform the principal about the serious situation at hand. Hindsight aside, to this day, I'm not sure if it was our personal relationship or the fact that I was a total moron, but I decided to intervene in this extremely dangerous situation.

As I slowly entered the AP's office, I calmly and quite slowly began to speak to this irate parent, hoping he'd recognize me and not freak out and start shooting. Luckily, "Charles Dillinger" did recognize who I was:

"Hey, Mr. Ross," he said as he caught a glimpse of me out of the corner of his eye.

Before I could respond, this irate parent continued, "This fucking teacher kicked my son in his stomach!" he said, obviously upset.

Expressing shock at my colleague's behavior, I began to cut the tension by taking the father's side in this dispute.

"You should press charges against the animal!" I stated in a shocked, though fabricated, tone of voice.

"Shooting him is not the solution to this problem," I continued.

Finally, after about five minutes, which felt like five years, he began to lower his gun, while warning my friend, "Don't you ever put your hands or feet on my son again!" he snarled.

He then came over to me, shook my hand, wished me well, and left. Just like that, it was over.

Without being melodramatic, I must admit that for the next couple of minutes I wasn't sure which one of us would have a heart attack. My friend, Max, was as white as a ghost and shaking uncontrollably. After convincing him to sit down, I proceeded to pick up the phone to call Principal Pell and inform him of what had just occurred. Max begged me to put the phone down. He pleaded with me not to let anyone know about this incident. Of course, out of respect for our friendship, I acquiesced to Max's request. After he partially regained his composure, Max went downstairs to Leonard Pell's office to inform him that he was sick and was going home.

All of these years, I've kept my word to Max and never told anyone about this incident. Not even my closest friends at I.S.24 knew about this event. Talk about getting up close and personal? I had witnessed or been directly involved in many disturbing incidences in my life, and this one definitely was right up there with the best of them. Thankfully, I had, and still have, excellent control of my sphincter muscle, or there could have been another tragedy.

Throughout this entire book, I will constantly emphasize the fact that you, the average layman, have no idea what kind of environment I found myself teaching in. I am not trying to demean your intelligence or life experiences, but in all honesty, could any one of you have guessed that the aforementioned lunatic that had held a gun to my friend Max's head was none other than a veteran New York City police officer? This was an individual whose sworn duty was to protect the public and who, in a fit of rage, had almost gone over the edge. Here was a highly decorated police officer, who, if turned in, would have immediately been suspended from the force for illegally drawing his weapon, and eventually charged with such felonies as kidnapping, false imprisonment, and a host of other crimes. Undoubtedly, he later would have been fired. There's no doubt that he also had a good chance of doing some serious jail time, if my friend pressed charges against him.

Later that evening while reflecting on the day's events, I realized that if I had followed correct procedure and reported what was going on with a call to 911, the result could have been disastrous. Just imagine what might have occurred during a hostage crisis, police vs. police. The possible scenarios are mind-boggling. To this day, I thank G-d that I never made that call. For the last time, does anyone still want my old job?

When you take some time and analyze the few experiences I've discussed, I'm sure you can understand how pissed off I was, listening to some jealous imbecile castigate my colleagues and me for having holidays and summers off. Well, uninformed and jealous fools, "Life is a bitch," and in most instances you don't die; but I have to tell you that on a number of occasions, I came awfully close!

As I've tried to impart to the reader, life at I.S.24 was on par with trying to survive in a combat zone, and as in combat, there were many injuries. I cannot count the number of times I gave medical assistance to students and teachers who were injured as a result of a fight or other mishap. The frequency of such occurrences eventually resulted in my becoming apathetic towards the sight of blood and its associated gore.

Many teachers at I.S.24 began to feel like they were members of a "MASH" unit with Hawkeye Pierce being their inspirational leader. I must admit that years after my forced retirement, when my step-daughter came into the house screaming with her face totally covered with blood, I calmly took a towel, threw it on her face, and began looking for the injury that had contributed to this grizzly sight. Luckily, she only needed minor plastic surgery due to an unfortunate encounter with her sister's tennis racket. Undoubtedly, my past experiences with blood and gore in the trenches of I.S.24 helped me to maintain my cool and find the source of this bleeder. Her mother, formerly married to a doctor, could not bear the sight of this gruesome scene, even though she had seen many of her former husband's patients in dire straights. Pathetic as it seems, working at I.S.24 had some real world value. I always wondered how I would perform as a combat medic. Thank G-d I never was put in this situation but I fervently believe I would have been a credit to these savers of lives.

While on the topic of young ladies and injuries, many uninformed people in our society, especially those that wanted my job, perceive violence in our schools as primarily a "male thing." Being macho has been dramatized on the silver screen, as well as on our TV as if it is testosterone-related, thus inferring that most incidences of violence are male dominated. *Au contraire*, my dear friends! Some of the most vicious fights I observed, or wound up participating in, were between members of the female gender.

I cannot recall the number of times I had to take off either my sports jacket or shirt and cover a bare breasted youth whose clothing had been torn off during a no-holds-barred fight. As fortunate as it was, I learned quite early in my career to try, if possible, not to intervene when young "ladies" were involved in fisticuffs. Talk about heart? The ferocity exhibited by these girls goes beyond comprehension. Only through experience was I able to anticipate an impending altercation. Too bad that no one ever "explained" this to me at Brooklyn College.

The first time I saw one of my female students smearing Vaseline on her face, I asked if there was a problem I could help her out with?

"No, Mr. Ross. I'm just using it as a moisturizer," she replied with this innocent look on her face.

I would soon learn that girls used Vaseline to minimize possible facial scarring caused by clawing and gouging during a fight. It seems I never learned this in an education class! The violence and ultimate damage that many girls inflicted on one another was at times worse than what I saw watching a professional boxing match. Many times, it looked like either or both combatants had an unfortunate meeting with a tiger. In no uncertain terms, they tried their best to mutilate each other. Talk about having "heart." These girls defined the word!

One of the best pugilists during my entire teaching career was Stephanie Bryant. Usually attired in a black leather jacket, Stephanie took on all comers, male or female. One of Stephanie's favorite lines was:

"Mr. Ross, I'll kick anyone's ass!" and she meant it, too.

Stephanie took no prisoners. To say I adored her would be an understatement. Stephanie had the most vibrant personality of any female student I ever came in contact with. Funny, animated, exceptionally intelligent, she personified the "Modern Woman" (fighting omitted, of course). She carried herself with such dignity it often bordered on elegance.

Despite so many attributes, Stephanie had one major personality flaw: an explosive temper.

During the year that Stephanie was a student of mine, I managed to keep her temper mostly in check. She never caused any grief in my class, especially since everyone was scared to death of her, boys and girls alike. Unfortunately, whenever she was out of my sight, all bets were off!

Stephanie and I enjoyed a very special relationship. I was always reinforcing the fact that she was a bright and beautiful young lady. She knew that I was sincere and meant every word when I praised her. I tried with all of my being to put her on a pedestal and was successful most of the time. Sadly, there were a few times when she either fell or was pushed from her royal throne.

One such occurrence happened one day when Stephanie left my room to go to lunch. It seems that two boys, and may I add two stupid boys, decided to ruffle Stephanie's feathers by intentionally banging into her. By the time I happened on the scene, which couldn't have been but a few minutes later, there stood Stephanie in her victory pose, hovering over the two boys she had mercilessly decimated. I was to find out that these two clowns had done this to Stephanie on numerous occasions, and she, much to her credit, had kept her composure. This time, she finally let her emotions get the best of her, and all hell broke loose.

In all honesty, there was no way I could be angry with Stephanie for her actions. The truth was, these two fools got what they deserved. Come to think of it, I could never be totally infuriated with her because Stephanie had the most infectious smile I have ever encountered. She was one of a kind, and to this day, I think about her with the fondest of memories.

During my entire career, there was only one other female student that could compete with Stephanie as far as combativeness goes. Unlike Stephanie's exuberant and lovable personality, this student promulgated an aura of outright viciousness. It's only through the good graces of G-d that these two individuals didn't attend I.S.24 in the same time frame. You can't imagine the utter chaos that would have ensued. Although I believe Stephanie would have been victorious in any confrontation, the following episode should give you some insight into a girl named Tanya.

One day, I went down to the main office and, by chance, encountered one of our assistant principals seated at a table. He appeared to be both irate, yet on the verge of tears. As I was soon to discover, he had sent for

Tanya during one of her seemingly endless outbursts, and the result of his intervention was disastrous to put it mildly.

John Saxon was approximately 55 and not a feeble physical specimen. At about six foot two and weighing in at 190 pounds, Saxon was an imposing figure to many of our students. I guess to Tanya, he "wasn't all that" since I would learn that she had physically picked up Saxon and thrown him out of his office. She then proceeded to barricade herself in his office, and our principal was now waiting for the police to extract her from Saxon's domicile.

I must admit that when I heard the facts surrounding Tanya's exploit, even I was impressed. I thought I had witnessed or had heard of every form of unacceptable behavior during my stay at I.S.24, but this event even caught me off guard. I was in awe of Tanya's physical prowess, as well as the brazen nature of her action. This youngster had no fear whatsoever. If she had been a male, she would have been lauded as a "kid with a huge pair of brass-balls."

Once Tanya was removed from Saxon's office, the fallout from this incident moved at super sonic speed. The immediate results of this mind-boggling event were easy to anticipate. John Saxon, the "school disciplinarian," saw the respect, toughness, and manliness that he had worked so hard to attain destroyed in a matter of minutes by a 15-year-old student. Everything he had accomplished during his lengthy career went down the drain, including the high esteem he was held in by his colleagues. Tanya, after her eviction, was immediately suspended and later transferred to a new school. Another student in the district, who had also been expelled from "his" school, replaced her. One fact was undeniable; we got the better of the deal!

Although John Saxon physically recovered from his ordeal, psychologically he was never the same. A broken man, he would retire at the end of the school year. I'm positive that anyone who found out about this incident never questioned his right to holidays and summers off. I'm equally positive that, if given the opportunity, Saxon would have said, "Here, take my job," and under his breath muttered, "And shove it up your ass!"

It is rather pathetic that I could write a tome about the violence that permeated I.S.24. So many variables came into play, and the results were often devastating. Adding additional fuel to this perpetual fire was the overcrowding that existed at I.S.24. It caused constant irritability, especially during the warmer months, and only added to everyone's stress level. As smart as some of us were, no one knew when a pitch battle would erupt. The only constant was that both teachers and students were in a perpetual state of alert. The ultimate result of such tension was simple: As the years passed by, many teachers edged closer to total burnout.

For some students, the fallout from this never-ending violence at I.S.24 was just as damaging. Fear of bodily injury led a number of students to stay home for extended periods of time. Some would drop out altogether or transfer to another school using a relative or friend's address as their official residence. Unfortunately, everyone, be they a student, teacher, or administrator, lost. Teachers saw some of their nicest and brightest students staying home for fear of getting robbed or getting their asses kicked in. The administration lost, since it was their responsibility to keep order in the school, thus lowering teacher absenteeism, which reached new highs each and every year due to their need to "catch a break" from the ever-present insanity which had long since infiltrated our school. The reality of this entire scenario was the fact that this vicious cycle was self-perpetuating, and the future looked just as bleak.

Hopefully, we're at the point in time that, when you see a teacher enjoying a holiday or their summer vacation, you can look at this individual and think, *You really did earn this respite. By the way, you can keep your job. I definitely don't want it!*

P.S. Don't Mess With Me!

The late 60s and 70s, besides being noted for "free love," drugs, and the war in Vietnam, saw a tremendous growth in the martial arts industry. Due to overexposure by both the TV and cinema media, all forms of these arts, especially karate, reached what was thought to be prohibitive heights of popularity. As if hypnotized into thinking that they were martial arts experts, many students, although having never taken a lesson, professed to be black belts in karate, Tae Kwon do, Go Ju Ryu, etc.

When our students would get into altercations, it seemed at least one participant would assume a stance from one of these various forms of fighting and proceed from there. I always wondered how poorly they would fare against a true student of these arts. My curiosity would be answered in 1974.

The middle of the 1974-1975 school year saw the enrollment of two Asian students at I.S.24. Staff members assumed that their parents had taken over the ownership of the Silver Dragon, the neighborhood's only Chinese takeout business. Our assumption later proved to be correct. These two boys were the first, and ultimately the only students of Oriental heritage, to ever grace our building. Not trying to be accused of stereotyping, I must confess "the twins" were extremely well behaved, quite intelligent, and unfortunately, short. This lack of height and their oriental features made them the brunt of both verbal and physical abuse.

Experience should teach any individual that, in the real world, anyone could reach his or her so-called breaking point. When this occurs, control of one's emotions, disciplines, etc. can come to a screeching halt. As five students would soon find out, you can only push an individual, or in this case, "the twins," so far until you reap the rewards of your actions. The sight of five students in horizontal positions, bleeding and in a few cases incoherent, is testimony to the deserved beating inflicted on them by the "two short kids." The fact that each one of these five juvenile delinquents had been a constant disruption to school harmony only added to the beauty of their near annihilation. Sadly, I was only privy to the outcome of this massacre. Those that witnessed this mini-conflagration expressed utter disbelief in the twins' martial arts abilities.

As details of the incident spread through the school populace, respect became the order of the day. Needless to say, nobody messed with the twins for the rest of the year.

Although numerous positives came out of this scuffle, unfortunately there was a downside, too. The fact that two children had to lower themselves to a combative state in order to secure an environment that was conducive to both their safety and education is quite sad. The shame they brought upon their family's honor, due to their suspension, negated their great accomplishment. After evaluating the cause and effect of the entire incident, I came away with only one regret; no one had a camcorder to record their magnificent triumph.

Further analysis led to another dubious reality. Two docile, well-behaved youths had been introduced to such a violent environment that in order to survive, they had to bring shame upon their family and the tradition of such an old, respected culture. Imagine going against centuries of tradition and honor in order to survive. It truly boggles one's imagination. Are you sure that you'd want a job that can bring out the worst in individuals and dishonor that which is held so sacred? It really makes you wonder.

CHAPTER FIVE

I'm the Captain of the Ship

The fourth year of my career at I.S.24 started with a drastic change in our school environment. Retiring after G-d knows how many years, Principal Sidney Cohen was replaced by Claude Jennings, a.k.a. "The Great Educator." For the first time in many years there was an air of electricity exhibited by our entire staff, in regards to an administrator and the onset of a new semester.

To say that an exemplary reputation preceded this individual would be an injustice. Being led to believe that he was a reincarnation of Joe Clark and George S. Patton, at the first U.F.T. meeting of the year, our staff agreed to go far beyond the purview of our union contract and assist Mr. Jennings in any way possible. Any individual who could improve the educational environment that we had been drowning in for so long would get our maximum assistance. All of us hoped that Claude Jennings would be the man that we so desperately needed to turn things around. The question that had to be answered was: would he be someone we could deify or a demagogue we'd have to crucify? One fact was certain; we would surely find out.

Our first staff meeting with Mr. Jennings was like a breath of fresh air. Irrespective of a heavy Southern accent and some non-Northern phraseology, everyone was impressed with his leadership qualities. Expressing his vision for the school's future and articulating his full backing of the teaching staff, most of us left this meeting invigorated and quite optimistic. With an enthusiasm so uncharacteristic of a Sidney Cohen, the next few days with Jennings were dynamic. Preparation for the first official day of school proceeded at a blistering pace. Monday would hopefully be the beginning of a new era. At last there would be an atmosphere conducive to teaching and learning. No longer would we be policemen or an army platoon engaged in a holding action until reinforcements arrived. Finally we would be TEACHERS!

Monday morning arrived and proceeded like clockwork. Students were ushered into the gymnasium and grouped into classes. Each class was then taken to their official room and seated. All of this was accomplished with unprecedented speed. Within minutes Jennings' voice was booming over the P.A. system, welcoming our pupils and emphasizing what was expected of them. To say the least, his words were quite inspirational. Then, as if we were participants in an episode of *The Twilight Zone*, Jennings uttered words I believe no member of our staff would ever forget:

"I wants all of yous to come to school with shined sneakers!" he stated.

As I tried to maintain an air of professionalism, "shined sneakers" caused an electrical malfunction in my brain. It took every bit of inner-fortitude not to burst out laughing. I was stupefied! Was this the same man who had impressed my colleagues and Sam Ross the previous days, or was this an impostor delivering an early April Fools' prank? I remember silently praying, *Please G-d, not another lunatic.*

During my ten-year residence at I.S.24, I worked for three different principals. Besides their differences in race, religion, educational background, etc., here were three men, although worlds apart from one another, trying to fill the "elite" educational position of principal. Could times have changed in such a radical manner that the flawed bosses of my professional career had replaced the principals I respected and feared during my formative education? What had gone wrong?

Sidney Cohen was my boss for my first three years at I.S.24, and he was the epitome of what I perceived a principal to be. Impeccably dressed, distinguished-looking gray hair, almost statuesque in appearance, he was "the principal." Being a raw recruit, it took a number of months before I realized that Sidney enjoyed the world of magic. Not only did he enjoy magic, but Sidney was also a magician in his own right. He was the David Copperfield of I.S.24, replete with props, illusions, and, sadly, delusions.

All of this becomes apparent when I try to describe my three years under the Sidney Cohen regime. Except for staff meetings, I rarely ever saw him. The guy basically didn't exist! I never saw him in the hallway during the changing of classes. He was never in the students' cafeteria overseeing the usual fisticuffs that took place. Auditorium Day rarely saw Sidney as a participant. The man who I eventually dubbed "the Ghost" was definitely a magician; he could make himself disappear! Your odds of a chance encounter with Sidney or a UFO were 50:50.

Sarcasm aside, I was able to ascertain from my colleagues that during an earlier period in his career, Sidney Cohen was a tremendous principal and administrator. As his time in the profession progressed, so did the inevitable "playing out the string." Towards the end of his career, only a ghost-like spirit remained.

Few teachers were privy to an audience with Sidney, and only his administrators had unrestricted accessibility to his sanctuary. As my own cynicism progressed, I seriously contemplated calling the police, so an APB could be issued. That's how rare sightings were of this once vibrant and dedicated individual.

At the end of his final year, the district threw Sidney a huge retirement party. Over 400 people participated in the festivities. Most people had a great time. Word has it that a number of participants awoke the next morning, hung over and seeking an answer to the question, "Was Sidney at the party?"

In all honesty, while I've embellished the Sidney regime with somewhat humorous dissertation, the fact remains that the essence of this characterization is totally genuine. Unfortunately, the school atmosphere and the well being of its staff and student population suffered greatly due to the "Ghostman's" inaccessibility and rare sightings. Without direction or leadership, misery reigned supreme.

Most of us were ecstatic when we learned Sidney was going to retire. Only those who had kissed his ass over the years, and had received tidbits for their loyalty, were apprehensive over his impending departure. In hindsight, our exuberance only showed how ignorant many of us were. You never know how good something is until it is replaced by something else. In this case, as bad as things were under Sidney Cohen, none of us could have imagined the nightmare we'd experience under the leadership of Claude Jennings, i.e. our new "Captain of the Ship."

In contrast to Sidney Cohen, Claude Jennings was "Mr. Public." Like one's shadow, it seemed that no matter where you were, he was right behind you. I fervently believe cloning had already taken place in the early 70s because it was humanly impossible for one person to be in so many places at the same time.

Jennings' superhuman energy, the great rapport he established with our student population, and his ability to lead, gained him the respect of our entire staff. Most of us believed that we finally had a principal we could all admire and go the extra mile for, irrespective of his call for "shined sneakers." Sadly, we had not learned a simple lesson that Sidney Cohen had tried to teach us in regards to the world of magic: What appears to be one thing can, in reality, be something totally different. We would pay the price for our ignorance.

Claude Jennings had been born and educated in the deep South. Little was known about his education and training, yet the revues on this man were spectacular. His reputation was so renowned that many of the requirements needed to ascent to the position of principal had been waived in order to secure his services. How this was accomplished, we, as a staff, couldn't have cared less. We were getting a "Blue Chip" educator, and we sorely needed his help.

As previously noted, Mr. Jennings had the devotion of the entire staff. In essence, we bent over backwards to help him succeed because his accomplishments, invariably, would make our jobs much easier. As the school year progressed, letters of commendation continuously poured in, extolling the job he was doing. Not only was be becoming a legend in his own time, unfortunately, he was becoming a legend in his own mind!

I'll never understand how the human psyche works when it comes to dealing with the issue of power. What is known is that individuals handle "might" in different ways. Some continue to be their usual selves, in most cases, the self that helped ingratiate them to those they've impressed. Others, unfortunately, become consumed with what I call the "G-d complex." With this complex comes a change in personality, which eventually alienates friends, co-workers, and those they once impressed.

Without a doubt, our school under Jennings' leadership had made a 180-degree turnabout. Teaching was finally the norm, rather than the exception. Both the faculty and student population enjoyed a serenity that was long since missing in our educational edifice. Lost in the total equation was the simple fact that the staff had helped Jennings attain his celebrity status. As Jennings became totally absorbed in self-aggrandizement, he began to bite the hand that had fed him.

The staff that had gone out of its way to help Claude Jennings now became his "whipping boy." The man who had once promised to back us 100 percent did a complete about face and took every opportunity to castigate and demoralize us. Now, the students were always right, and the teachers were at fault. His anti-teacher stance became so blatant that only a fool would fail to realize that such behavior could only lead to an all-out confrontation. This fool was too busy basking in his press clippings to see the handwriting on the wall!

Marvin Feinberg was a science teacher whose time to retire had definitely arrived. Hard of hearing, forgetfulness, and other maladies had unfortunately begun to affect his everyday classroom performance. Living in the past where teachers were respected and revered, Marvin could not adapt to the modern-day student. On the other side of the spectrum was Laura Rolls. New to teaching she was having a difficult time adjusting to her new environment and constantly sought help from her peers, as well as members of the administration. This was quite common with new teachers. Instead of rendering assistance to these two individuals, as well as others that needed help, Jennings decided to attack with one goal in mind—to make their lives so miserable that they would eventually resign.

Jennings forgot, or never realized, that almost 100 percent of our staff were members of the United Federation of Teachers. As with all unions, when even one of our members faced harassment, threats, or other forms of rebuke, the union leadership was supposed to help them in any way possible. The expression "in numbers there is strength" would soon be put to the test, as Jennings' power trip became totally irrational, and his abuse of teachers reached unfathomable levels. As the staff's frustration with Jennings' theatrics and abuse reached unparalleled heights, in direct contrast to our avid enthusiasm months earlier, our membership agreed to desist in aiding Jennings in anything above what our contract called for. From now on, we'd go by the letter of our contract—nothing more, nothing less.

Our contract specifically detailed the proper procedures that had to be followed by any school administrator desirous of ridding themselves of "unfit teachers." Egotistical Jennings not only didn't abide by the guidelines that had been agreed upon, but decided to invent his own procedure. In essence, he was breaking a union contract that had taken years of intense negotiation to secure. Yes, there were some bad teachers on our staff. Yes, some of them should have been replaced. Yes, yes, yes, but not by Claude Jennings, since he was not empowered with the right to unilaterally decide such issues as teacher competency or who should be fired. Proper procedure had to be followed, and he tried to circumvent this process. This power-crazed individual had now negated what originally had been respect and cooperation, and every aspect of life at I.S.24 went downhill.

We all know the expression that "time heals all wounds." Personally, I believe it's a bunch of bull, but maybe... At our last U.F.T. Chapter meeting, some members of our chapter expressed their optimism that our summer hiatus might help abate the hostility that had built up during the school year.

Hopefully, Jennings would have a reality check and clearly understand that no individual could run our school single-handedly. Maybe he'd realize we all needed each other to accomplish anything positive and would reverse the self-destructive course he had mysteriously opted to embrace.

My summer vacation, which, in essence, was a revitalization of my physical as well as emotional well-being, was invigorating to say the least. Spending time with my family in a more relaxed and serene environment was "just what the doctor ordered." Short trips, plenty of fishing and just relaxing was a prescription no doctor could possibly have written. Great success in the stock market also made this summer more enjoyable than the previous three. As the saying goes, "All good things must come to an end." With the summer vacation flying by and the new school year fast approaching, a calm and happy individual was beginning to exude signs of tension, as exemplified by my snapping at the most inane occurrences. My old friend, diarrhea, began "rearing" it's ugly head as the first day of school approached.

The thought of having to break in a new group of students, as well as trepidation's about Jennings, began to occupy my mind with increased frequency. Natural intuition led me to believe that this would be a year to remember—one way or another. Was I optimistic as far as Jennings was concerned? Not really. Could I forget Jennings' past actions and give him the benefit of the doubt? Yes. Did I really believe he would change for the better? Unfortunately, no.

Our first day back to work would set the tone for the entire school year. As was the norm, a staff meeting was called for in the library by our principal. Expecting nothing, yet hoping for a conciliatory speech, I sat down as an "upbeat" Jennings strode to the podium to address the entire staff. Immediately, his presence created an aura which was a far cry from the preceding year. All of us were hoping Jennings would express his desire to start anew and let bygones be bygones. Were we wrong!

With arrogance more perverse than ever before, Claude Jennings began his oration by welcoming us back and expressing his hope that we had enjoyed our summer vacation. Not being neurotic, I realized that by the tone of his voice, he was like Crazy Horse inviting George Armstrong Custer and his Seventh Calvary over for a barbecue. Then, like a tyrant enthralled with his power, he went on a diatribe that was nothing short of a declaration of war! After stating that he knew we were out to get him, Jennings imparted these infamous words:

"I'm the captain of this ship, and if I go down, you're going with me!" he raged. While reviling us and accusing the staff of everything imaginable, we all sat in a state of shock. When he had finally finished his verbal tirade, he stormed out of the library. The first thought to enter my mind was, *Now that was conciliatory.*

The school year would be as explosive as any in the history of I.S.24. As the year progressed, Jennings' paranoia reached new heights. Terrible teacher ratings, berating teachers in front of their classes, abusive language, the calling of illegal meetings under the guise of emergencies, and constant violations of the union contract, all expedited the inevitable—chaos. As tension heightened, our students took full advantage of the situation at hand. Fights, fires, and confrontations escalated, reaching unimaginable heights.

During one week, the Fire Department was at our school about eight times. One morning, after three false alarms, Jennings announced on the loudspeaker:

"If the fire alarms go off again, no one is to leave the building. Failure to heed this warning will be dealt with severely! "he warned the staff.

My attitude on this matter was simple: if the damn alarms went off, my class and I would get the hell out of the building. What could this "nut job" do to me? How was I supposed to know that this alarm didn't signify a real fire? Furthermore, I had every legal right to leave the building in order to insure my students' safety. Finally, I really wanted to see which other teachers, besides myself, had the guts to walk out.

As if by divine providence, the fire alarms went off within an hour of Jennings' order not to vacate the building. I lined up my class and told them:

"We're out of here!" I said in a sarcastic tone of voice.

Much to my amazement, only one other teacher had the courage to leave the building with his students. It didn't take more than five minutes before Jennings was out there berating us and threatening us with all sorts of nonsense. After listening to his anal outburst, I responded to Jennings' threats in a calm, confident voice.

"Do whatever you have to do and I'll have the union file a grievance against you!" I warned him. Continuing with my calm demeanor, I told Jennings, "I will personally bring you up on civil charges and I'm going to report your actions to the head of the New York City Fire Department."

Deciding it was time to end this game of threats, and to totally piss off this idiot, I lowered my voice and said, "If the fire alarms go off again, I'm going to leave the building with my class, again!" this time getting right up in his face.

If looks could kill, I definitely would have joined "my friend" George Armstrong Custer. I knew from that moment on that I was on Jennings' "shit list." To tell you the truth, I considered it an honor.

Although appraised of the events going on in our school, the district superintendent had great trepidation about getting involved. Besides his approval of Jennings' appointment, he too had been basking in the glory as I.S.24 made such a dramatic turnaround. To admit that he had made a major mistake would have been too much for his ego to accept. Of greater importance was his fear of the newspapers getting wind of the true conditions at I.S.24 and how they would crucify him and the office of personnel at the board of education. The *New York Post* in particular would have had a field day with the incompetence of both of these institutions. As hard as he tried to keep this explosive time bomb under wraps, the newspapers would eventually find out about the situation at I.S.24. The ultimate joke of this entire debacle was the city's dailies castigating everyone except Jennings. You just had to love it!

Before the onset of the explosion that would tear at the very foundation of I.S.24, Jennings, much to his credit or outright lunacy, decided to take on all comers. Directives from the district office were totally ignored when he felt they were insignificant. Politicking in the neighborhood enabled Jennings to align himself with the so-called "political troublemakers," and as his political base grew, so did his self-perceived air of invincibility. Now he was even disregarding directives from the board of education.

Jennings' use and abuse of power neared its apex with his enlistment of "school goons" to patrol the halls, staircases, etc., and ultimately keep the entire school population under his rigid control. Assaults on students by his "goons" became an everyday occurrence. Nothing but thugs themselves, they were given the power to patrol, detain, and kick the shit out of whomever they wanted, whether they had done something wrong or not. The only prerequisites to be chosen to be a member of "The Goon Squad" were that you had to be big, strong, and nasty. Good grades were not applicable when seeking entrance. Gang membership was a definite plus. To say the least, any semblance of normalcy was now spiraling out of control, and all hell was about to break loose.

Under the auspices of a covert like CIA operation, the local school board, with cooperation from the district superintendent, who finally had to accept the dangers of the existing situation, and Mario Danzio, our union district representative, held a late-night, non-publicized meeting, and voted to have Jennings removed as principal of I.S.24. With Jennings' firing accomplished, all that had to be done was to inform him of his ouster and have the police on hand if he didn't leave peaceably. This, of course, would take place in the morning.

When Jennings was informed of his dismissal, he wouldn't leave the building. With the police on their way to carry out the notice of dismissal by the local school board, Jennings, in his last act of defiance, turned on the school's P.A. system and told the student population to, "RIOT!" Needless to say, all hell broke loose!

To this day, I have no idea if Jennings finally left the building on his own volition or by police escort. The truth depended on with whom you spoke. In the meantime, anarchy was everywhere. Our school was like a war zone. There were fires, assaults on teachers and students, and destruction wherever you looked.

During Jennings' final loudspeaker outburst, I was marking papers in my classroom. My initial reaction was, *Thank G-d they removed the idiot.* Then, as if a bomb had detonated, I heard this loud sound in the hallway and went outside to investigate its origin. I couldn't believe it! There must have been 200-300 students running full speed as I stepped into the hallway.

Through all of the noise and mayhem, I was able to discern one voice. "There's Ross! Let's get him!" screamed one of the youngsters in this group

For whatever reason, I slowly reopened my classroom door, picked up a chair, and stepped back into the hallway.

It was as if I was watching a cartoon in slow motion. The rioters in the front stopped when they saw me with the chair, and those in the back started banging into those ahead of them, not knowing or seeing why the stampede had come to a screeching halt. If the event weren't so unnerving, I probably would have laughed my ass off.

I'm not sure if it was due to the chair, my reputation, or what have you, but everything seemed to stop as if stuck in a time warp. The quiet was deafening! I had no place to run or hide and realized I could be severely injured or possibly killed.

"I know you mother fuckers can kill me, but before I hit the ground, five of you bastards will be dead!" I yelled.

As we stared at each other, each second felt like an eternity until a voice broke the silence. "Ross is the only cool teacher in the school. Let's go!" said one of the ringleaders.

With that statement, they proceeded to run down the staircase and destroy anything or anyone in their path. I, on the other hand, with my heart racing and sweat pouring down my face, opened the door to my room and sat down. It felt great that I was considered the coolest teacher in the school, but somehow, the translation was lost due to the insanity of the situation at hand.

Cop cars began arriving within minutes as fighting spilled out into the street. Some neighborhood residents got involved in the melee without even knowing what was going on. Finally, with a large police presence, the fighting abated. All students were ordered out of the building and told to go home. The staff was told to remain inside until order was totally restored.

Within an hour, a directive came down from the district office telling us that the school would be closed the remainder of the week and that we should report back to work the following Monday. Under a police escort, teachers and administrators were led to their cars. Never in my ten years at I.S.24 was I so glad to get out of the neighborhood, although I must admit that the bus ride with "Jesse James" ran a close second.

As I was to find out at a later date, the remainder of that week was filled with meetings between community leaders, representatives from the police and fire departments, local school board members, representatives from the board of education and the clergy. Their main goal, of course, was to diffuse a volatile situation and restore order to both I.S.24 and the neighborhood. Ultimately realizing that Jennings was out and that nothing could precipitate his return, community leaders accepted the best offer they could obtain from the local school board and the district superintendent. With the approval of the board of education, a deal was reached and finalized with the appointment of a new principal, recommended by Charles Rogers, the district superintendent.

I remember thinking how despicable and repulsive this entire scenario was as truckloads of supplies arrived at I.S.24 the following week. For years we had been under-supplied, and teachers had to scrounge around for the most basic of supplies. Now, due to the removal of a principal and a full-scale riot, our school looked like it was a participant in the Marshall Plan, which was used to rebuild Europe after World War II. Supplies, supplies, and more supplies. All part of the deal to placate community leaders and assist the new principal. I remember thinking: *Could you imagine what we would have gotten if someone died during the riot?* It was a damn disgrace!

Although everyone seemed pleased with the new agreement, the police, taking no chances, were everywhere when school resumed the following week. Prior to the commencement of classes that Monday morning, an emergency U.F.T. meeting was called. Our chapter chairman, Allan Banister, informed us about the deal that had been struck and gave us a short biography about our new principal. We would learn that Leonard Pell had worked for many years at the district office and had always been very cooperative with our union. He had shown that he was pro-teacher, followed the union contract to the letter, and was an overall "good guy." Given the circumstances leading up to his appointment, only one thought entered my mind. *This Pell guy has to have a big pair of cohones (balls)!*

Not being a total idiot, I surmised that at least two variables had to be in play for Leonard Pell to accept this precarious appointment. Either he'd been promised the world or he had no choice in the matter. Of course, both scenarios were true, as I would soon discover. The bottom line was, if Pell didn't accept the job, he'd never be offered another principal position again. Sure, he could have kept his cushy job at the district office, but he was smart enough to realize his boss, the district superintendent, would have made his life one filled with misery.

When Leonard Pell entered our library, he was greeted with a standing ovation. He began his first staff meeting like an individual who had been sentenced to death, yet given the option to choose his poison. Although I had never met the man, I clearly sensed the uneasiness that pervaded his demeanor, mainly due to the circumstances that had led to his appointment.

In front of us stood a man, approximately six feet tall, 185 pounds, 48-50 years of age. Here was an individual with the unenviable task of having to appease an extremely distrusting staff, despite what our chapter chairman had told us, a back-stabbing sistrict superintendent, as you'll later discover; and a community wary of anyone from the district office. As if all of this wasn't bad enough, he had to restore order to a school that had experienced rioting the previous week. For whatever reason, considering the fact that I had become totally anti-administration, I felt instant compassion for this man. Knowing we've all, at sometime in our lives, been caught between "a rock and a hard place," his attempt at a "stiff upper lip" was quite meritorious.

Without trying to get ahead of myself, Pell would survive many years at I.S.24. Whether you liked the man or not, you had to admire his resiliency and the skill he displayed placating so many factions who never trusted him or each other. If one had to evaluate what Pell's greatest asset was, unequivocally, it had to be his backing of his teachers. Never, in my dealings with him as both a teacher and a chapter chairman, did he ever take the side of a student over any member of his staff. His attitude was "the teacher is right, and the student is wrong." This put him in good stead with the staff. His philosophy was a far cry from that of Claude Jennings, whose true colors, once unveiled, were dangerous to everyone associated with I.S.24.

Leonard Pell and Sam Ross, as you will find out in greater detail, would butt heads on numerous occasions. Every confrontation was due to union business. My distrust and outright hostility towards this man would reach unimaginable heights. Having so many years to reflect on our relationship, I've softened my opinion about his actions on numerous matters. I've come to realize that on many occasions, through no fault of his own, he found himself in no-win situations. However, there were times when he could have made a decision but was gutless for fear of offending someone or some group. At times it seemed as if he was sitting on a wooden fence, leaning towards one side, then the other, until all he could decide on was which doctor to go to so he could have the splinters removed from his ass.

Yes, 22 years is a long time. I wish I could inform you that Leonard Pell is in the best of health and enjoying his family and a well-deserved retirement. What he endured as a teacher, his years at the district office, and his ultimate sentence to I.S.24, gives him this right. I'm sorry to say I have no idea where he is and how he is doing. The passage of time has left me void of information about this very complex man. Admittedly, I could make a phone call and find out about such matters, but something inside of me tells me to "let sleeping dogs lie." Who knows, maybe some day.

CHAPTER SIX

Administrators: Us vs. Them

It is a noted fact that many individuals during their incarceration in a penal institution will try to assimilate as much knowledge as possible from fellow inmates if their intent is to continue their criminal careers upon their release. Upon further examination, why would anyone seek guidance from a source that has already failed, as attested to by their own incarceration? Isn't it logical to wait for your release, and then seek out someone who has eluded law enforcement for years?

Basically using the same logic, why would anyone purchase stocks recommended by a broker who, for whatever reason, is constantly picking losers? Doesn't it make sense to search for a broker who has a proven track record of making money for his or her clients? With these analogies as a background, I would like to discuss one of my favorite topics: administrators.

When one mentions a school administration, they are referring to individuals who are at the top of the school's brain chain. They are the movers and shakers, as well as the initiators of the events that go on in the educational facility. Previously I discussed my interaction with three principals from I.S.24. Now, it humbles me to ask you to join me as I enter the world of the assistant principal.

Before introducing you to a number of assistant principals I worked under during my tenure at I.S.24, I feel it is pertinent to give you the contents of a theory I formulated very early in my career regarding these individuals. I fervently believe that my conclusions have withstood the test of time and are still valid in the educational environment that exists today.

Undoubtedly there are, and hopefully will always be, exceptions to my theory, and I'm thankful for that. I wholeheartedly concede that there are some brilliant and accomplished AP's who warrant only admiration from their colleagues, as well as from those teachers who are under their tutelage. Unfortunately, there are a far greater number who are outright incompetents that bring denigration to themselves and the title they hold.

Here are the essential components of my theory on assistant principals:

1. Many individuals become AP's in order to secure a higher salary and prestige. Since this is common in the business world and most professions, there is nothing wrong with having and achieving such a goal.

2. An extremely high percentage of those individuals that attain the title of assistant principal could not teach their way out of a paper bag when they were in a classroom setting.

This, without a doubt, is the controversial aspect of my theory. On-the-job experience has led me to deduce that many AP's are classroom rejects who aspired to their present position in order to escape from the rigor and turmoil of classroom life. Having experienced almost total burnout myself, I cannot denigrate these people for their need to get out of the classroom. What I find totally despicable is the fact that, like the incarcerated criminal who tries to further his education by learning from another detainee, we as teachers are now expected to go to these classroom dropouts for guidance and assistance.

I always found it reprehensible that these classroom failures, better known in my vernacular as "pencil pushers," are often given the responsibility of observing teachers presenting their lessons in class, and then writing up a report called an observation critiquing their performance. Part of their responsibility in observing your lesson is to inform you of your strengths and weaknesses in regards to the lesson you presented and your ability to teach. They are then required to help you with your deficiencies so you can improve your lesson presentation, enhance your teaching abilities, and improve your classroom management. All of this is pretty asinine when you consider the fact that, in many instances, their performance in the classroom was quite pathetic in its own right!

My take on this entire mess is quite simple. Just because a teacher takes the necessary administrative courses, and passes a license exam, does not qualify that person to observe and critique members of the teaching staff, or successfully carry out the responsibilities their new job demands of them. Hopefully, the following events will give the reader greater insight into what transpired at I.S.24 during my ten-year tenure. Of course I cannot write about every incident that took place, but I believe you'll get a sense of the environment we were teaching in as well as the assistant principals who were supposed to be our saviors.

Please believe me when I state that I never was predisposed towards confrontation when I began my teaching career. Unfortunately, being thrust into situations where help was needed and little was rendered, cynicism replaced optimism. Although some tried valiantly to be of assistance, their mediocrity, combined with the arrogance and unprofessional performance of their colleagues, led to what I call the three D's: distrust, disgust, and outright dislike. What could have been a smooth working professional staff became an "Us vs. Them" relationship. This, more than anything else, led to a breakdown in school structure and the students eventually bore the brunt of this constant friction.

Linda Stolle was a seventh grade AP and unfortunately for me, my supervisor for a 3-4 year period. Lazy, slovenly dressed, always looking like she had been caught in the middle of a hurricane, this member of the administration was supposed to be my mentor and someone I could go to with any problem. Rarely ever lifting her humongous behind off her overly snug chair, it was a miracle to see Linda on patrol or helping with the changing of classes. Adding to this unflattering character study was the never-denied allegations by numerous members of our staff that before her appointment as assistant principal, Linda Stolle was a horrendous teacher.

Being as fair-minded as possible, I decided I had no right to make a snap judgement about her abilities until I witnessed her possible ineptness in person. Much to my dismay, any thought of her gaining my trust and respect vanished quite rapidly. Watching her cover a class, due to teacher absenteeism, was an abomination. To watch her being pelted with all sorts of objects, laughed at due to her slovenly appearance, and being treated like a piece of garbage instead of an AP was outright repulsive. How was I to respect such an incompetent? Although still clinging to the slightest bit of hope, it was the following event which made her an everlasting enemy and could have cost me my job.

One morning while teaching my top science class, Ms. Stolle appeared at my door and stated, "Mr. Ross, I'd like to speak with you now!" in a nasty tone of voice.

Showing no inclination towards professional courtesy, I decided to ignore her, as she was not following proper protocol. In a more sarcastic tone, she repeated her request to speak with me. Trying to diffuse a possible conflict in the making, I calmly and professionally told her, "Ms.

Stolle, I'm in the middle of an important lesson and if whatever has to be discussed is not an emergency, I'll speak to you after I dismiss my class."

This again was standard procedure and professional courtesy.

Returning to the blackboard to continue my work on a chemical equation, I felt someone grab my forearm. Immediately I made a fist and turned. To my amazement, there was Ms. Stolle, who had somehow snuck up behind me, forcing my now clenched fist to hit my jaw each time she slowly enunciated each of the following words

"I-said-I-want-to-talk-to-you-now!" she stated with such animosity.

Although each shot to my jaw was nothing more than a minor tap, just imagine what it was like being forced to hit yourself in your jaw nine times.

It is almost impossible to put into words the feelings of shock and rage that erupted in my being. Weighing in at about 300 pounds, Stolle was pretty strong, yet as soon as the shock of her action wore off, I freed my arm from her powerful grip and proceeded to throw her into the blackboard.

Fighting a raging urge to slap the shit out of her, I decided to leave her alone. I had never in my life raised my hands to a woman, and I wouldn't allow this despicable embarrassment to dignify this type of behavior on my part. As she lumbered to the door, my students threw papers and garbage at her as well as spewed out some serious verbal abuse. I was really impressed with their loyalty, yet not enthralled with their vocabulary. (That's pretty funny coming from me.)

It took a couple of minutes before things settled down in the classroom. After we cleaned up the mess on the floor, I warned my class that it would only be a matter of minutes before I was summoned to the principals' office. I extolled them to respect whoever would be taking over the class until I returned. It was really uplifting when a number of my students expressed their concern about my well being.

"I will be fine! You know me. I'll be back in twenty minutes," I told my students. Even with this assurance, quite a few were worried that I'd lose my job. I really loved these kids! Besides their intelligence, they were just a pleasure to be with. Any teacher would have found it an honor to have them as their class!

Within a matter of minutes, a fellow colleague arrived and told me, "Leonard Pell wants to see you in his office."

Given a great send off by my kids, in the form of a standing ovation, I began my trek down to the first floor. Along the way, I decided that I would go on the offensive as soon as I entered Pell's office. Although seeming to always back his teachers, I couldn't make up my mind what Pell's take on this incident would be. Stolle was still an AP, therefore one of his people.

Upon entering Pell's office and before he could utter a word, I went on a verbal rampage. Since I hadn't been treated in a professional manner, I decided to throw out any vestige of normal protocol. Basically pretending to be having a fit and totally out of my mind, I looked Pell directly in his eyes and, using his first name, stated, "Leonard! If that piece of shit ever walks into my classroom again, I'll throw her right out of the fucking window!" I screamed, showing no respect to my new principal or his despicable associate.

This was really funny considering Stolle's size, my inability to lift her, and the fact that bars and grating were attached to each window to deter break-ins or, I guess toss-outs.

I continued. "How dare she embarrass me in front of my class, and where did she get the nerve to lift her hands to my person?" I shouted like a maniac.

With the look of blood draining from Pell's face, I turned to Stolle and told her, "I don't give a shit if you place a letter in my file! As a matter of fact, I don't give a shit if you call the district superintendent or the fucking FBI. I'm really considering filing assault and civil charges against you. I warn you, stay the fuck away from me!" My rage now reached its pinnacle.

With that, I stormed out of Pell's office. Realistically, what could either one of them do to me? During this entire episode, neither Stolle nor Pell uttered a single word. Although not thrilled with my vocabulary, it did add to the dramatic effect I was seeking.

When I returned to my class, I was again given a standing ovation, which was greatly appreciated. My kids were elated that I hadn't been fired. Of course, when they asked me what had happened I replied, "Not much."

They were pretty sharp kids and already had figured out that I must have gone off the walls. When the bell rang, I thanked them all for being so great and received a load of "low fives" as they left the room.

Later in the day, I received a memo from Pell's office requesting my presence. Not regretting my earlier performance, I decided to enter his office in the most professional manner and proceed from there. After knocking and being told to enter, much to my surprise, Pell complimented me on my earlier performance. With his statement, "That was great!" he requested that I sit down and relax.

With this being our first personal encounter with each other, I really respected the man for backing me up. He could have caused me some serious grief if he wanted to, with being fired a definite possibility.

As I stated earlier, Pell was pro-teacher. As I also related to the reader, Leonard Pell and I would really get into some heavy confrontations when I became chapter chairman. At times, our relationship, or lack there of, would border on open warfare. Even when this occurred, I never forgot how he backed me during the preceding incident, but as chapter chairman of I.S.24, I represented our union membership, and this responsibility made it impossible for us to be friends. It was my job to fight for everything our membership needed and against anyone who posed a threat to us. Besides, there was no way that I'd have even one member of our chapter questioning where my allegiance lay. The reality was, it was "Us vs. Them," and this would never change at I.S.24.

In direct contrast to Linda Stolle, Sandra Elliot was extremely well organized, had been a great teacher, and commanded respect from the entire student body. With my ascent to an eighth grade teaching position, Sandra became my immediate supervisor. Our relationship was purely professional and quite refreshing. Already into my eighth year of teaching, I was not adverse to any new ideas or techniques, which would make my life easier.

Although Sandra was accessible to those teachers in need of her assistance, was constantly patrolling the halls, and always helping out where needed, I noticed what I considered a flaw in her personality. Again, I must reiterate that I was really impressed with her professionalism, understanding of our students' needs, and overall work ethic. Unfortunately, she would not accept any input from staff members as far as implementation of new ideas, especially changes in the curriculum. This would eventually lead to some tense moments between us. The bottom line was, Sandra was too rigid as far as procedures, curriculum, and many other aspects of her job. The more I interacted with her, the greater was my belief that she was a borderline obsessive-compulsive personality.

At times, I really felt badly for Sandra Elliot. She could never deviate from this straight and narrow path, even if it was warranted. Making matters worse was her belief that the students came first, and we as teachers were nothing better than second-class citizens. Although giving her the benefit of the doubt, due to the tremendous respect I had for her, I intuitively knew that we were on course for a head-on collision. Unfortunately, my students would be caught in the middle of what eventually would be a struggle for supremacy.

Before explaining the overall situation which led to our eventual confrontation, it is pertinent that the reader be cognizant of the following realities that were in play at I.S.24.

A. During my eighth year at I.S.24, I taught what was classified as a "self-contained" class. These types of classes consisted of students who, due to behavioral problems, did not fare well in the mainstream school population. A self-contained class meant that the students were kept in the same classroom with the same teacher for all of their subjects and only left this setting to go to gym and lunch.

The students that comprised these classes were from every spectrum of the educational ladder. Some could read on a college level whereby others couldn't read a first grade primer. What they all had in common was discipline problems. In order to improve safety conditions at 24, these students were removed from mainstream classes and placed in this self-contained setting.

B. Of equal importance was the fact that, for five consecutive years, our school had the distinct honor of having the lowest reading scores in the entire city of New York. There we were, right on the bottom of the list published by the New York Times. Imagine, five years in a row, dead last! What a disgrace!

Since my students were with me most of the day and I didn't have to worry about when a period began or ended, I decided to change the normal reading practices that had failed so miserably year after year. My rationale was simple: Let them read whatever they wanted to read! What did we have to lose? We couldn't fall any lower in the ratings. Even if they used longer paper, we'd still be last. It was tragic that most fifth graders read better than a majority of my kids. Something had to be done!

Every morning, like clockwork, my students would come into my room and start reading. Advanced readers were paired with slower readers in a one-on-one setting, giving them the personalized attention that they needed to improve their reading skills. My responsibilities in this non-authorized experiment were few, due to self-imposed limitations. Basically, my job was to supervise the classroom groupings and make sure things were running smoothly. As often as possible I would sit and help the most illiterate of my students, and they really liked this personalized attention. The last ten minutes of the session, each child wrote a couple of lines about what they had read. Their partner helped with this if help was needed. Beyond any doubt, the best part of this entire process was the fact that each student could read what he or she wanted. X-rated materials, of course, were not allowed.

I was like a broken record when my kids came into class each morning. All they knew was that the first thing they did to start the school day was to read! Never did I deviate from this rule! Bring in whatever you'd like to learn about, and read it. Cartoons, the sports section, a teen magazine, etc. Read, read, and read some more!

As far as I was concerned, if my concept on teaching reading was correct and it helped these young people to improve their reading and writing skills, I didn't give a damn what anyone else thought about it. The old practices had failed miserably, so why not try mine and see if I could be successful?

Sure enough, word reached Mrs. Elliot, and to be as kind as possible, she did not approve of my experiment which deviated from the curriculum. I was sent a letter informing me that I had to follow the strict format of the eighth grade curriculum or there would be repercussions. By now, I know you realize I couldn't have cared less about Elliot's threat. Big deal, another letter in my file—so what! The more the merrier! Besides, if Leonard Pell took her side in this dispute, he could always "punish me" by having me teach mainstream classes. There was no way in the world that this would happen!

After months of participating in the "Sam Ross theory on reading," city-wide reading exams were given. Much to my delight and Sandra Elliot's chagrin, results showed reading scores for my kids soared 2-3 grade levels. You would have thought that Sandra would have been somewhat satisfied with these spectacular results, but now that you're practically insiders into the workings or non-workings of I.S.24, you know that she was totally bent out of shape.

Summoned to her office, I was immediately accused of giving my students the correct answers and informed that they would be re-tested the following week. This was outright lunacy! Why punish my kids for doing so great on these exams? Sure, she didn't like my reading program. So what? Why take it out on my kids who had busted their butts for so many months and were finally enjoying reading?

By the time I had finished telling "my readers" that they were going to be re-tested due to Elliot's desire to kill my reading program, my kids were totally pissed, and that's putting it mildly. She was, in all honesty, lucky that one of them didn't kick her ass in! I couldn't believe the "follow the syllabus stupidity" that such an intelligent and caring individual was trying to shove down my throat.

Every day leading up to the re-test was filled with motivational speeches on my part and questions such as, "How could that bitch do this to us?" on the part of my students.

I knew that if I could calm them down and rebuild their self-esteem, everything would work out to their benefit. Convincing them of this was another matter altogether.

Finally, the day of the reading exam was at hand. I reassured my readers that they would do just fine on the test. When Elliot arrived with the exams, I was informed in front of my class that I had to leave the room while testing was going on. Upon hearing this, my kids were ready to explode.

"Relax and show them how smart you are," I implored my students.

"Do it for yourselves, not for me," I practically pleaded.

"You'll do fine!" I said as if my banishment was inconsequential.

With that, I walked out of the room, pissed off at the entire world!

Being totally honest, I didn't sleep well that evening since I knew their test scores would be on Leonard Pell's desk the next morning. I kept praying that my kids hadn't choked due to the unnecessary pressure of having to take the exam a second time and do as well, if not better, than before. I also hoped they hadn't said, "Fuck this test!" in response to my being told to leave the room.

The next morning, there was a letter in my mailbox informing me to report to Leonard Pell's office. As I entered his hallowed sanctuary, there was Pell and an upbeat Sandra Elliot. She had the look of a hunter with its prey in her cross hairs. In this case, the prey was me.

When Pell opened the envelope from the district office, a huge smile came over his face. He informed me that my kids had done even better on the retest. You could have scraped me off the ceiling that's how happy I was for both my students and my method of teaching reading.

Nothing could dampen my feelings of grandeur as I bolted out of Leonard Pell's office to find my students in the schoolyard. Having to wait for them to show up for homeroom was much too long a delay with the news I had. They needed to know now, how great they had done and how proud I was of them. Not even the searing gaze of Sandra Elliot would deter me from this goal. My students instinctively knew they had done well just by the way I was running toward them. Either that or I had totally flipped out and was looking to kill someone. The huge smile on my face assured them it was the former.

Later that morning, I thought about Sandra Elliot. Being pro-student, I knew that inwardly, she was happy that my kids had done extremely well on the exam. On the other hand, as far as "radical me" was concerned, part of her had wished that my class had tanked the exam so she could lambaste me for my innovative techniques, as well as the fact that I wouldn't listen to her and follow the curriculum to the letter. I knew that from this day forward, I'd be matching wits with this cunning antagonist. It was truly a shame that we couldn't at least coexist. We both cared so much about our kids and only wanted the best for them. Sandra's problem was the fact that she was too rigid, which made it impossible for her to deviate from the "letter of the law" as mandated in the board of education in regards to the curriculum.

I sincerely believe that if Sandra Elliot and I could have worked together, we could have accomplished so much more, especially for those students with limited reading abilities. Unfortunately, this would never happen. During summer vacation, I learned that Sandra Elliot had transferred out of I.S.24. Unfortunately, our school had lost an excellent administrator and mentor to many of its students. I never found out why she had transferred, and I hoped it wasn't due to the friction that existed between us for the rest of that school year. If only she had learned to lighten up a bit. Between us, we could have made such a difference in the lives of so many children. Unfortunately, she never realized how alike we were. Sadly, she couldn't change who she was, and I wouldn't change to appease her or her belief in how things should be done.

Oh, by the way, if this sounds like the movie *Stand and Deliver* you're correct, but, if you think you've caught me in a lie, guess again. My experience occurred long before the movie appeared on TV in the late 80s. The movie itself retold the story of Jaime Escalante and his Chicano students and how they shocked the academic community with the results of their 1982 national calculus exam. My kids only shocked Sandra Elliot and those at the district office. To me, their accomplishment was just as great as Escalantes' kids. Too bad that others didn't have as much faith in them, or in my reading program, as I did!

Matt Polsky was one of the most simple, yet complex individuals I ever met during my career at I.S.24. Utterly brilliant would be an understatement. I guess I acquired an immediate affinity towards him when I shockingly watched the man do the Sunday *New York Times* crossword puzzle in less than half an hour. I loved to do the puzzles every day, but Polsky put me to shame. To watch this man put in answer after answer with such speed reminded me of a master artisan creating a work for the ages.

Before becoming an assistant principal, Polsky was a social studies teacher. On many an occasion, I had the opportunity to observe him teaching a class due to teacher absenteeism. The man had the uncanny ability to mesmerize students. Without a doubt, he was the true exception to my theory that AP's couldn't teach their way out of a paper bag. When you were given a write up after he observed one of your lessons, there was no way to vilify the man if he pointed out areas you needed to improve in. Bottom line, the man was just incredible.

Matt was as affable as anyone I had met in the teaching profession. Always accessible to students and teachers, there were times we just sat and spoke about politics, history, and numerous other topics. As brilliant as he was, what I respected the most about the man was the fact that he never spoke down to anyone. Unfortunately, it was his affable nature that seemed to be his greatest liability. No, I had nothing to do with his transfer just in case this thought has crossed your mind.

Due to the stressful environment the teachers at I.S.24 found themselves mired in, and the lack of support we received from the school's administration, the "Us vs. Them" mind set that most teachers at I.S.24 had adopted, eventually claimed Matt as a victim. In an ideal school setting, I fervently believe that Polsky would have been the perfect administrator. In ours, he became a "fence sitter" whom nobody seemed to trust. Here was a poor guy who just wanted to be liked by everyone. I honestly believe he didn't have a mean bone in his body. Unfortunately, if he was too nice to our staff, the administration got on him. If under certain instances he had to be forceful with a teacher, we, the union, got on his case. This poor guy was in a "catch 22" situation, and no matter what he did, he could never win. As time wore on, I could see this dilemma sucking the educational life force from Matt's being.

Upon reflection, even today I'm still amazed that everybody was fighting everybody. "Us vs. Them," the union vs. the administration, our school vs. the district office, and on it went. The irony of the entire mess was the fact that there were no spoils of war to be had. It's not as if we were in the corporate world whereby screwing someone could reap great rewards. In essence, we all had nothing, and there was nothing attainable to warrant such strife. Pitiful, if you ask me.

I recall walking into Polsky's office one day, seeking an answer to a question that bothered me, especially in Matt's case.

"Matt, what the hell are you doing here?" I inquired.

Before he had a chance to answer, I kept up my third degree. "You have so much to offer people. You could be a college professor and get all the respect you deserve. You could work directly out of the board of education, writing up programs or formulating a new social studies syllabus. The private sector would love a guy like you. Why do you need this garbage? Here you are in the middle of a war, and no matter which side wins, you lose!" I adamantly stated.

Matt's reply was one which many of my co-workers would use sometime during their career at I.S.24. "I got caught up in the system," was the simple reply from this brilliant individual.

In essence, Matt explained, "Every time I'd think of leaving, we'd get a raise, thereby making it easier for me to pay alimony and child support. Adding to my dilemma was the decent medical coverage I enjoyed for me and my family," he stated defensively.

Finally, Matt had met and married a wonderful woman who also was an educator and just so happened to be part of our staff. All of these factors, plus others, I'm sure, which he didn't reveal, had relegated his remaining in a system that wasn't worth the sweat off his brow. Despite my utter disdain for AP's, Matt was one I felt great empathy towards. I sincerely hope that today he is working somewhere that his talents are truly appreciated or enjoying a well-deserved retirement.

Ben Johnson was the most colorful AP I ever dealt with. Ben was born on one of the Caribbean Islands and migrated with his family to the United States. Entering the teaching profession after college, he eventually scaled the educational ladder and was finally appointed as acting AP at I.S.24. After quite a few years, he received his permanent assistant principal's appointment to our school, and deservedly so. I adamantly believe that the delay in his permanent appointment was precipitated by three factors: He had an accent, he was black, and he was "independent." In essence, Ben Johnson had a trait I found lacking in most administrators: A pair of balls. His problem, if one wanted to characterize it as such, was the fact that he wouldn't take shit from anyone.

I personally didn't consider this no-nonsense approach to be a flaw in Ben's character, but rather a major attribute. Ben treated everyone equally, which was in direct contrast to most of his administrative colleagues. At least you knew where he was coming from, which couldn't be said about many of his backstabbing cohorts. Here was a man that constantly patrolled the hallways and staircases. Carrying what looked like a miniature nightstick, Ben was out there looking to get involved in any fracas that might erupt. Our students, even those with diminished mental capacity, stayed out of his way. When I later became chapter chairman of I.S.24, I was privy to administrative meetings, and to tell the truth, everyone, including the principal, was petrified of Ben, especially when he was in one of his moods. With Ben, it was never "Us vs. Them," but rather Ben against the world.

Ben and I really didn't have much to say to each other, except the informal acknowledgment of nodding our heads when our paths crossed. If we managed a "hello" or "what's up," it was a major conversation. Realistically, there were two reasons why we didn't have much contact with each other: I never sent a student to him for discipline, and we were located on different floors from one another. Although he later told me he respected me for the job I was doing, until we became "neighbors," just a simple hello would suffice. I always knew one reality check when it came to Ben; you never wanted to get on his bad side.

Like everything else at I.S.24, our relationship would eventually change, and in this instance, for the better. The year after Ben's appointment, I was given an official room right next to his office on the third floor. One afternoon after early dismissal, I heard the sound of a saxophone emanating from Ben's office. Much to my surprise, there he was playing some serious jazz. When he saw me, he motioned for me to come in and sit down. After he had finished his piece, I told him that I was very impressed. My father was a professional musician, and soon we were discussing many aspects of the music business and his playing. In ten minutes, we said more to each other than all the previous years combined, and a newfound bond was formed. On many an occasion, I would lend Ben music books, and for this he was extremely appreciative. Besides our love of music, I believe that Ben really liked me due to the fact that I was one of a select few that he would goof around with. Adding to this relationship was the fact that I, just like Ben, didn't like his colleagues.

Having a room next to Ben's office was an experience in itself. At times you could feel the walls shaking, which is amazing since they were made of concrete, steel, and plaster. It seemed that no matter how much Ben was respected and feared, there were always some fools trying to make a name for themselves by attempting to kick Ben's ass. As hard as they tried, none were ever successful. If they somehow managed to get in the first punch, Ben made sure he got in the last one!

At this juncture in my book, I'm sure you aren't shocked by the endless physical confrontations I constantly refer to. Have no fear, there will be many more! If by chance you get the impression we were nothing more than thugs ourselves, I ask you to never lose sight of the environment we found ourselves in. I, too, find it reprehensible that many of my colleagues, myself included, had to engage in physical confrontation in order to maintain some semblance of order in our school. I fervently believe that 99% of us never went looking for physical altercations. Most of us had our own children and would have been irate, to say the least, if their teacher so much as laid a finger on them. What was so sad was the fact that most of us just wanted to teach. I cannot tell you how many times teachers, as well as students, were assaulted in our school. You didn't have to go looking for trouble; it found you.

We've all heard of the expression "tough love." Well, people like Ben Johnson or a Sam Ross must have been doing something correct, judging by the number of former students who visited us long after their graduation. Whether this was the result of an altercation, a moment of compassion, or just the giving of time to listen to a problem, something warranted such visits. In retrospect, maybe it simply was the fact that they knew we cared.

Although there were numerous assistant principals that I had to deal with during my tenure at I.S.24, I chose these individuals just to give you a flavor of the broad spectrum of personalities and attitudes that existed there. Although a majority of the assistant principals I discussed were presented to you in a somewhat positive light, a greater percentage of this exclusive fraternity was incompetent. When I transferred to I.S.302, I was not shocked to find that the same level of incompetence was prevalent there, as well.

Unfortunately, the "Us vs. Them" phenomenon also existed in this new educational environment. Again I encountered petty infighting, mistrust, and in some cases, dislike bordering on hatred. After a while, I began to question if this, "Us vs. Them" attitude was ingrained in the system itself? I concluded that this scenario also existed in the corporate environment and other venues where individuals vied for leadership roles, advancement, monetary gain, etc. What I found to be the difference between the mistrust and infighting in our schools as opposed to that in the corporate world was one undeniable fact; our children always suffered the repercussions.

To this day, I wish this "Us vs. Them" mentality could possibly be changed to "we." Hopefully, someday this will come to fruition because as of now, "we" does not exist. Imagine, more than two decades since my retirement, and this attitude is as blatant as ever. When I speak with today's teachers, it's still:

"This damn assistant principal is such a...."

or

"This administration is so full of...!"

When I hear such incessant complaints, one thought comes to mind: *Will this Us Vs Them bullshit ever change?*

There is not a semblance of doubt, on my part, that this mistrust, lack of respect, and in some cases, outright hatred, is ingrained in the system itself. How or if it will ever be exorcised, I have no idea. Personally, I don't hold out much hope that this will ever happen.

Trying not to be a total pessimist, I have come to realize in recent years that there may be one avenue that might be used to possibly decrease this perpetual animosity. I honestly believe that the answer lies in administrators being held to the same criteria of accountability that everyone wants to see imposed on our teachers. Maybe, just maybe, this double-edged sword can at least put a damper on one of our educational system's most divisive forces.

CHAPTER SEVEN

Survival of the Fittest: The Staff

Anyone who has ever doubted the existence of an all-knowing, all-seeing Supreme Being had only to spend one year teaching at I.S.24 to reconcile this age-old question. Of course there was never a sighting of the Almighty, nobody discovered a new cloth of Turin, there was never an Immaculate Conception, or any other significant religious revelation. Irrespective of your religious persuasion or beliefs, either due to the reality of where we taught or the near insanity that most of us experienced on an daily basis, even an atheist had to eventually believe in a Higher Power. How, you may ask, could one possibly reach such a conclusion considering what I've already read about I.S.24 and what I'm sure will be introduced to me in the upcoming pages? The main reason I knew there had to be a Supreme Being was simple: Only a Higher Authority could bring together a teaching staff as off the wall, yet as spectacular, as that which existed at I.S.24.

No one could ever convince me that the group of individuals that comprised our staff was assembled by "the luck of the draw." No way could so many have been so unlucky! To this day, I find it inconceivable that such a conglomeration of individuals could have haphazardly been brought together to constitute what would eventually form the teaching staff of I.S.24. There are not enough adjectives in the English language that can describe these individuals who, in some cases, were my colleagues for ten years. No, I've never doubted there was a G-d because only this spiritual entity could accomplish such a spectacular feat!

Before I discuss the staff which I had the distinct honor of being a part of, I feel I would be negligent if I didn't impart to the reader a belief that, to this day, I feel still holds water: Teachers are born, not made! Undoubtedly any individual can be taught technique, nuances, and countless other aspects of this profession. Unfortunately, no matter how much education you attain or number of degrees you can accrue, I believe with all of my heart that one fact cannot be dismissed: You are born with the innate ability to teach!

For an individual to be a successful teacher, he or she must have various character traits in their personality that will help them to achieve this goal. These traits, I believe, are G-d given and are biological in nature. Just as the genes on a chromosome determine what a person looks like, what intellectual capacities they may possibly attain, and what sex they are, there must be a genetic code which incorporates the characteristics that will allow an individual to be a great educator.

Not everyone can have this genetic capacity. The tools necessary to be a doctor, lawyer, athlete, and so on, are not found on every microscopic band that constitutes a chromosome, yet it is on some of these bands that we find the combination necessary to be successful in these various professions. Where this information comes from is a matter of conjecture, but one fact cannot be denied: If it is not G-d given, then at least G-d knows where and how it originated.

In order to comprehend the stress and anxiety that my co-workers and I experienced during my ten years at I.S.24, only one simple fact must be bared: Out of the 25 teachers that started their careers with me, only five remained after a five-year period had elapsed. Twenty individuals, for whatever reasons, resigned from their chosen profession, and what remained was the "cream of the crop!" Unfortunately, what was lost were the hopes and aspirations of twenty people. To see a young woman put on roller skates and skate out the front door of our school, never to return, was heartbreaking. The fact that she had only lasted three days was an abomination. All of her schooling, endless hours of study, and so many dreams, gone! I can't conceive of any other profession which could incur such a loss of manpower except a combat unit on the verge of annihilation. As the title states: My Life in the Trenches…

The staff of I.S.24 consisted of people from all walks of life. All had a common purpose: teaching and survival and not necessarily in that order. In retrospect, I would pit our staff against any and all comers as far as ability, intelligence, and overall performance were concerned.

One of my major objectives throughout this book was to make sure the reader remained aware of the insanity we encountered on a daily basis at I.S.24. In order to continue to exist, each and every one of my colleagues developed techniques that they hoped would insure their continued viability, as well as their capability to impart knowledge. I adamantly believe that it was these techniques, as well as our united dislike of administrators and those in positions of power, that were core ingredients in helping us remain a viable staff.

Those in power could never comprehend that I.S.24 was our home from at least 8:00 a.m. to 3:00 p.m., five days a week. Broken windows, doors, drugs, robberies, assaults, graffiti, and so many other disheartening elements contributed to the environment we all found ourselves a part of, yet this was where we lived, and we defended it against all adversaries. To survive, each and every one of us became "a piece of work," and to this day, I consider it an honor to have been a part of this insane conglomeration of individuals!

As is the case with most concentrations of people, our staff had within it numerous factions, cliques, and sects. There were the pot heads and pills users, as well as the gays and heterosexuals. Mixed in were the intellectuals, the jocks, the nerds and ass-kissers. We had Blacks, Whites, Hispanics, and representatives of other ethnicities. Then there were those who were adamant that they were totally sane, and everyone else was nuts. No matter where you fit into this mix, you soon realized that we all had a common goal: Do our job and get back home in one piece. As diverse as we were, one key factor always remained a constant: When we were threatened, we closed ranks and became a single and quite formidable entity.

It is with deep regret that I cannot write about all of the sacrificial lambs that I worked with during my ten years at I.S.24. To do so would turn this book into a massive tome. What I have attempted to do is to give the reader a better feel for what, at times, was the outlandish behavior of some of my co-workers. Some of the funniest situations and stories that have occurred during my lifetime emerged from this group of rejects, undesirables, and what many deemed insane individuals. I ask that you never forget that through thick and thin, all we had was each other, and there was no doubt that a number of us were skating on some really thin ice.

One of the nicest and most hilarious colleagues that I had the honor to work with was Phil Selkin. Openly gay and proud of this fact, Phil was the epitome of formality. If he just met you five minutes ago or knew you for ten years, you were always addressed as Mr., Mrs., Miss, etc. Phil's favorite word when describing anyone he didn't like was "beast." To this day, when I see or hear this word, Phil's name immediately comes to mind. His expressive nature, jowl-like features, and vocal tonality gave him a magical flair.

When I began teaching at I.S.24, as previously noted, I was given a science program. At the first science department meeting, I was introduced to the vice-chairman of the department, Phil Selkin. After the debacle of my first bus ride home from I.S.24, I was informed by Phil that he lived in my neighborhood and that until I could purchase a car, he would pick me up and take me home from work. Not being homophobic, I thanked Phil for being a lifesaver but found it necessary to inform him that I was 100% heterosexual.

"Oh, Mr. Ross..." Phil replied.

From that moment on, I considered Phil a friend and a wonderful colleague.

Every ride to or from school was an adventure with Phil. As time passed and I got to know him better, I realized that Phil was one complicated piece of work. He was charming, quite intelligent, sophisticated, and extremely well versed in the arts. What overshadowed all of these attributes was his personification of proper etiquette. Equipped with all of these attributes, Phil had the innate ability to make anyone feel like a barbarian.

As the school year progressed, I realized that it was the norm for Phil to come to work impeccably dressed, never use vulgarity, and always speak the "King's English." It didn't take an Albert Einstein to ultimately realize that Phil did not belong in this environment of mayhem. I could picture him being the curator of a museum, hanging out with William Shakespeare, or being a member of the royal family of England. If one believes in reincarnation, then Phil did some serious shit to be sent to the hellhole he found himself teaching in.

As culturally correct as Selkin could be, he inadvertently would throw you a curve ball from out of nowhere, and you would be totally unprepared. One day on our way home, Phil, who drove a red Cadillac, said, "Mr. Ross, I have something to show you." This was accompanied with an impish look.

Having no idea what to expect, except a possible dissertation on the architectural history of the buildings on Eastern Parkway, Phil proceeded to get into the Eastern Parkway service lane. As he slowed to 5-10 miles per hour, prostitutes came running towards our car offering their services from $10-$25. Eventually waving them off with almost pompous snobbery, he began to chuckle in such a high pitch that his jowls appeared to expand and contract. With his final wave and high-pitched "ta ta," I started to laugh so hard that tears started to roll down my cheeks. Then, in a stoic yet reflective mood, he stated, "They love red Cadillacs!" as this huge grin spread across his entire face.

After this experience, nothing Phil Selkin ever did would totally catch me off guard. One fact would always remain constant: It would be done in good taste and with the utmost etiquette.

In direct contrast to Phil Selkin, and located at the other end of the cultural spectrum, was Robert Collins. Totally void of manners, brusque in nature, culturally deficient and exuding the persona of a madman, Collins instilled instant fear in anyone he came in contact with. Short hair, military demeanor, forearms like tree trunks, and an overall aura of meanness were characteristics that added credence to this illusion. Collins was definitely the type of person you didn't antagonize because you had no idea what he was capable of. Thankfully, he didn't fly off the handle too often and wasn't free with his hands.

Although the possessor of many characteristics that could irritate anyone, Bob had one in particular that irked even the most docile of my colleagues. Phil Selkin would definitely classify Bob Collins as a "beast" just by this action alone. It seemed that whenever or wherever we had lunch, Bob would eventually ask, "Do you want this?" or "Are you done with that?" in such an urgent way that one would think he hadn't eaten in 48 hours.

One day, I was having lunch in the teachers' cafeteria and shooting the breeze with a number of colleagues, including Bob. Then, out of nowhere, a couple of fingers gouged out some of the mashed potatoes from my plate. Immediately seeing it was Bob, I became so enraged I screamed, "You're a fucking animal!"

I then proceeded to pick up the rest of my potatoes and throw them in his face. I figured, *if you want to be an animal, I'll treat you like the savage you really are!* It didn't take me too long to realize the error of my ways, so I immediately got up and ran the hell out of there before the crazy bastard got hold of me and crushed me to death. Needless to say, I stayed out of Bob's way until things eventually cooled down a bit.

As crazy as Collins was, he had so many attributes. Bob was an excellent teacher, tremendous disciplinarian, great innovator, etc. I always believed that if I found myself in a dangerous situation, I'd want him covering my back. Collins always amazed me! If a fire broke out, Bob would be there trying to put it out. If a brawl erupted, there would be Bob trying to separate the combatants. If one of our female students was in distress, there was "hard-ass Bob" trying to console her in a fatherly fashion. In retrospect, Collins was one piece of work, yet irrespective of the mashed potato incident, I did consider him a friend and definitely respected him as a teacher. Thankfully, he couldn't read minds because on many an occasion when I saw him, I'd think, *Well, here comes Mr. Potato Head.*

Steve Wright was basically a nice guy. Unfortunately, he was the butt of many a joke due to the fact that he had changed the pronunciation of his last name, so the student population wouldn't goof on him. Much to his chagrin, many of our students, who were literate, knew how to pronounce his name correctly, so inadvertently, the only person he was fooling was himself. Numerous staff members, as you should realize by now, were merciless and always called him by his correct name. They did this so our illiterate students could hear it and use the correct pronunciation, further antagonizing Steve.

In no uncertain terms, Steve was an exceptional teacher. Like all of us, he did have at least one major character flaw: he was too free with his hands. Either due to an over-caring nature or lack of female companionship, Wright would be constantly seen with his arm around one of our female students, especially if she was Spanish. He was constantly being warned that he could get into some deep shit if he didn't stop this type of behavior. Steve never seemed to comprehend that we were truly his friends and didn't want to see him accused of being a pedophile, which he wasn't, or anything remotely resembling this accusation. Sadly, during the time that I knew him, he never refrained from this hands-on activity. Although this was just part of Steve's caring nature, unfortunately times were changing and such "caring" was met with skepticism.

The bottom line, as far as Steve was concerned, was the fact that he wasn't a lucky guy, as the following incident will bare witness to. One morning a member of our staff, all six feet four inches and 230 pounds or so of him came running into the main office. "I've been robbed!" he screamed almost inaudibly.

After calling 911, we calmed him down and asked what had happened. He related to us that, as he approached our building, this little kid popped out of nowhere.

"Give me your money!" he demanded.

My friend, laughing due to the size of this felon, told him, "Fuck off or I'll shove my foot up your ass!" and he began to laugh.

Before he realized what had happened, another youngster, basically his size and weight, had snuck up behind him and had put a gun to his head.

"Give the kid your money!" he said in a deep threatening voice.

My friend immediately complied.

To say the least, we were all somewhat shaken by the incident yet not totally freaked out since robberies were not uncommon in Bed-Sty. Any new occurrence just added to one's apprehension. Unfortunately, the longer you taught at I.S.24, the more emotionally immune you became to such events.

I'm not sure if it was this ever-growing cynicism or the fact that I was a sick bastard myself, but the behavior I exhibited five minutes later, after calling the police, was totally uncalled for and unacceptable! It was at this precise moment that Steve Wright came lumbering into the main office.

"Call the police! Call the police! You'll never guess what just happened!" he said, totally out of breath.

I calmly looked at Steve and said, "Let me guess. You were nearing the building when this little kid came up to you and said, 'Give me your money!' You probably said, 'Get the hell out of here before I shove my foot up your ass!' Then before you knew it, a big guy was behind you with a gun pointed at your head and he said, 'Give the kid the money!' in this deadly serious monotone voice."

The look of astonishment on Steve's face was indescribable. It was as if he were trying to decipher if I was a psychic or the whole incident had been a set up. When he started to ask, "How did you...?" a number of us started to crack up.

Finally, he was told what had previously happened and that the police were on their way.

Through the years, whenever I've thought of this incident, I've realized how lucky I was that Steve didn't get up from the chair we had provided him and try to kick my ass. Although Steve was not a violent person, I definitely could have pushed him over the edge with my insensitivity and outright stupidity. I definitely was a low-life when Steve really needed my help. I began to realize that I was becoming totally immune to any event that occurred in the neighborhood, be it inside the school building or outside on the street. Little did I realize that I was exhibiting all of the symptoms of burnout.

In retrospect, I must give Steve his due. No matter how many times I apologized to him, the result was the same. "Fuck off!" would be his reply.

It took more than a year for us to start speaking, and I deserved every moment of his silence. Hopefully, he is in good health and finally has met someone who's as caring an individual as he is. He definitely deserves such happiness.

84

At this moment in time, since this book is basically an autobiography, I feel I feel it would be remiss on my part if I didn't share with you a special event that occurred at I.S.24, of which I was a primary participant. There were many other places in this book where I believe I could have recounted this story, but I decided to put it in this chapter because I consider it a classic and because I was also a member of *The Staff.*

The next to the last day of my second year of teaching, I met up with two of my best friends who happened to be speaking with a teacher's aide. Although I had seen her around the building during the school year, I never had an occasion or a reason to speak with her. I guess it was her adulation of her sexual exploits that led me to say, "You're full of shit!" in a sarcastic tone of voice.

I must inform you that even at the age of 21, I was always respectful of women, never denigrated them, and held them in the highest esteem. Whatever the reason was for my uncharacteristic outburst, one fact couldn't be denied: Here was a young woman, describing such sexual exploits that even Larry Flint of *Hustler* magazine would have found it difficult not to blush.

When she turned to me and said, "Who the fuck are you?" in this arrogant tone, I figured *Well here's a class act,* and asked her the same question.

Knowing one of my friends was married and the other engaged I figured that this young "lady" was throwing out such bull because she knew these guys wouldn't cheat on their other halves. Being single at the time, I decided to call her bluff and prove to my buddies that she was full of it.

"What do I have to do to prove to you that I'm telling the truth?" she asked in an annoyed tone.

With these words of encouragement, I went and unlocked my classroom door and asked her to come in. To say the least, even clothed she had an incredible body. I've always loved Spanish women and still think they are the sexiest women in the world. With this in mind, I covered all of the windows in my room and, as nonchalantly as possible said, "Take off your blouse!"

She didn't hesitate for a second. "What now?" she inquired of me.

"Remove your bra!" I told her, trying to remain cool.

Her bra came off in a heartbeat. By now, my friends were getting a little antsy due to their commitments, and when she responded to my request to remove her jeans, they were headed to the front door. When I finally asked her, "Well, what about your panties?" I thought, *This will finally end this game.*

Her response to my question, a.k.a., order, was so daringly blatant, I've never forgotten one word of it.

"You know, you've got a big fucking mouth! Let's see if your balls are as big as your mouth. I'll be here tomorrow at one o'clock. (By then our kids would have been dismissed and have started their summer vacation.) Let's see if you have the balls to show up!" she stated matter of factly.

With that said, she slowly put back on her skintight dungarees, followed by her bra and blouse and left my classroom.

As I stood alone, I was utterly floored. I couldn't believe what seemed like such good fortune. Here was this owner of an incredible figure, boldly daring me to make it with her the next day. Just imagining what would be in store for me tomorrow at 1:00, I felt like the luckiest guy in the world. This only happened in books or XXX movies and rarely in the real world. I was the happiest man alive!

The final day of the school year mercifully arrived. It had been a long year, and today I had something to look forward to besides the beginning of our summer vacation. As was our custom in the science department, the lab technician had brought in liquor, and we all were getting "happier" as the morning wore on. While everyone was looking forward to our end-term party, I was looking forward to a "special party." Speaking with my friends who had been in the room with me the day before, they both believed that my date would not show up. I, being a macho male asshole, knew one thing: I'd be there!

Although feeling the effects of the alcohol, as the morning wore on, I began to ask myself, *If this young lady is so easy, what the hell am I doing? Who knows what type of diseases she may have?* Of course, I dismissed such thoughts, especially after the liquor took greater control of my brain cells or what was left of them. Finally, I decided to go for it.

After what seemed like an eternity, the last official bell of the school year rang. In the process of handing out report cards, I wished my students a great summer. I told them how much I enjoyed being their teacher and thanked them for being who they were, a great bunch of kids! With their last chore of pushing the desks to the walls and putting the chairs on top of them accomplished, I escorted them down the stairs and out of the building.

It had been one hell of an arduous and debilitating year. As much as I liked my kids, the accumulated insanity that existed at I.S.24 had exacted a tremendous toll on my overall being. Now freedom was at hand, and I was going to enjoy every second of it. The first order of business was to go up to the science lab and have a few more drinks with my friends. Then I'd take care of the unfinished business that I had started the previous day.

By the time I was able to get my key to open the locked door to my room, I was feeling no pain. The alcohol I had consumed had done its job, and although not disoriented, I definitely was in a great mood. The moment of truth had arrived, and Sam Ross would "rise" to the occasion.

As I opened my door, there to my utter amazement was the most incredible naked body I had ever seen. The broad smile on my visitor's face expressed to me how pleased she was that I had the "balls" to back up my "big mouth."

I must admit that after this day, a teacher's desk would take on a new meaning as far as I was concerned. During our tryst, individuals having master keys to the school's various classrooms interrupted us on two separate occasions. With deep regret, nothing was consummated since I didn't want a member of the custodial staff, no less an administrator, to surprise us during the incredible love-making session we were both enjoying. We would later find out that numerous other couples had paired off and had gone to various locations in the building to enjoy themselves in the same pleasure-seeking manner. Unfortunately, it seemed that we were the only couple that was constantly being interrupted: just my luck.

By the time we finally showed up at the end-term party, it seemed everyone was aware of what we had been engaging in, as evidenced by the thunderous ovation that greeted us. I felt like I was attending my coronation as "The King of Sex." Some king, by the time I got home and my head hit the pillow, I must have said to myself countless times, *Idiot, what did you do? She was so easy! No protection....*

Even with an abundance of street smarts, as well as a wealth of common sense, alcohol and a stupid male ego had let me be enticed by a gorgeous, yet promiscuous, young woman. When I awoke the following morning and went to the bathroom, I almost passed out from the severe burning sensation I experienced when I urinated. The only word I could utter and which basically explained the entire situation was, "Fuck!" which seemed to be my word of choice for everything.

By Sunday, the appearance of Lorena Bobbitt would have been welcome, that's how severe the burning had become. A visit to the hospital did not confirm syphilis or any other form of venereal disease. That would have been too easy. Rather, I had caught a severe urinary tract infection, which would eventually spread to my prostate gland and plague me with prostatitis until this very day. After a shot and a script for antibiotics, I was soon on my way home.

After I filled my prescription and fixed my checkbook, all I could think about was what a jerk I had been!

As I stated in this book's prologue, every event I'd relate to the reader would be true. I felt it wouldn't be fair to discuss events that occurred in regards to my co-workers without showing stupidity on my part. The only positive to come out of this entire experience was the fact that when I taught my students about safe sex, I had firsthand knowledge of the ramifications one could suffer when you don't practice what you preach. Of equal importance was the fact that, when I related this story to my students, of course omitting certain details, they were impressed with my real-life experience, as well as my candor. I'm pretty sure they were also struck by the reality that Sam Ross, their teacher, could be such a dope!

Returning to my cohorts, Nick Capino was one of the most likable teachers on our staff. No matter where his allegiance lay during a dispute, no one could really get mad at him. Nick was an anachronism. He was a throwback to the 50s where guys hung out in their clubhouse. Here they could and would get drunk, tell a load of bullshit stories, practice harmonizing, or for some, just chill out.

Nick was basically an enigma. As a teacher, our kids respected him, and despite his hard-ass aura, they realized he really cared about them. They all described him as "crazy," yet in the same breath, they knew they could talk to him about anything (sound familiar?). We, on the other hand, saw another side of Nick's personality. To us, he was a "Toys-R-Us Kid" who didn't want to grow up. Just hanging out was his greatest enjoyment and form of entertainment.

Nick had many attributes, but the most special trait he possessed was his ability to tell a story. He exuded a certain panache when describing an event that would literally put you on the edge of your seat. Not only was this a great attribute as far as his being a teacher, but it served him well in his everyday life.

One day, I was sitting in the teachers' room when Nick walked in. I almost fell over when I looked at him. He had a bandaged forehead, facial cuts, stitches, a black eye, and an arm in a sling.

"Nick, What the hell happened to you?" I asked.

"Sam, you'll never guess what happened. I was driving my new car on the Belt Parkway, and this fucking tree ran out in the middle of the road and hit me!" he answered as straight faced as possible.

I almost soiled my pants from laughing so hard.

Nick was very lucky that he totally recovered from this mishap, but like all of us, he seemed to have a curse that would follow him. Years later, a friend told me that Nick had been hurt in another accident. It seems that the roof of Nick's clubhouse caved in and fell on his head. Now, now, let's not laugh. I was told he suffered blackouts and headaches for quite a while. Fortunately, he recovered from this mishap and later got married. One condition of his marriage was that he had to give up his membership to Toys-R-Us.

"Joe Q. Public" rarely takes into consideration the fact that teachers are subject to various childhood diseases due to their constant interaction with their pupils. While colds, influenza, etc., are always contracted, it is the more dangerous illnesses, such as chicken pox and the measles, that when caught can have serious ramifications for adults. Never in my wildest imagination did I expect one of my colleagues to catch an illness which was so highly contagious that, until the incubation period passed, I was completely neurotic.

Jeff Donlevy and I had started our teaching careers at the same time. We often had conversations about our job, families, etc. Although not the best of friends, we both enrolled at Brooklyn College and took a few graduate courses together. One evening, Jeff didn't show up to class and was also absent from school the next day. When I saw Mike, who was Jeff's best friend, and inquired about him, he told me Jeff's testicles had swollen up like an elephant's balls, and he was going to the doctor. Jeff would be diagnosed with a highly contagious childhood disease known as the mumps. In males, this illness can be quite debilitating, depending primarily on how much swelling occurs in the testicles. Of greater consequence is the fact that it can cause sterility.

To say that I was off the walls due to my fear of catching the mumps is putting it quite mildly. The fact that Dianah and I wanted to have children left us both extremely concerned. Since Jeff and I sat next to each other in our grad classes, I assumed there was a distinct possibility that I could catch this menace. I don't remember how long the incubation period was, but I do remember scrutinizing my balls for a number of weeks. Luckily, Jeff recovered with no side effects, and thankfully, my balls remained their normal size.

There is no doubt in my mind, or whatever remains of it, that teachers who survive their first couple of years eventually are the cream of the crop in our profession. I personally was fortunate enough to become the best of friends with an individual I consider the best teacher I ever had the honor to work with: Jerry Lester.

I originally met Jerry during my college days and was totally surprised to see his face when the regulars reported to work that Monday, the first day for the 1969 school year. Being new and not knowing a soul, it was a great comfort to see a friendly face. It was just a matter of time before we were practically inseparable. We were so close that years later, Dianah, my future wife, had to answer about 50 questions that Jerry had made up in order to get his blessing for us to be married. Of course if Dianah had answered every question incorrectly, I still would have married her, but this just gives you an idea of how close we all were, since we could fool around in such a manner.

If there is such an animal as a "master teacher," Jerry earned this title, hands down! Jerry represented all that was good in the teaching profession. Not only was he a devoted teacher, but he was loved and respected by all of his students and colleagues. In the ten-year span that we taught together, no one ever had anything negative to say about this man. If there was ever a teacher that deserved bonus pay, Jerry was the ideal candidate.

What set Jerry apart from his colleagues is very difficult to put one's finger on. Any ill-conceived idea that he was six feet plus, weighed in at 220 pounds, and ruled by intimidation is totally bogus. At five feet six inches and 150 pounds, any number of our students could have easily beaten him to a pulp, although he did show off a scary temper. The fact that his students felt they could talk to him about anything, i.e. drugs, pregnancy, criminal activity, only added to his "master teacher" mystique. Just like a puppy can warm the coldest of hearts, Jerry was able to break all barriers to have the goodness of even his most belligerent kids' rise to the surface.

After much thought, the answer to the question of why Jerry was such a great educator is very easy to discern. He was born to be a teacher! He had compassion, practicality, patience, sensitivity, and numerous qualities which, when combined, made him the special person he was and hopefully still is. Many fine teachers had some of these qualities. Jerry was blessed with all of them!

It is so gratifying to see that teachers are finally getting the recognition they so richly deserve and have worked so hard to attain. The Teacher of the Year Award presented by the President of the United States is a nice gesture towards recognizing the blood, sweat, and tears so many of my colleagues put forth each day of the school year. Being presented with this award would grant Jerry Lester the ultimate honor he so richly deserves.

Knowing Jerry and many other wonderful teachers I had the honor to work with, the greatest reward they received was when a former student would come to visit and let them know how they were doing. To hear that they were married or had a good job was extremely gratifying. If they told us that they had graduated college, were employed in the corporate world, and were making a great living, this too was so invigorating. Unfortunately, when we heard that a former student was homeless, in jail, or was dealing drugs, it hurt quite deeply. Some wondered where they had failed and hoped they would be more successful in the future! I learned not to take such realities personally.

I could easily write a book about the teachers I worked with, including their effect on their coworkers, schools, and students. I will continue to discuss some of my other colleagues in the following chapters, just in a different context. Be that as it may, one of the greatest gifts we as parents can give to our children's teachers is a simple letter, or even a short note, thanking them for the help and concern they've shown our offspring. I know how rejuvenated I felt when I received either one. There are so many caring and talented individuals in the teaching profession. Every teacher that falls within these parameters deserves a pat on the back, greater financial gain, and just a plain heartfelt "thank you."

CHAPTER EIGHT

Substitute Teachers: G-d Bless Them!

Life experience leads me to conclude that one of the most difficult jobs anyone can possibly aspire to, besides parenting, is that of being a substitute teacher. If one had to outline the prerequisites necessary to be successful in this educational endeavor, the following qualifications would only touch the surface:

1. A college degree.
2. Thick skin.
3. Love of being abused!
4. Capacity to accept degradation and dehumanization.
5. A hidden propensity towards mental illness.
6. Low self-esteem.

Being a substitute teacher is the most unrewarding, dangerous, and strength-sapping position in the field of education. Those that work in either junior or high school classrooms are subject to all types of abuse with both physical and mental being at the top of the list. When I covered classes in New York, you were paid $8.00 a coverage. Today it's between $20-30. I realize people need money. I empathize with their need to support themselves and their families, but for an individual to walk into a classroom with 25-40 students, whom he or she knows nothing about, takes a pair of brass balls or loose screws, depending on your gender.

During my career, I met substitute teachers from all walks of life. If given a chance to teach by the classes they covered, many turned out to be excellent teachers. Others were like fish out of water, flopping and gasping for air. No matter how hard they tried, they were overmatched and subsequently overwhelmed. I eventually realized that many of those that were successful had some sort of gimmick which helped them immeasurably in gaining the cooperation of the students they were trying to educate. On the other side of the coin, some gimmicks were nothing more than a prelude to disaster.

I had met Rasah Sahimi in the main office while in the process of punching in and getting ready for the day's "festivities." Sahimi was a pleasant elderly gentleman who proceeded to inform me that he was going to be a substitute teacher at our school for the rest of the week. Right off the bat, I knew our kids would eat him alive, mainly due to his age and accent. The fact that Jerry would be out for the week due to a bout with the flu lent to the distinct possibility that Mr. Sahimi would be teaching right next door to me.

When Mr. Sahimi showed me the classes he was assigned to cover, I immediately recognized that he had been given Jerry's program. Without any doubt, I knew that this was going to be one hell of a week. All I could foresee was noise and chaos, and that was being optimistic.

As the morning progressed, it appeared that Mr. Sahimi was doing an adequate job since it was pretty quiet next door. I even began to question my assumption that he'd be eaten alive. Stupid me! The old expression, *never count your chickens before they hatch* raced around my brain as the first sounds of hysteria emanated from Jerry's room. In a matter of seconds, I was at the front door of room 306.

As I entered Jerry's classroom, an extraordinary sight caught my attention and left me nearly speechless. I thought that I had seen just about anything possible, as far as teachers using visual aids, but the scene that greeted me was the most grotesque that I had ever encountered. Even my fertile imagination couldn't have conjured up something as nauseating. There, before my eyes, was Mr. Sahimi standing at the sink, washing his glass eyeball he had just removed from his eye socket. Where this glass eye was once nestled, a disgusting, moist, empty hole was now visible.

During the process of washing his eye, Mr. Sahimi kept looking up at the class, enabling all of the students, especially those near the sink, to get a "bird's eye view" of this hideous sight. Every time he did this, the girls let out ear-piercing screams, and all you heard from the boys was the word "Daaaamn!"

After I was able to secure some semblance of order, I asked Sahimi, "What the hell are you doing?" although trying to contain my rage out of reverence to this mans age:

"I thought if I removed my eye, the class would quiet down and I would be able to teach the lesson that Mr. Lester had left me," he responded.

93

My G-d, was he wrong!

In all honesty, I was really impressed by Sahimi's innovative approach. Unfortunately, this anatomical performance led to a total breakdown of what would be considered a normal classroom environment. As I've stated on numerous occasions, I was a pretty good disciplinarian, yet no matter what I tried, nothing could deter further hysterical flare-ups from recurring as the period wore on. For the remaining 25 minutes, both classes learned absolutely nothing due to Sahimi's brain fart. Wait, Jerry's kids did learn a little something: how to remove, wash, and reinsert a glass eyeball. Needless to say, Mr. Sahimi's services were not requested for the remainder of the week.

Bert Paladin, who subbed for an extended period of time, deserves special recognition due to his rare technique of getting his pupils' attention. Paladin, as we nicknamed him, was extremely impressed with his muscularity and professed to our students that he was a weight lifter. One day, while on patrol, I passed Paladin's classroom and immediately noticed how quiet it was. *A substitute with a quiet room?* This thought was mind boggling in it's own right. As I watched, I noticed he was flexing his arm muscles, and the kids, especially the girls, loved it.

Even when he took off his shirt and seriously began posing, I thought *Whatever works for him is fine by me.* I guess I was taken aback when he started to unbuckle his belt for the expressed purpose of showing off, what I hoped, were his thigh muscles. It was at this point that I walked into his room to stop this exhibitionist. What I found astonishing was the fact that Paladin didn't think he was doing anything wrong. After explaining to him that he could be brought up on various charges by the principal or district superintendent, have his license to teach revoked, or possibly be jailed, with great reluctance he began to get dressed. I remember thinking, *Gee, I love this job!*

As the fame of 24 spread throughout the substitute teachers' world, getting subs to cover classes for absent teachers became quite difficult. Although most had the six qualifications I previously presented, few had the desire to be permanently injured or possibly killed. Thankfully, there was never a death at I.S.24, but the possibility definitely existed. As the pool of substitutes dwindled, regular appointees began vying for these coverages.

As insane as it sounds, many teachers fought tooth and nail for these coverages. You must remember, our pay was deplorably low, few had summer or after-school jobs, and this added income could definitely supplement our archaic regular salaries.

There, I've admitted it! I was one of those crazies since I fought for as many coverage's as possible to supplement my lousy salary. There were days that I was able to secure 3-4 such assignments. These, plus my regular workload, had me in the classroom the entire day. When the passing bell rang, I'd choke down some food and get ready for my next class.

One year, I managed to accrue over 600 coverages. Paid semi-annually, when I received my check, I was ecstatic, yet I never lost sight of the fact that this was nothing but " blood money!"

Of the 700-800 or so classes I covered due to teacher absenteeism, one stands out above all the rest. Due to my reputation, even the most difficult classes gave me little trouble. I'd be an outright liar if I said that there never was a fight or other incidents during these babysitting ventures, but they were kept to a minimum. On the day in question, I walked into a sixth grade class and asked that everyone sit down. Since most of the students knew or had heard of me, they quickly adhered to my request. Of course there still were the shufflers, who walked real slow to show everyone how cool and tough they were. This was to be expected. It was during this seating process that I heard an almost inaudible, "Fuck you," from one of the boys in the class.

As previously stated, only two students had ever said "fuck you" to me. Now, here was this diminutive, almost elf-like twerp expressing such a thought. When I asked him to repeat what he had just said, he did so with both defiance and dignity.

Reflecting back on the good old "Donald days," I asked this student, whom I would later find out was named Willie, to step out into the hallway. Rather than berate him and mostly due his diminutive size, I decided to lift him off the ground with one hand and pin him against the wall.

"Don't pull your shit with me!" I said to this youngster.

When I released my grip on him, Willie fell to the ground and landed on his ass. As he righted himself, I started to laugh. Then, in a flash, he made a B-line to the staircase, and I instinctively knew "Daddy" would be right up to see me.

As I opened the classroom door, there stood a gentleman nattily dressed in a three-piece suit. After formally introducing himself as Willie's father, he inquired, "Why did you punch my son in his face?" while staring at me with this angry gaze.

Immediately realizing Willie had lied to his dad, my retort was, "Looking at my size and that of your son, do you honestly believe if I punched him in the face he would have been able to get off the floor and come running home to get you?" I replied.

Then figuring that "all is fair in love and war" I continued. "Did you raise your son to call a teacher a white motherfucker?" I asked Willie's father.

The sound of Willie's father's open-hand slap to Willie's face sent chills down my spine. Although he deserved some form of punishment, I didn't want the kid to be maimed. The look of shock on Willie's face, before the onset of tears, made me feel even greater remorse. On the other hand, the fact that he had lied added some solace to my fabrication of his statement.

The rest of that day and night, I thought a great deal about what had transpired with Willie. Morally speaking, I had done the wrong thing by lying. Reality-wise, I was able to show Willie that anyone could make up a story, and mine was much better than his. He had indeed said "fuck you" to me and I wasn't going to let that slide.

The next morning when Willie appeared at my door, I excused myself from my class and stepped into the hallway. The first words out of Willie's mouth were, "Why did you lie to my father?" he asked me with this puzzled look on his face.

When I posed the same question to him, there was utter silence. I guess he finally realized I had out-slicked him, and he apologized for what had happened. I explained to him how lucky he was that none of my eighth graders had heard about this incident because they would have beaten the living shit out of him! I also let him know how lucky he was to have parents that cared so much about him, and instead of saying "fuck you" to a teacher, or to anyone for that matter, he should say and do things that would make his parents proud of him.

As in the past, you can psychoanalyze this entire episode and form your own judgements as to whom to affix blame. No matter what your determination, one fact speaks volumes about the entire incident: Willie visited me every day for the rest of that year! What is ironic is that two years later, I would be Willie's eighth grade teacher and totally adore him. His charm, wit, and intelligence were exceptional and remain with me to this day—so much for first impressions. By the way, I still feel terrible that he was slapped so hard by his father.

When I think back on the coverages I took at I.S.24, I can't help but remember how often I saw a substitute teacher mentally, and at times physically, destroyed—such misery in order to earn a day's wages. Unfortunately, I cannot give an accurate account as to the number of subs that walked out of a classroom in the middle of a period, never to return to I.S.24, but the number was outrageous! While I felt, and still feel, a great deal of compassion for these individuals, who knows; maybe they were the lucky ones. They got out while the going was still good. Others stayed on and finally succumbed to a miserable existence, mainly due to financial considerations. As wages and benefits increased over the years, many became trapped in an economic web. With families to support and other financial responsibilities, few had the option or the courage go walk away from a job which at times could dehumanize those with the most altruistic intentions.

As is stated in the heading of this chapter: *Substitute Teachers: G-d Bless Them.* No words could better express how we should feel towards these unique warriors. They truly are a special breed apart from other members of the work force. They deserve as much financial and monetary compensation as possible, considering the danger and frustrations their job entails. Unfortunately, I believe they will never get the respect they so richly deserve because when they are in front of a strange group of youngsters, they are seen for what they are: substitutes, i.e., an individual covering for the regular teacher who is absent. By definition alone, this puts them at a distinct disadvantage! To overcome this initial setback is so difficult. To do this on a continuous basis is nearly impossible!

CHAPTER NINE

Drugs in the Schools: Anyone Want a Joint?

Although I grew up in some pretty rough neighborhoods, I was never interested in drugs. While most of my friends drank and smoked pot, my drug of choice was sports. The high I experienced from competition, and my desire to win, had to be better than what drugs had to offer. I did have my first serious encounter with hard liquor at the age of ten but hardly was a constant drinker. This was due to my love of athletics and the fact that I had grown up in a house plagued by my father's alcoholism. I had promised myself that this evil would never exist in my life.

To this day, I vividly remember the experience of throwing my father, who was drunk at the time and abusing my mother, into a wall and putting a knife to his throat. Nor can I ever forget how hysterical I became when I realized that I almost committed such an insidious act as slitting his throat. I still can picture myself, a 15-year-old, racing down eight flights of steps, crying uncontrollably and running as fast and as far as I could until I nearly collapsed. The hatred and the love I had for this man still tug at my very existence. When he wasn't drinking, he was the greatest father any child could possibly hope for. When he was on a drinking binge, I felt he was the biggest piece of shit G-d had ever created. The disgusting language he used to abuse my mother will never be forgotten on my part. To say I have forgiven him for this abuse since his death in 1983 would be too charitable, but I still love him with all of my heart and miss him with all of my being!

The only consolation of this entire mental trauma was the fact that I swore I would never put my future wife and children through this living hell that I experienced. This is not to say I've never been drunk. Undoubtedly, I have. Like most teenagers, I tried and experienced the side effects of liquor. As an adult, I have been drunk on a couple of occasions, but I thank G-d and, ironically, my father's memory that the numbers of these lapses have been minimal in totality.

My years at I.S.24 saw students and staff members alike, embracing alcohol and drugs. Although there was minimal heroin and cocaine use, pot, speed, and many varieties of stimulants and depressants were readily available. Unfortunately, the disparity between student and teacher use was not that great. Orders for any drug were easily filled irrespective of whether the buyer was a student or a teacher.

Hopefully at this point in time, you realize I was never out of touch with what was going on in the real world. Before setting foot into I.S.24, I knew there would be drug use by both my students and colleagues. Never, and I emphatically mean never, did I anticipate that drug use would be as rampant as it was amongst my fellow educators. The fact that many of my coworkers were part of the so-called "Drug Generation" cannot be denied. They ranged from the "Flower Children" who opposed the war in Vietnam to those that couldn't cope with the hostile environment of I.S.24 and its surroundings. So many factors contributed to the use of drugs by staff members, yet if anyone asks, "What was the primary catalyst that lured drug-free teachers into a life of use, if not abuse," the answer is simple: the job itself!

During my entire career as a New York City schoolteacher, the news media failed to educate the general public as to the many dangers we as teachers faced on a daily basis. Just as many in our military took to smoking and mainlining drugs to try to erase the horrors of the war they were participating in, we, your children's teachers, were also fighting a war. Each day I would ask myself which student might have on them a knife, or possibly a gun, or who's going to be assaulted today? In rapid succession, you would try to figure out how many fights there would be, whose car would be vandalized or stolen, and on it went. Just like a soldier who wants to win or survive a battle, we as teachers wanted to win our "little battles" and help educate our pupils. Sadly, this was easier said than done!

Waking up and realizing that it wasn't Friday, although you were already bent out of shape, was more than many of my colleagues could handle. Quite a few were idealists and thought they could change the world. Oh, how wrong they were! Eventually you realized that if you won small battles, you were doing a good job. If you didn't adapt to this reality, you were destined for failure. So many teachers, such good, caring people, were suffering a slow death each day they punched their time cards, because they couldn't reconcile the fact that what they wanted and what they could possibly attain were worlds apart. As their failures mounted and the cold-hearted reality of I.S.24 was unmasked, for many, drugs became the only outlet to insure survival. This ungodly truth, along with the responsibilities of raising families, paying bills, and all of the other problems that people face in their everyday lives, led to one foregone conclusion: The drugs continued to flow.

In a span of ten years, I saw some of the most caring people suffer complete burnout. Unfortunately, one of my best friends was institutionalized because he couldn't cope. His glazed eyes profoundly expressed the look of being in another world. He was like a zombie when he finally snapped. Drugs such as marijuana and Quaaludes, which he and many of my colleagues hoped would allow them to cope with the enormous pressures they found on the job, only helped to accelerate their demise. Careers were destroyed, marriages irreparably damaged, and self-esteem driven into the depths of despair, and still the drugs continued to flow.

On the other side of the spectrum, I would estimate that at least 50% of the student population had tried drugs with about 20-25% being more than casual users. Many of these students were in our slower classes, and as the class designations went lower, drug use increased substantially. Whether it was from their overall frustration with school, which included the inability to read on grade, poor study habits, or just the many obstacles that society put in their paths, nothing could change the fact that too many of our students were using drugs, and we had a major problem on our hands.

Most of our users chose marijuana as their drug of choice. Their reasoning was simple: It was easy to get and it was cheap. Right across the street from our school was a bodega, i.e. a small grocery store where you could buy nickel or dime bags of pot with no hassle. Of greater significance was the fact that you could buy one joint for a dollar, which was an entrepreneurial coup, if you ask me. This basically assured anyone in the neighborhood that if they wanted to get high for a couple of hours, all they needed was a buck. Absolutely brilliant!

Everyone in the neighborhood knew that the police were aware of the sale of pot at the bodega. The fact that they never raided the place meant business was always brisk. I just assumed that Five O, i.e. the police, were after some big fish rather than some end of the line street dealer. Besides, if they closed the bodega down, three stores over was the dry cleaner, and a person without an iota of common sense had to realize that all of the youngsters visiting his establishment weren't just picking up their parents' dry cleaning. Like the bodega, his doors remained open and the traffic in and out was brisk.

My attitude on student drug use was what you'd expect. I didn't condone its use, but I wasn't a DEA agent either. It was standard policy that if a student was caught with any drugs, they would be suspended for one to two weeks. Unfortunately, no matter what ramifications he or she faced at home, this youngster now had more of an opportunity to get high on whatever their drug of choice was, to sell their shit on the streets, or possibly engage in other criminal activity.

During my eighth year at I.S.24, as already mentioned, I taught a self-contained class of upwards of 35 students. Again, the only time they left my classroom was to go to gym and lunch. The equation was simple: restricted movement equaled a reduction in fights and other forms of unacceptable behavior. The bottom line of this entire program was contain the incorrigibles and keep them out of the mainstream.

One morning I awoke as "sick as a dog." I called the school to let the appropriate people know that I wouldn't be in. The following morning, by the time the late bell rang, only 15 of my students were present. Unless there was an outbreak of malaria, I knew something was wrong. When I asked one of my girls where everyone was, she replied, "You know how much we love you, Mr. Ross."

Right then I knew "we" were in trouble. She proceeded to tell me that as soon as everyone heard I was going to be absent, "They went crazy and got suspended."

Knowing I wasn't getting the entire story, I asked another one of my students what had happened.

She related to me that when some of my kids found out that I wasn't coming in, they went to the bodega, bought some beer and pot, and decided to have a party in one of our lesser used staircases. When they were caught, 18 were suspended for one week.

Although each and every student deserved to be suspended in accordance with the student code of conduct, realistically, what did this form of punishment accomplish? The simple truth: Absolutely nothing! Understand that most of my kids didn't give a crap that on their record was a notation: "Suspended due to the use of drugs." They were all too happy to be running the streets and having a ball. Most didn't care that their parents, or whomever they lived with, were notified that they were suspended. As a few had previously told me, they had gotten beatings before with hands, belts, wire, hangers, bats, and so many other items. So what!

The reader must understand that my kids weren't worried that this incident would keep them out of college. For most, it was a foregone conclusion that they wouldn't be accepted into any college, so what was the big deal? Just finishing high school was a super accomplishment in their eyes. They cared about what was happening now, not five years down the road. Their outlook on life was just as simple: Survive each day. Try not to get robbed, beaten up, stabbed, shot, or killed. To most, college was just a fool's dream, and they lived in the real world!

Out of the 18 students who were suspended, not one, to my knowledge, gave up drinking or smoking pot as a result of that suspension. The only positive in suspending these kids was the fact that they were out of the school building for a week, and therefore couldn't cause any problems. Unfortunately, you now had a number of unsupervised teenagers out on the streets, and in one instance, the ramifications would be devastating for many innocent pedestrians.

While on his "forced vacation," Jesus Apontelone hooked up with three friends and went for a ride into Manhattan. While there, they decided to hold up a jewelry store. The ensuing police chase led to their vehicle veering out of control and cutting down numerous innocent bystanders. The final tally of this disaster was 12 people injured, 4 youths incarcerated, and so much pain and suffering. As in most cases, suspension had accomplished nothing.

I cannot count the number of times that students of mine nodded out in class due to their use of drugs. I could have had them suspended in a heartbeat. So what! You've just gotten a glimpse of how unsuccessful this avenue of behavioral modification was anyway. My attitude was, if they weren't causing any trouble in class, leave them alone and keep them in the building. At least I knew where they were and hopefully was able to keep them out of further trouble.

When the effects of whatever drug they were on had worn off, I would get into it with them, down and dirty. There would be lectures, cursing, expression of disappointment, and any realistic threat that I thought might be beneficial in deterring drug use. To suspend was so easy, but to fight them tooth and nail showed more concern and love than any suspension could. Did I change the world? Of course not! But some kids, for the first time in years, stayed straight long enough to come to school on a regular basis, and that was good enough for me.

Throughout this book, I've tried to emphasize how important it was to gain the trust of one's students. No matter how wonderful a teacher you were, if you didn't have this important asset, you'd never accomplish much when it came to dealing with the problems of the students who needed your help the most. Just the fact that my kids offered me free weed or other drugs on a daily basis shows how much they trusted me. This meant that I could accomplish more with them than something as stupid as a suspension.

The trust I was able to develop with many of my students was very special. Ultimately, it allowed them to express to me their innermost thoughts and feelings, including their hopes and dreams. This expression of such private matters was not available to many of their parents, no less my colleagues. Just knowing that they were letting me into "their world" was such a triumph. Of course, I walked a thin line when it came to such affairs. They had to know, and respect the fact, that I wasn't their buddy, yet I cared enough about them, so they could speak to me on a multitude of topics. At times, it was extremely difficult not to go over this line, and in most cases, I was successful.

Before you erect a statue in my honor, recognize the fact that there were so many failures on my part. No one but a "Higher Authority" could totally change the reality that existed in this world of cruelty and mayhem. I was happy with little successes, rather than being foolhardy to think that I, Sam Ross, a simple layman, could change or erase all of the ills of a society that my kids found themselves pressured by. This fact was never more apparent than when I crossed paths with Willie Grayson.

It was during the start of my second year at I.S.24 that a youngster named Willie Grayson entered my classroom. Willie stood out immediately. He had one of the most magnificent smiles I had ever encountered, appeared quite affable, and was dressed to the nines. From the moment I met Willie, I just knew that he would either be one of my best pupils or someone who would cause a world of hurt in someone's life.

As the term progressed, I noticed Willie was nodding out with greater frequency. Originally I deceived myself with the rationalization that Willie had an after-school job and was putting in incredibly long hours. I basically knew that I was playing head games with myself, but I hoped I was wrong. Glassy eyes, slurred speech, constant nodding out, banging into chairs, desks, walls, and other students led to only one conclusion: Willie was using.

When I confronted Willie with my suspicions, he said, "Yo, Mr. Ross. I'm only smoking some weed and chillin' out," as he fashioned this great big smile.

"Everything's fine at home, as well as at my job," he continued.

Knowing my kids, just the phrase "just chillin' out" was a telltale sign that things were not right at all.

As determined as I was to get Willie to stop his drug use, which I knew consisted of more than just smoking pot, nothing worked. With Willie's consent, I enlisted the assistance of the school's drug coordinator, and he "played her like a fiddle." It as only a matter of time until Willie began to be a no-show.

Following proper procedure, all of Willie's absences were reported and numerous calls were made to his house. Eventually, truant officers were sent out to find Willie, but they also drew a blank. Ultimately, the police were called in because Willie had just disappeared, and no one knew where he was and if he was okay. It was at this point that I unfortunately had to write Willie off. Other students desperately needed my help, and I already had learned that you couldn't save everyone no matter how much you liked them

It's with a great sense of sadness that I must report that Willie doesn't smile much these days. You see, while ripped, i.e. stoned, on some drug, Willie got into a shoot-out with some of New York's "finest," and shot and killed a police officer. The kid with the great smile will spend the rest of his life incarcerated in an adult facility. Willie Grayson, who could have been someone very special, it not too special these days. He has what two million other Americans in this country have—a prison uniform with his own I.D. number.

When I look back on my years at I.S.24 and to a lesser degree I.S.302, I'm thankful that only a small percentage of our students did hard drugs. There is no denying that on numerous occasions I found used syringes hidden in various school apertures, but most of the heavy drug use was found in the high schools.

During the school year, former students would come back to visit me and let me know what was going on in such schools as Boys and Girls High School, Bushwick High School, etc. The picture they painted was not a pleasant one. Word about former students using, dealing, and occasionally overdosing became commonplace, but this news hurt just the same. I knew many of "my kids" would eventually succumb to the pressures of the streets, yet it never lessened the pain I felt for them, their families, and all concerned.

To take the plight of my former students personally and say I failed as a teacher would be ridiculous. Undoubtedly, there were outside influences that steered them into getting involved in some serious shit. Maybe it was just a conglomeration of everything: school, the family, the neighborhood, peer pressure, the need to be accepted, etc. There were far too many ingredients available to turn good children into their own worst enemies. No, I didn't fail these kids—society did!

During the ten years I taught at 24, I spent from 1-2 weeks each semester talking exclusively about drugs. Accessibility to a drug kit containing all types of educational reproductions was a powerful tool in trying to educate my kids. I answered any and every question as honestly as possible, yet in many instances, my kids new more than I did. As I said before, "I didn't exist in their world. I was just a visitor, trying to do as good a job as possible." The truth was that I didn't face the pressures they did every day of their lives. Yes, I could understand their plight, but I didn't have to live it. The bottom line was that when school let out, I went home to my own crazy neighborhood with its own problems. They just walked out of the front door of the school and were home, and their environment was a hell of a lot worse than mine.

Today our great nation faces an enemy that has always been active within our borders but was never seriously addressed. Recent years have witnessed this enemy infiltrate borders once considered impenetrable. What was once contained in our slums, ghettos, and poorer neighborhoods is now a national nemesis, becoming stronger every hour of every day as it victimizes all strata of our society. What must we as a nation do to fight this insidious cancer that now has no boundaries and is color-blind? How do we defeat something, which presently looks immune to every roadblock we can throw in its way?

Sam Ross, a mere speck in this battle for supremacy, cannot give you the definitive answers you are looking for to eradicate this "virus" that spreads unabated. All I can do is tell every American that we must fight what might be the most difficult and costly war in our history. To every parent or individual that loves a child, any child, I beg of you to take notice of this wonderful creation. Look at the way they act. Know who they hang out with. See if they have unexplained wads of money or new and unaccounted-for jewelry. Open your eyes! You might not like what you may see, but it's time to stop hiding and making believe that there isn't a problem. Use any and every mean at your disposal to get the help your children need to combat this illness. Call 911, AA, D.A.R.E. or use any other avenue that can help you intervene on your child's behalf. There are so many nonprofit organizations that are better equipped to handle this problem than we are. Now is not the time to be a hero. Recognize the fact that your child may have a problem, and no matter how small it is, fight them with all of your being. Stop trying to be their buddy or friend, and be their parent. Save them because in many cases they do not know how to save themselves.

No one, I don't care who they are, can promise you success in this fight for your child's life. Those in the know can promise you misery, feelings of hopelessness, outrage, and the possibility that your child may die with or without your intervention. The greatest tragedy in life is for a parent to bury his or her own child. This is happening somewhere in the United States at this very moment. Hopefully, it will not happen to you!

Please, no matter how difficult this war can be, you must never surrender. Let the truth be told that, those who are so unfortunate as to have to bury their child will not feel better knowing that they fought as hard as they could. Nothing will make you feel better! Never forget, you fought to keep them alive, not to soothe your conscience should the unthinkable occur.

I implore the reader, do not be inclined to think that I speak to you on a higher plane than that which you find yourselves ensnared in. Understand that I am not preaching, but begging because like so many parents, I too was a participant in this war. It took place in my own household. At times, I felt so lost and thought of myself as a total failure. Eventually, I realized that blaming myself would not change the reality of what was at hand. I knew that I would never stop fighting for my child, and I challenged every movement this young teenager made. I remember my feelings of desperation, although my daughter told me she was only "experimenting" and was not involved with such drugs as cocaine, meth, or ecstasy. What I knew was that this experiment could become a lifelong and possibly a life-taking addiction.

I must admit to everyone that I was extremely lucky to have the help of someone who became one of my best friends. I will forever owe a huge debt of gratitude to this little friend who helped me rid my daughter of this destroyer that was trying to claim another victim. Yes, I was given a pledge of no more drugs if this little friend could be part of our lives. Not only would there be no more drugs, but also no cigarettes, drinking, etc. I'm still in awe of how this diminutive little angel changed both of our lives, hopefully forever.

December 02, 2004 marked the three-year anniversary of my daughter being drug, cigarette, and liquor free. She promised me she would do this if I bought her something she wanted so badly. It was on this day that we brought home Mya, her miniature Daschund. Imagine, all the heartache, worry, misery, and fear, solved with the purchase of the cutest puppy imaginable. I sincerely hope that everyone could be as lucky as I was in finding the answer to my prayers. Any parent in this gut-wrenching situation must never give up hope, since you'll never know what may be the catalyst that can turn you child's life around. Fight, pray, hope, cry, but never surrender! Your child, or whoever this lost soul is, needs you, although they may not realize it at this moment in time. With all of the misery you will experience, never lose sight of one reality in the entire fiasco: You need them also!

CHAPTER TEN

Sex in the Schools: Babies Having Babies

She exuded an outer and inner beauty well beyond her 15 years: articulate, charming, poised, caring, and so much more. All teachers pined for such a true treasure. She would enter my classroom and invigorate me during the most trying of times. She circumvented any prejudice toward race, religion, color, or language. In essence, she was the daughter any parent would pray to have. Never did I expect her to come over to me one day, this diminutive angel, and say, "Mr. Ross, please don't be mad at me, but I have to tell you something. I'm pregnant." This was spoken in the soft, precious voice I'd grown to love.

Sure, I had street smarts. Undoubtedly, I didn't live in a plastic bubble. But Sandra? My G-d, anyone but this golden child. This beautiful, almost spiritual creation of two loving parents had in the flash of a second sent my heart spiraling down into a black abyss. Shocked could not describe my feelings. For one of the few times in my life, it took all of my strength to fight back the tears now welling up. I knew I had to be strong for Sandra because her fear of my rejection was minuscule in comparison to the difficulties that lay ahead. Forget all of the wonderful attributes and accolades I could bestow on this magnificent child. The ugly head of the real world had reared its uncompromising self, and the luster of such a precious gem was lost forever. She, like so many before her, became part of the world of "babies having babies."

Sandy, as I called her, was part of a wonderful family whom I'd gotten to know and respect over the years. I remember her bringing her youngest brother up to school to visit me at the tender age of three. Eventually, he too would become one of my students. Later in his teens he would represent the

United States as a boxer on our 1984 Olympic Boxing Team and win a gold medal. Subsequently, he would become a professional fighter and a world champion at approximately twenty years of age.

Sandy was part a lovely, caring family with all of the ingredients most families could only hope for. What had gone wrong? Why Sandy of all people? Why, at the tender age of 15, was she going to be a mother in less than nine months?

Before we can possibly find the answers to these questions, certain facts about the real world must be explored. Babies having babies has always permeated every segment of our society. There are no boundaries to be found as far as this reality goes. To think that teen pregnancy is a new phenomenon is ridiculous.

The study of historical morality shows us that for generations the rich sent their pregnant daughters away to have their "bastard children," thus protecting the family name and status in society. Girls of parents without such financial means were considered sluts or whores when confronted with the same dilemma. Irrespective of their race, religion, or background, they were pieces of trash, frowned upon by our "moral society." When one of these young girls was with child, you would hear, "How could they let her..." or "If that was my daughter, I'd..." Well, America, whether you like to hear it or not, those children who were called sluts and whores were, are, and always will be our daughters!

The spectacular rise in teen pregnancy, I believe, can be traced to at least one irrefutable fact. As our society has progressed, parents and family members have noticeably less time to spend with their children. Although I thoroughly detest the phrase "quality time," mainly due to the fact that it is inappropriately used to explain away all the ills of our society, on this social issue, it does play a key role. Modern reality demands that far too many families must depend on at least two incomes, just to keep pace with the financial demands our society places on its people. The tremendous influx of women into the work place has helped to destabilize the family unit as we once knew it. Where it was once common for the father to work and the mother to remain home and raise the children, today's pressure-filled environment and the desire of women to be independent has seen this institution undergo revolutionary change. Although this change has brought about many positive ramifications, "quality time" has been a major casualty. In order to fill this void in their lives, many of our babies are having their own babies.

How many of you are aware of the fact that if you asked a pregnant teen, "Why did you get pregnant?" her response might be, "I wanted someone to love and someone to love me back." I guarantee you that the old answers of "I made a mistake," or "It was an accident," have dwindled as the new answer of "I wanted someone to love and someone to love me back," has soared.

You may ask, "Is this what happened to Sandy?" In all honesty, with her strong family unit, I really don't think so, but who knows? Unfortunately, I was so shocked and devastated, I never asked her this question. In regards to the other "Sandra's" of the world, some of which were my students, I did ask this question and the answer in a majority of their responses was yes.

Unfortunately, as our society surges into the 21st century, we will hear this answer with increased frequency as greater pressure is placed on parents to work longer hours in order to earn the money necessary to maintain the basic needs of the household. As the family unit further deteriorates, our children will not only continue this trend of out-of-wedlock births, but we will see more children indulging in sex and at a younger age.

In today's society, so many of our "babies" are experimenting or are constant participants in a new sexual revolution that goes far beyond the comprehension of most of our adult population. Many parents who know about this promiscuity have "thrown in the towel" rather than persist in trying to teach their children to refrain from such activity. It is this ambivalence that further fuels this out-of-control wildfire. Their attitude of "I can't watch her 24/7" gives the parent, or whomever is responsible for this child's welfare, the excuse to absolve themselves of any guilt they may experience should their child become pregnant. The following event, although definitely out of the norm, does reflect the defeatist attitude many parents have fallen victim to in regards to this social problem.

While on patrol in the school basement, a member of the teaching staff encountered a seventh grade student having sex with five boys. While one young man was zipping up his fly, another was in the midst of a pleasurable experience, and three others were waiting their turn. All six students were quickly ushered upstairs, and their parents, or whoever was responsible for them, were contacted and informed that they had to come up to school immediately!

Upon her arrival, the young girl's mother was escorted up to Ben Johnson's office. As stated earlier, my classroom was right next to Ben's office, so I could hear this entire scene play out. As a matter of fact, it was Ben who let me know what had occurred in the basement and to be prepared to hear his entire dissertation when the mother arrived. Adding further impetus to this possibly explosive situation was the fact that this mother had to leave work early, was about to get the shocking news, and would then have to take her daughter home since she was being suspended. Sadly, this parent had no idea that the ceiling would come crashing down on her head as she entered Ben Johnson's office.

Ben was a pretty slick guy when it came to matters that could lead to a student's "untimely death." Upon her arrival, Ben immediately offered this irate mother a chair and let her chill for a while. After a few minutes had passed, Ben began to explain that her daughter had cut her fifth period science class and had been caught in the basement having sex with five boys. With steam already exiting this poor woman's head, Ben also let her know that her daughter was now being suspended for two weeks due to her behavior, or lack thereof.

By now, I was right outside Ben's office, and from the look on this woman's face, I thought she was going to kill her daughter. This "mother " then turned to her daughter and in the most disgusted voice that she could muster, stated: "I don't want you ever cutting science again!"

Talk about apathy? It couldn't have been more blatant. I was not only shocked, but also totally disheartened and embarrassed that a so-called adult could be so stupid! Here, you're being told that five different boys are laying your daughter, and the best you can come up with is, "I don't want you ever cutting science again." Unbelievable! If her response hadn't been so asinine, I probably would have had tears running down my cheeks thinking of this poor mother and what misery had fallen right into her lap. Now, it took every bit of my inner strength not to burst out laughing in response to her idiotic retort. In all honesty, if someone told me this story, as a lay person, I'd say they were full of shit! You may say it if you'd like, but I guarantee you, it's the truth!

During my stay at 24, students were discovered having sex in closets, staircases, and any conceivable place. No matter what their chronological age or how sexually developed they were, a majority lacked in mental maturity what their bodies had an abundance of. The following should give you an idea what I'm talking about.

As disgusting as it sounds, some of these so-called mature girls found nothing wrong with throwing their used tampons or sanitary napkins into the class radiators. It is impossible to describe the putrid stench that emanated from these items as the heat rose through the radiators to warm the room during the cold winter months. The only way to get this horrific smell out of the room was to open the windows and let the cold in. Now, besides stinking, it was freezing. This process finally ceased when the tampon or Kotex pad was recovered from the radiator. I'm sure you can guess whose job it was to recover this vomit-inducing item...Sam Ross! I never asked any student to volunteer for this revolting undertaking. I could never ask this of another human being.

To reinforce your understanding of how immature some of our sexually promiscuous "babies" were, the following story should further your enlightenment.

One morning, after the late bell rang, I walked into my classroom to see all of my students at the window screaming at someone or something. What immediately caught my attention was the fact that the sound was not just coming from my kids, but from other rooms as well. It almost appeared as if the entire building was tilting.

With my kids screaming for me to come over and see this, I sort of had an idea of what to expect, but experience had taught me never to expect anything. What I did know was that it had to be something special the way the girls were freaking out. This automatically ruled out the possibility that maybe some woman or guy was walking around their apartment naked or that a couple was engaging in sexual activity and had forgotten to shut their Venetian blinds, or whatever item they used for privacy. No matter what it was, it had to be "better" than these mundane actions. As I looked out the window at the tenement across the street, there, in all of his glory, was the individual I would dub, "The Mad Masturbator."

The Mad Masturbator was a young man in his mid-thirties who lived on the third floor across the street from our school. As would be his custom for weeks to come, he would awaken between 7:30-8:15, go over to the window, which faced our school, stretch, then whip out his penis and masturbate. When he repeated this activity the next day, we called the police. We were told that as long as he wasn't harming anyone with his actions, there was nothing they could do. We would eventually learn that "MM," as I often called him, had recently been released from a mental institution, and his actions were not deemed sufficient to return him to the mental facility he had recently departed.

Day after day, my immature babies watched this same event unfold. Although practically scripted, after a week, I wondered when they would tire of watching MM's daily ritual. Every day they screamed out the window, making disparaging remarks or doing anything to distract MM from his desired goal. Instead of acting their ages, many of my wards exhibited the mentality of ten-year-olds. Yes, they were physically able to have their own babies, yet as previously alluded to, many were immature babies themselves. Considering that at least 70% of the students in my self-contained class were indulging in sexual activity, why were they so fascinated by this sick individual's method of sexual gratification?

As one of my more mature girls asked me, "Mr. Ross, what's wrong with everyone? We do this to our boyfriends all of the time, so why watch this guy? I just don't get it!" she said in this confused state.

"Guess what? Neither do I," was all I could say to her.

As quickly as the "Mad Masturbator" appeared, that's how quickly he disappeared. Soon, we all began to wonder what had happened to him. Just like everything else, he had become just another part of "the neighborhood." Eventually, word would filter down to us that someone in the neighborhood took exception to MM's daily routine of self-gratification and shot him.

My initial reaction to the shooting was, "Oh well, one less problem!" now displaying my own insensitivity. Upon further consideration, I realized how cynical I had become since he was just a sick, harmless individual who needed some serious help. There was no need to be angry at MM. He couldn't control his actions. The person that deserved to be shot was the jerk that had placed him in an apartment directly across the street from a school. Whoever this fool was, I'm sure he / she knew about MM's behavior. They just didn't care, and this apathy could have cost MM his life. No one at our school ever found out if MM had recovered from his gunshot wounds. All we knew was that he was never seen again, and another chapter in the history of "the neighborhood" had come to an abrupt end.

Being as fair and honest as possible, I would be remiss if I failed to inform the reader that quite a number of my sexually active students were both physically and mentally mature. Numerous indulged in sexual activities because they truly believed they really loved their mate. In many instances, these youngsters were far more mature than many of their contemporaries from around the country. A number of these young ladies were helping to raise their younger brothers and sisters, as well cooking, cleaning, going shopping, etc., so their parent, parents, or whomever they lived with could go to work and earn a living. These were no longer immature little girls, but rather young women who, unfortunately, had their childhood torn right out from under them.

The first time I saw Sandra with her newborn, a number of thoughts and observations came into focus. Immediately, I saw a beautiful baby being held by an extremely gorgeous and proud mother. Sandra's original look of shame had been replaced by one of pride and accomplishment. Being a parent, no matter what one's chronological age, gives the individual a feeling of grandeur, and Sandra definitely exhibited this emotion.

On the other side of the equation, I thought about all that Sandra had sacrificed by becoming a teenage mother. Although lucky to have a great family who would help in raising her child, Sandra just didn't realize what she had forfeited. She had lost both her sexual innocence, as well as a huge portion of her own childhood. Instead of being a somewhat carefree individual, just trying to experience the trials and tribulations of being a teenager, Sandra now had responsibilities that women twice her age found difficult to handle.

Anyone who has ever had a child knows of the many pitfalls that need to be overcome to raise such a wonder. Although the parent or parents may be chronologically mature, have the financial resources and other ingredients necessary to raise a well-rounded child, I have always believed that few individuals, even those with the previously mentioned assets, have or understand the true prerequisites needed to start a family. All of the books, theories, help lines, and other resources available do not necessarily give the person the qualities necessary to assume the role of parent. No book can tell you if you have what it takes to handle a baby's crying, the endless sleepless nights if your child has colic, the doctor visits, shopping, etc. It's great to be an optimist as to the parenting abilities that you think you possess, but don't be surprised when you find out that you're not as prepared as you thought you were.

I believe that only one fact can convince me, as well as any potential parent, that they are ready for the insane world of raising a child: EXPERIENCE! Only after going through the rigors of being a first time parent can anyone convince me that they are ready to have a child. To totally understand the ramifications of a single act of love or passion, entails understanding the responsibilities this act may present.

Yes, Sandra's baby was magnificent, incredible, and every positive adjective I could possibly think of, but could she ever regain the youthful experiences she would miss in order to raise this baby in a responsible manner? Did she have the know-how necessary to comprehend the enormous task she had now embarked upon? Unfortunately, I believe the answers to these questions are no! Sandra never told me she wanted to have a baby because she wanted someone to love and to love her back. She already had this with her parent(s) and siblings. Others, unfortunately, were not so lucky!

During my ten years at I.S.24, I would "guesstimate" a minimum of 50 young ladies "showed" they were pregnant. Just think, an average of five per year, which in the entire scheme of things wasn't too bad, or was it? Of these 50 pregnancies, how many of these would-be parents had the where-with-all to deal with the enormous responsibility of raising a child without having the safety net that was accorded to Sandra. The answer, no matter what you believe, was a few at best.

I cannot desist in reiterating the irrefutable fact that many of "our babies" are having babies because they are not getting the love and attention they so desperately need. This is the truth, whether you want to hear it or not. Teen pregnancy, like drug use, crosses all boundaries, be they geographical, racial, social class, etc. Yes, you will still get the answer "I made a mistake." Unfortunately, this response is being heard less often as this problem increases. Those in the know, be they government officials, think-tank participants, or anyone that can help with this ever-growing social crisis, had better figure out why so many of our children do not feel loved and need their own child to satisfy this feeling of neglect. It's great to have programs to deal with this social reality, but too many deal with the problem after the fact. We had better deal with causality before tens of thousands of newborns become part of our ever-increasing population. We, as a society, cannot continue on this unabated path. Let our teens be teens and leave the responsibility of having children to our so-called adults. Too much is lost when this natural order is reversed!

CHAPTER ELEVEN

Trips to the City

Some of the fondest memories I have from my teaching experience relate to the class trips I shared with my students. In most instances, we were never afforded the luxury of a school bus, this of course due to our "elite standing," or lack thereof, in our district. In most cases, our only mode of transportation was the use of mass transit, and usually the subway was our only option. There were times when four or five classes went on a trip together, and trying to contain this many students on a train was quite difficult. With experience, I learned that going alone with my class was a much easier and enjoyable outing. When I think of all of the possible scenarios that might have occurred, I'm quite proud to say that I never lost a student, and not one of my kids was ever arrested. I've often wondered if teachers from "better schools" can make this claim.

To say that each trip was an adventure would be an understatement. Something inadvertently would always occur. One time, we were on the train, heading into Manhattan, when I noticed that a woman with beautiful, long, blond hair had dropped her pocketbook and was unaware of this fact. After picking it up, I tapped her on her shoulder:

"Excuse me, Miss, you dropped your pocketbook," I informed her.

As she turned around, she was really a he, and my kids went wild. They started laughing and goofing on this guy all the while calling him some unflattering names. As for myself, I must have turned every shade of red imaginable due to the embarrassment I caused both of us. I learned a quick trip lesson: Never tap someone on the back and say, "Excuse me, Mr., Miss, Ma'am, etc." You just don't know the gender of the person until they turn around, and in some cases even this doesn't help. Just say, "Excuse me...."

During my third year teaching, I decided to take my class into the city and catch a movie, which dealt with a topic we were learning about in class. I informed the cinema's manager about our plans and was told that if 16 students showed up, we'd get a group rate. Anything less meant we'd have to pay full price. When my students returned their trip slips, I counted 18 students who were given permission to go on this excursion.

Trip day finally arrived, and unfortunately, only 14 of my students showed up. When we reached the theater, no matter how hard I tried, the manager would not give us a discount. I was always pretty good when it came to bargaining with people, but this guy wouldn't budge an inch. You would have thought the money was coming out of his paycheck. Since I didn't want to disappoint my kids, I figured we'd scout around until we could find a movie or some other form of entertainment that met our budget. As luck would have it, we found a theater that was showing a "Spaghetti Western" starring Lee Van Kleif. The fact that karate was involved made this flick the perfect entertainment medium.

As we entered the theater at approximately 9:15 a.m., I thought *I'd drop dead!* The place was jam-packed. There had to be at least 500 people waiting for the movie to begin. The reason I almost dropped was simple: There had to be at least 300 people smoking pot, drinking, shooting up, and whatever else you can possibly imagine.

I told my kids, "Let's get out of here!" all the while feeling badly for them.

Carlos then asked me, "Yo, Mr. Ross, what's your problem? It's just like the movie theater where we live!" he said as a matter of fact.

After mulling over Carlos' words of wisdom, I realized he was right, and I told my kids we would stay. When everyone was seated I told my kids, "Nobody goes to the bathroom or to buy food by themselves." And they knew I meant every word of this warning.

Although my kids looked at me as if I was nuts, they all agreed.

Incident #1 was pretty funny. Some guy, stoned out of his mind, entered the row in front of us, falling all over people and saying, "Excuse me, excuse me...." while looking for a seat.

Finally reaching an apparently empty seat in the middle of the row, he sat down. The next thing we saw was this other guy get up and punch our stoned friend upside his head. What he had thought was an empty seat was occupied, and the seat's occupant did not appreciate our friend sitting on his lap. Well, to get back to the aisle, our buddy tripped over the same people he had encountered on his way in. My kids were rolling from laughter as our friend was kicked and punched by those he again stumbled over.

As we began to watch the movie, it didn't take but five minutes for incident #2 to occur. It seems that this dude behind me, ripped on some drug, started to nod out and rest his head on my shoulder. This happened about four times, and each time I pushed his head off of my shoulder, my kids laughed harder than the previous episode. Finally, this guy nods out on my shoulder, and I give him a shot to the head with my elbow. He goes flying backwards with a thud. My students were now totally hysterical with laughter, especially when he let out a grunt but didn't wake up.

When the movie ended, all things considered, my students had thoroughly enjoyed themselves. Furthermore, our enjoyment was enhanced due to the fact that we all were high from all the weed that was being smoked during the movie's longevity. To tell you the truth, I was flying from the pot fumes that permeated every part of this huge movie theater. I don't think anyone that had watched this movie left without at least a "buzz," if you know what I mean.

Outside the movie theater, we noticed some guy with blood pouring down the side of his face. Paramedics were in the process of bandaging up another patron and still two others were taking care of an overdose victim. Police on the scene had two guys in handcuffs and were speaking to someone about what had occurred. It was at this moment in time that a police sergeant came storming over to me totally pissed off. Without any form of acknowledgment, this lunatic goes off the walls.

"Are you nuts? How dare you bring your class to a movie like this!" he raged. For a second I was startled, and then I remembered what Carlos had said earlier. Looking at the officer almost eyeball to eyeball, in a smart ass tone of voice I stated, "Hey, look at these kids! Do you think the movie theaters in their neighborhood are any better?" I said matter of factly.

At this point I think you could have fried an egg on this officer's head, that's how angry he was. His face became so red, I thought he might have a stroke from high blood pressure. Finally, he managed to blurt out, "Get the hell out of here!" all the while looking like he wanted to kill me. Admittedly, irrespective of Carlos' logic, I really had made a stupid decision staying in this environment. Thankfully, none of my kids were injured, or worse.

After eating lunch at Nathan's across the street from the theater, I realized that we still had time to kill before we were due back at school for dismissal. I told my kids we had some time to walk around the city, check out the stores, buildings, etc. It was while we were walking down 42nd Street that incident #3 took place.

During our little sightseeing tour, I had gotten into a conversation with some of my students about the city when I sensed that something was wrong. Turning around, I noticed that six or seven of my students were missing. Looking back up the block, I saw my missing wards talking to a young lady in a doorway. As I neared my wayward youngsters, I heard them propositioning this girl, who just so happened to be a prostitute. Using their street smarts, my kids were trying to find out if she would lower her price for…

As I yelled at them, "Get the hell over here," inwardly I was laughing my head off.

As I've said before, nothing my kids did surprised me. As a matter of fact, I was very proud of them since I felt that they were doing a good job of bargaining. I knew that the more they became adept at this art, the better off they would be in this everyday aspect of their lives. Besides, this hooker was much better looking than those on the Eastern Parkway and the surrounding areas of our school.

To see the look of amazement on a child's face when he or she discovers something for the first time is one of the many rewards I enjoyed as a teacher. On trips to the Museum of Natural History, the Brooklyn Museum, the Museum of Modern Art, etc., my kids at times were mesmerized. The panoramas at the Museum of Natural History were mind-boggling, especially when I explained that every leaf, twig, piece of dirt, etc. was hand made and that it took up to 15 years to complete one exhibit. The dinosaur display blew their minds due to the immensity of the skeletal bones.

Nothing needs to be said about their reaction to the nudes found at the various museums we visited, as well as others previously mentioned. Trying to figure out an abstract painting and what the artist was trying to express was always an adventure. My kids came up with all sorts of explanations, ranging from the sexual mode to alien invaders. I thought it was great because they were using their gray matter. Whether their interpretation was correct was irrelevant. It was the thought process that was important. Besides, who knows if my interpretation was any better than theirs.

One of our trips to the Brooklyn Museum had special significance as far as I personally was concerned. I was very familiar with the museum since I had frequented it practically once a month since the age of 12. The museum had one of the world's greatest Egyptian collections, and since I was interested in deciphering hieroglyphics, this place was a dream come true.

As I previously stated, something always happened to us on a trip, and this adventure was no exception. After viewing many of the museum's exhibits, I decided it was time for us to eat lunch. We went down to the cafeteria, and my students either purchased lunch or ate what they brought with them. Being too lazy to pack my own lunch, I had decided to eat the museum's food. I opted for a hamburger and fries and put ketchup from packets on both. Right away I knew something was wrong with the ketchup. After two bites, I tossed the entire meal into the garbage. Without a doubt the ketchup was rancid!

No matter what I ate or drank afterwards, nothing could get rid of the terrible taste the ketchup had left in my mouth. By the time we finally boarded the train to get back to school, I was suffering from severe stomach cramps. At the first stop, I ran off the train and threw up my guts in a trash can. Every stop thereafter was a repeat of the original episode. Initially my kids thought this was pretty funny, but after the third time, they felt sorry for me and showed great concern. I seriously felt I was going to die. Here we had gone to a great museum for the expressed purpose of furthering and enhancing everyone's knowledge and the primary memory of this trip would be their teacher upchucking. I guess it was a successful experience because my kids would never forget what food poisoning was. By the time we arrived back at I.S.24, I must have barfed at least ten times. With little strength left, I remained at school at least two hours after the school's population had been dismissed. When I felt strong enough, I began the long ride home. To this day, I have never had ketchup or, for that matter, any condiment that comes in a packet.

During a three-year span, one of my favorite trips was to Battery Park with my self-contained class. Due to the fact that Principal Pell wanted us out of the building as often as possible as we neared the end of the school year, I took my kids on a trip every Friday to the park. No matter how often we went, my students always wanted to know if we would ride the Staten Island "Fairy." For 25 cents, we could ride the ferry as many times as we wished, and my kids loved it. Afterwards, as if on cue, we'd get on the line to go out to the Statue of Liberty. Unfortunately, as also was the norm, we never managed to get out there due to the impatience of my students having to wait on line for up to two hours before our turn arrived.

On one of our Battery Park excursions, my friend, Jerry, joined us with one of his classes. After the normal "Fairy Ride," our kids either ate their lunch and/or ran around the park enjoying the safety and freedom Battery

Park offered. Some of Jerry's kids had never seen a park this size, and they were having a blast. We, on the other hand, were looking at the magnificent women who entered the park to enjoy their lunch break. I cannot tell you how much I enjoyed this extra perk that the park offered.

While observing the park's beauty, Jerry and I noticed that a crowd of people had congregated and were watching something with intense curiosity. We decided to investigate, just to make sure none of our children were involved in whatever was attracting this ever-growing crowd. Much to our surprise, a group of businessmen and women were watching our students climbing a tree and indulging in other forms of harmless fun such as doing cartwheels, flips, etc.

When one of these so-called "professionals" stated, "Look at those monkeys swinging from the trees!" I felt my blood pressure surge.

Knowing the use of fisticuffs was totally unprofessional and might get me locked up, I decided to go over to this gentleman and call him the asshole that he was. As I should have anticipated, in a matter of seconds, one word led to another, and we were close to getting into it when two of my kids pulled me away. If my students hadn't intervened there would have been a free for all, and this was still a possibility.

When one of my kids asked me if the guy had called them "monkeys," I didn't respond.

Not answering really pissed off a number of my students, as well as some of Jerry's. Now they were ready to kick ass. On the brink of inciting an all-out riot, it was now my responsibility to defuse a volatile situation. Thankfully, Jerry and I were able to calm down our students and bloodshed was averted. I couldn't believe how stupid I had been. Reflecting on the entire incident, the only asshole in the park was me!

To this day, there is no doubt in my mind that our kids would have put a severe hurt on some of these "professionals." Thankfully, this melee was diffused because, even if our students were just defending themselves, they would have been arrested since they were black and Spanish and not wearing Armani or Calvin Klein fashion ware.

Speaking of "real monkeys," for as long as I can remember, I have always loved and been fascinated with the animal kingdom. During my 12 years in the teaching profession, there were always various forms of animal life in my classrooms. Many of my students brought in their own pets, i.e. snakes, mice, rabbits, rats, to show their classmates, and before you knew it, my rooms looked like mini zoos. It was early in my career that I realized that many of my students shared my love of nature. It would become a foregone conclusion that a trip to the zoo would be an annual event.

One day, before a scheduled excursion, a colleague of mine told me a hilarious story. He had taken his class to the zoo earlier in the day and cautioned his students not to harass the animals. Despite his warnings, his kids began tormenting these incarcerated "felons." By the time they reached the gorilla cage, his students were totally abusive and out of control. When they caught sight of the gorilla, they started screaming at him, throwing papers, and engaging in activities that would irritate a human, no less a caged animal of such intelligence.

Before anyone realized what was about to happen, the gorilla, obviously upset, went to the corner of his cage, picked up a pile of shit, and threw it at one of his tormentors. Bull's-eye! The kid was hit right below the chest and the shit splattered just under his chin and down to around his crotch. If this had happened today, I could see this as an episode of "Those Amazing Animals" with the title, "Kid Covered with Gorilla Shit after Attack at the Central Park Zoo." Without a doubt, it would be their highest rated show ever aired.

I also pictured this incident being reported on ESPN. "We have a final score from the Central Park Zoo: Gorilla 1, Student 0." Meanwhile, I was in tears from laughing so hard.

The next morning before we left for the zoo, I warned my kids not to piss off the animals by screaming at them or throwing objects. When we finally reached the zoo and started making the rounds, everything went off without a hitch. Eventually, we reached the gorilla cage, and there he was, sitting in a tire. In all honesty, this was the nastiest and ugliest gorilla I had ever seen. He looked pissed off at the entire world. A quick glance let me know there wasn't any feces in the cage, thereby allowing me to relax.

I don't know if it was because the gorilla looked so mean or because he was so ugly, but within a matter of seconds, my kids, who had just been great up until this moment, disregarded my warnings and started to taunt this animal. What unfolded was an event that appeared as if it was occurring in slow motion.

The gorilla, obviously annoyed, ever so slowly extricated himself from his tire and began to walk towards one of my students, who was being totally obnoxious. Knowing that he couldn't reach out and grab the kid and there was no shit around to throw, I remained quite calm. At the worst, I figured he would spit at my student, and to tell you the truth, he deserved it.

When the gorilla reached my student, he turned his back to him and let out a fart that was deafening. The indescribable smell of this explosion of high-octane gas caused one of my girls to throw up immediately. If forced to describe its aroma, the best I could conjure up was that it emanated from the bowels of hell.

Not withstanding the stink, within seconds I was hysterical from laughing so hard. My ribs would kill me the rest of the day because I just couldn't stop. This entire event was a classic! Being sprayed by a couple of skunks couldn't have compared with the smell from that devastating fart. It took almost two days to get the stench of that weapon of mass destruction out of my nostrils. I used nasal spray, Vicks vapor rub, a nose inhaler, and still this stench lingered. I thought I was going crazy, but my kids told me they were having the same problem. It was as if that fart was made up of gas and glue so when we first smelled it, the molecules stuck to the inner lining of our nostrils.

In the meantime, the gorilla, proud of his accomplishment, slowly walked back to his tire, sat down, and maintained his "pissed off at the world" disposition. I must admit that upon closer inspection, he did seem to exude a sense of great satisfaction. I, on the other hand, acquired a far greater respect for animal intelligence than I had ever thought possible.

A short epilogue to this event is in order. After years of complaints and demonstrations by animal rights groups, as well as your average citizen, the Central Park Zoo was closed for renovation. When it reopened to the public, there was a vast improvement in animal accommodations. Unfortunately, the gorilla passed away a few years later, a sad ending to a very sad existence. The only positive aspect to his death was the salvation of some unsuspecting individuals' nostrils.

When memories of this trip recur, I recognize the importance this experience had on all concerned. Undoubtedly, many of our other trips offered greater instructional and educational value, but the Central Park escapade reached a much higher spiritual plateau. My students took away the understanding that one should respect another's feelings, rights, and territory, be it human or animal. This is not to say that they didn't know this from life on the streets in Bed-Sty, but now it had been explained to them in a different context.

I, in turn, witnessed the caring nature of some of my most hardened, street-savvy students. I was taken aback by the empathy they showed towards many of these imprisoned creatures. In some respects, it was much greater than that shown to fellow human beings. I always knew that, under their gruff exterior, many of my kids were caring individuals, but I never before had realized the magnitude of their concern.

Unfortunately, like many trips in life, reality set in when we departed for the train that would take us back to I.S.24. Again, we were in the "real world," and although we had enjoyed a brief respite from its tumultuous character, nothing had changed during our absence.

CHAPTER TWELVE

War in the Rank and File

Following in the family tradition of being active unionists, one of my first actions after reporting to I.S.24 was to seek membership in the union that represented my fellow colleagues: The United Federation of Teachers. Like most labor unions, the U.F.T. had its own agenda with a common purpose: the betterment and protection of its members. Inherent in this cause was the ever-present need to secure increased financial reward, better working conditions, and procurement of the best possible health benefits. Equally important was the "watch dog" responsibility of our leadership in making sure that the board of education, the city of New York, and New York State complied with all contract provisions we had won in the past through collective bargaining agreements, or as a result of our membership going out on strike.

Under the astute leadership of Al Shanker, our union grew to be a powerful force in city, state, and national politics. In city elections, not having the backing of our membership was tantamount to political suicide. With the teachers' union often aligned with other municipal unions representing police, fire fighters, sanitation workers, etc., the U.F.T. rose from a fledgling organization in the early '50s to the powerful organization it is today.

In order to comprehend the war that tore at the fiber of our school's existence and that had ramifications that reached the highest levels of our union's leadership, it is important to have some insight into the internal structure of the U.F.T. At the top of our union's hierarchy is the president and his or her executive board, consisting of six vice presidents, a treasurer, secretary, and assistant secretary. Every aspect of union policy emanates from this executive board. They are the major participants in negotiating contracts with the city of New York and the board of education, as well as protecting members from any illegal activity of school boards, city agencies, etc. This executive board also helps determine how vast sums of money are invested, as well as how our financial strength and power are used in backing those politicians or organizations that champion our positions on numerous areas of contention. Of course the aforementioned are just a few of the multitude of responsibilities delegated to this branch of our organization.

At every level of our union's hierarchy, there are people who make sure our contract is not violated, members are not harassed, and union policy is carried out with speed and optimum efficiency. Power is delegated from our president and executive board as follows:

1. Just as there are five boroughs that comprise New York City, so too are there five union borough representatives. Whether they represent the Bronx, Brooklyn, Staten Island, Queens, or Manhattan, they are the most important union official in the borough. They coordinate all union activity and delegate authority throughout the borough. This individual will handle any problems that cannot be dealt with on the district level. They will monitor every aspect of union activity in the borough and carefully keep tabs on those individuals or institutions that might try to circumvent the proper procedural courses of action as agreed upon in the collective bargaining agreement.

2. Each borough is divided up into school districts. This district is comprised of a number of schools from each grade level: elementary, junior, and high school. A District Representative is the elected spokesperson for all of the teachers who work in this specific school district. There are 32 school districts in the city of New York; therefore 32 representatives occupy these offices.

The district rep's job is to disseminate union information to its members, as well as make sure there are no contract violations by nonunion personnel, organizations, the district superintendent who is the head of all schools in the district, principals, assistant principals, etc. Of equal importance is the fact that they represent teachers at grievance hearings, as well as assume a multitude of other responsibilities.

3. Union members in every school in the city of New York elect their own school "leader" known as the chapter chairman. The chapter chairman represents teachers in their dealings with the school administration, district office, etc. The chapter chairman and his executive committee (vice

chapter chairman, sergeant at arms, delegate to the delegate assembly of the U.F.T., etc.) are the protectors of teachers' rights in their school.

The chapter chairman is to report to the district representative any contract violations, i.e. oversized classes, illegal teacher observations, unnecessary staff meetings, poor teacher evaluations, etc. They are the eyes and ears of the district rep in particular and the union in general. The chapter chairman, if well versed in all aspects of the union contract, can be extremely influential in determining the school's daily agenda. Conversely, steady conflict between a chapter chairman and a principal, or his administrators, can cause tremendous tension in the school environment. Ultimately, this can lead to open hostility and an atmosphere not conducive towards learning.

Simply put, there is a chain of command with leaders who are responsible to the membership and to their higher ups. This abbreviated organizational structure, as I've described it, insures that our members are protected, policy is disseminated, and our union works at optimum efficiency.

On a number of occasions, I've either mentioned or alluded to the fact that our staff at I.S.24 was a conglomeration of individuals which were representative of all strata of our society. As diverse as we were, we did have one common thread that united us as a staff: a powerful union membership. We fought tooth and nail with the school administration and the district office in order to protect our rights and to secure a more positive environment for our students and ourselves. Politics were always present, infighting was the norm, but when the common good was challenged, we all united to form a very formidable opposition. Nobody, internally or externally, was going to shit on us without a fight, and did we fight!

Towards the end of my sixth year at I.S.24, a number of my colleagues approached me about running for the office of chapter chairman. Having shown no inclination of seeking a union position in the past, numerous actions and activities by our school's union leadership had begun to irritate me and had me questioning my inactivity in union business. As my years at I.S.24 accumulated, these annoyances became quite disconcerting. All I knew was that the job of chapter chairman in our school, as well as in all schools, was to represent all U.F.T. staff members, and in my eyes, this was not being carried out in the proper manner. The more knowledgeable I became on the inner workings of this elected position, the more I perceived this office being abused by the individual that occupied its seat of power.

All I have ever asked for in my life is that everyone is treated equally and with the utmost respect. In this case, it was equality in teaching programs, securing after-school and summer jobs, etc. As I became more cognizant of what was correct union policy and what in reality was occurring in our school, my frustration with those in power reached new heights. With the passage of time, it became apparent to other union members that the time might be right for a change in leadership. Never did I anticipate that I would be at the center of this upheaval!

Having had so many years to analyze why I became involved in this "blood letting," I've realized that three irrefutable facts gnawed at my guts, causing me to seriously consider a run for the office of chapter chairman in 1975.

1. The fact that our chapter chairman, Allan Banister, had secured a short teaching program, no greater than 12 periods a week. This really ticked me and many other union members off since this position became available out of nowhere. Please understand, at least as far as my position on this matter was concerned, I was not jealous of this cushy program per se. In my heart, I truly believed that as a chapter chairman, you should be in the trenches like those you represent. I personally felt that Banister, although having seniority for this position, had violated a trust with the school's rank and file by accepting a position that somehow had been created to perfectly match his credentials. I believed it was an abuse of power and did a great disservice to the union office he held. This entire appointment smelled fishy, and many of my colleagues felt the same way.

2. The increasing perception that Banister, our elected leader, was "in bed" with the administration, which was and always would be our enemy. I was of the opinion that a chapter chairman should never be perceived as being one of the principal's buddies or constantly be seen hanging out with administrators. Not only did it look bad, it was bad! Many members, myself included, didn't want this type of individual to represent us in our constant confrontations with our proverbial enemies.

3. The blatant arrogance emanating from Banister and his inner circle of friends who thought they were better than everyone else alienated many union members, including yours truly. The unadulterated truth was, they made many of their fellow union members feel like low-lifes and outcasts. The longer I wrestled with the idea of running for chapter chairman, the greater was my desire to rid our school of those with their "holier than thou" attitude.

During the pre-infancy stage of testing the waters for a possible candidacy, I was keenly aware that seeking such a position entailed making the greatest of sacrifices and insured maximum disruption of family life, as Dianah and I had known it to be. Acknowledging the fact that if I ran and won, I'd be the representative of approximately 130 teachers, as well as 18 paraprofessionals (teacher assistants) and the entire secretarial staff of the school was quite a daunting prospect. The fact that I had never held a union position meant that my education would consist of on-the-job training. This in itself presented a tremendous hardship, knowing that my inexperience could lead to disastrous consequences for those who had chosen me to be their representative when dealing with the school administration and the district superintendent and his crew of back-stabbers.

There was no doubt in my mind that if I ran for my school's chairmanship and won, most of my free time would be consumed with meetings, helping individuals with their problems, implementing union policy, and making and receiving phone calls at all hours of the night, etc. All of these factors would only add further turmoil and chaos to an already tension-filled family life.

So many stressful events had occurred during our first year of marriage. It was amazing that Dianah and I still had our sanity. This was a tribute to our faith and inner strength, although at times we both felt we were teetering on the verge of nervous breakdowns. The pressure of being a good husband and family man, attending night school to get credits towards my masters degree, and just dealing with the responsibilities imposed on me by life itself, put a tremendous strain on my existence. The fact that I was even contemplating running for the office of chapter chairman could only lead to one conclusion: I was even crazier than I thought I was—or was I?

Having never been accused of being an individual that looked at life through rose-colored glasses, I innately realized that, if I ran, the campaign would be an all-out war. Being a student of history, I knew that if you are going to wage war, you must never underestimate the capabilities or possible devious behaviors of your opponent. I must admit that even with this awareness, I never expected the low-life tactics, threats, and ramifications that would be hurled at me. I could comprehend such behavior if this was a national election, but in essence, this was nothing more than a piss-poor school election—or so I thought. Soon I would learn that this insignificant contest would turn into a fight to the death. The reality of the entire ensuing mess was the fact that the "haves" had too much to lose if I was elected. Therefore, they would use any and every means at their disposal to destroy me.

In hindsight, I knew that the negatives far outweighed the positives in seeking this office. Why, therefore, did I embark on such an arduous undertaking, one that I knew would affect all aspects of my life? Why get involved in such a horrific struggle that ultimately led to stomach ulcers, sleepless nights, hypoglycemia (low blood sugar), dissension bordering on upheaval in my family life, and numerous other consequences?

As disruptive as the next two years would be, one non-negotiable principle constantly drove me and basically answered the previous questions of why I should run: Everyone should be treated equally and with respect. Be it idealism or outright stupidity, it was this belief that fueled the fire, allowing me to face head on all of the obstacles that could block my path towards victory. Of equal, if not greater, importance was the fact that my colleagues sought me out to run for the office of chapter chairman. Knowing my character, these individuals believed me to be an honorable person who would be fair with everyone. I just couldn't refuse their call for help.

With Jerry Lester as my confidant, I decided to have a meeting at my home with approximately 15 colleagues in attendance. The purpose of the meeting was simple enough: to discuss at length the possibility of my running for the office of chapter chairman. Before even commencing with this meeting, Jerry and I sat down and superficially went over the I.S.24 staff list. We concluded that only by winning the majority of votes cast by teachers from "The Annex" did we have a chance to be victorious and, might I add, it was a slim chance at best.

Although I.S. 24 consisted of grades K6-K8, our sixth grade was housed in a separate building called the annex. In order to save money, the board of education had decided to close the annex and incorporate the student population, teaching staff, and its administration into the main building. Having always been perceived to have a pristine existence, since they were far removed from the chaos we encountered on a daily basis, the annex staff feared retribution from our chapter chairman and his inner circle, upon their assimilation into the main building. The only possible way for us to win the election was for me, and members of my slate of candidates, to get about 75% of the annex vote. All of this would be irrelevant if I decided not to run. Although I had basically made up my mind to accept the challenge of being a candidate, this meeting was crucial as far as eliminating many of the trepidations I still had.

Being as discriminate as possible, I decided to invite to my home individuals whom I considered representative of various groups of disillusioned members of the I.S.24 staff. Of paramount importance was my belief that those who came could deliver the votes necessary for us to win what I knew would be a down and dirty election. Everyone would have input during this meeting and hopefully during my long tenure as chapter chairman. Of optimum concern was the need for this meeting to be kept under wraps. It was imperative that Allan Banister and Co. have no idea that such a meeting was in the works. I knew that if our opposition had gotten wind of this mini-conference, they would have exerted immense pressure on my would-be invitees not to get involved, or else!

To this day, I'm still not positive if my opponents knew about this impending meeting. One fact was a certainty: by Monday, they not only knew about it, but were also aware of everything that had transpired. To say that they weren't happy campers would be an understatement. Thankfully, at this moment in the entire scheme of things, our only advantage was the fact that they weren't taking my possible candidacy seriously. This would soon change.

With the meeting called for Saturday afternoon at 1:00 p.m., I awoke that morning filled with anticipation as well as apprehension. I had no idea how this scenario would play out, but an adrenaline rush was already kicking in. As zero hour approached, I began pacing back and forth, hoping that a majority of my invitees would show up for this skull session.

The fact that everyone I invited attended this meeting should give you an idea of how serious this entire matter was. Most of my guests had families and all had other responsibilities, yet everyone put whatever business they had on hold so that they could participate in this Saturday afternoon "pow-wow." Once it began, the session lasted approximately three hours. Of paramount importance was whether I would make the decision to run for office. Of equal significance was what I could offer these people, and the groups they represented, in order to secure their backing.

What I eventually proposed to this cross-section of union members was the least complicated component of this entire equation. I promised them fairness in regards to programming, after-school and summer jobs, hall patrols, and all other job-related issues at I.S.24. I also promised them respect, which meant listening to what they had to say and encouraging their input on union matters. Finally, I pledged a return to the days when they all felt that this was their chapter and not the establishment that now existed under the leadership of Allan Banister and his inner circle.

What I next guaranteed every attendee, I believe, they never expected to hear. I fervently believe that my brutal honesty as to the repercussions we would all face if we lost was one of the major reasons they decided to back my candidacy. In no uncertain terms, I let them know that we were going up against the establishment. Not only did we have to beat Banister and his cronies, but also our district representative, as well as the district superintendent and his gang of cutthroats. I guaranteed them that all of these forces would be aligned against us, and they would use any and all means necessary to insure our defeat.

I made it crystal clear to everyone in attendance that, should we suffer defeat, we would get the most horrific programs when the new school year began. My guests were told that they would get the most dangerous school patrols, be given coverages of the most out-of-control classes, and be subjected to all sorts of harassment within the limits of our contract.

Using a no-nonsense approach, I let it be known that this election would be an all-out conflagration with no prisoners taken. Again I reiterated that all I could give them was honesty, fairness, and equality. There was no denying Banister could get them jobs, easy programs, and other perks if they voted for him and his slate of candidates. If they voted for me and my running mates and we lost, a world of hurt would come crashing down on all of our heads.

The rest of that weekend was one of the longest and loneliest of my life. Fifteen people had opted to sacrifice so much on a mere novice when they endorsed my possible candidacy. Irrespective of what would happen to me, I knew I could possibly ruin many careers if I ran and lost. So much was at stake, and there was no way that I'd allow my ego to be a factor in this decision. I could do so much good for so many people who had been disenfranchised and basically screwed, or I could add further misery to an already lousy existence that most of us endured working at I.S.24.

Sunday night, after intense deliberation, I informed Dianah that I was going to run against Banister. Knowing me as well as she did, Dianah wasn't the least bit surprised. Although we had discussed my possible candidacy on previous occasions, I wanted her to know that I alone had made this decision. I tried to distance her from this process because if any physical harm came to me, I didn't want her carrying around feelings of guilt that she was partly to blame because she helped with my decision. Cautioning her to expect the unexpected only lent further credence to some of the bad vibes I still had about this entire situation. I'm proud to say that Dianah stood by me, knowing full well that, if I were elected, our lives would change, possibly forever.

With nominations called for by the week's end, my first order of business would be to assemble a full slate of candidates who would run for all of the other union offices to be voted on: vice chapter chairman, sergeant at arms, union delegate, treasurer, secretary, etc. After a long discussion with Jerry that Sunday night, I called every person who had attended Saturday's meeting and informed them of my decision to run for the office of chapter chairman. Nearly every individual that I asked to be part of my slate of candidates graciously accepted, knowing full well the ramifications if we lost. A number of people I spoke with seemed floored when I asked them their opinion about who they thought would be a good choice for a certain office. Some were flabbergasted when I agreed with their assessment. They found out that I wasn't kidding when I promised that this would be everyone's union, and they would spread this information to the rank and file.

From the moment I punched my time card on Monday morning, I knew word of our weekend meeting had already leaked out. Not knowing for sure who the informer was, yet not surprised there was a rat amongst us, the looks I received from some of my "friends" in Banister's inner circle would have led a brain dead individual to realize that the cat was out of the bag! During the next two days, quite a number of people approached me with:

"I heard you're thinking of running for chapter chairman." They'd inquired seemingly innocent of any ulterior motives.

Although I wanted to say, "You heard right," I skirted the issue.

I figured nomination day would arrive soon enough, and for now I'd keep them guessing, as if they didn't already know.

In the middle of the week, one of Banister's loyal soldiers told me that he would like to meet with me. As I entered his office, Banister got right to the point.

"I thought we were friends. Haven't I always been fair with you?" he asked. "I heard you might be running against me for the office of chapter chairman," he said with a disturbed look on his face.

"Why?" he inquired with a look of someone who had been betrayed.

I remember thinking to myself, *Are you full of shit!* Banister knew why! A number of us had warned him during the previous years that he was alienating numerous staff members with his arrogant attitude. Also, he had been informed on many an occasion that he was getting too chummy with the school administration and the clowns at the district office, and you know how most of us felt about those people.

I unequivocally believe that this self-indulgent egotist could not grasp the simple concept that someone had the balls to oppose his reelection. With only two days remaining until nominations and without the need to play "why games," I told Banister, "Not only am I going to run against you, but I'm going to beat you, too!" and he knew that I meant every word I had just spoken.

The stunned look on Banister's face spoke volumes. Then, like Dr. Jekyll and Mr. Hyde, that hurt look was replaced by one of arrogance and defiance. Furthermore, if looks could kill, my name would be on top of the unsolved murder list in all of Bed-Sty's homicide squad rooms. I swear, I felt that I could read his mind. It was as if he was thinking *I'm not worried about you winning this election, but where do you get the audacity to dare challenge me? I'll bury you and your people, you miserable...!*

Realistically, Banister and I both knew the "friends statement" was nothing more than a crock of shit. Yes, a number of us had gone to sporting events, parties, etc. I did this with other people who were just acquaintances. Jerry was a true friend! He was a person I could trust, confide in, and who had a closed mouth. Yeah, I was Banister's friend.... Come to think of it, I was! The question that had to be answered was—was he mine? The answer was simple: As long as I was beneficial to him. Once my usefulness was used up, I'd be cast aside like some worthless piece of garbage. He had done this to others in the past, so why would he change his spots now? In retrospect, the reality of this entire situation was that I had dumped his ass before he was able to dump mine, and his ego could never accept this. After his victory, Sam Ross would pay in spades for this indiscretion!

I must admit that Banister did know me somewhat. He knew in no uncertain terms that once I told him that I was going to run for chapter chairman, there was nothing he could say or do that would change my mind. As if reconciled to this fact, he looked down at some papers on his desk and tried to look busy. We both knew nothing else needed to be said.

Two days later, my name was placed in nomination for the office of Chapter Chairman of I.S.24. It was placed by Jerry and seconded by another friend. Others on my slate were also nominated and seconded. Alternating nominations for each office, Banister's people followed with the same procedure. Finally, it was official. The war was on, and I.S.24 would never be the same.

In order to win this election, every free moment of our time had to be used to speak with members of the rank and file. We had to let them know who we were, what we stood for, and what we would try to accomplish if elected. Since all of us taught full programs, campaigning for each other was a must.

Banister, if you recall, didn't teach more than 12 periods a week, so he had ample opportunity to reach out to every single voter and spend as much time as necessary to lock up their votes. Since the rest of his inner circle had great programs too, their ability to canvass, convince, and keep in line their purported backers far exceeded ours. We could not afford any down time. We had to nail down our solid backers, figure out who the fence sitters were, and ultimately convince them to vote for us.

The ensuing days consisted of constant meetings, nightly phone calls, continual analysis of who would or would not vote for us, as well as discussing all possible scenarios that might befall us and our campaigns. Our lack of free time, due to the rigors of teaching full programs, family responsibilities, and so many other time-consuming duties, took its toll on us. We had two weeks to pull off an upset of unimaginable proportions, the magnitude of which none of us at this early stage could possibly envision. Every second was as valuable as a piece of gold, and we used each and every one to our advantage. Within days, we were all feeling the strain of this non-stop action. Much to everyone's credit, we pushed on with ever-increasing ferocity. Too much was at stake if we lost, and none of us wanted to face this possible eventuality.

I wholeheartedly believe that our opponents' complacency and arrogance helped us immeasurably during the early stages of the campaign. Their message to staff members was:

"Who is Sam Ross?"

"What experience does he have?"

"In a crisis, who would you want to represent you?" was at the core of their verbal assault.

Besides these questions, they highlighted their strong union connections and how in the past they were able to restore teacher cutbacks, get individuals after-school and summer jobs, etc. With such self-aggrandizement, Banister and his crew convinced themselves that there was no way they could lose this election.

In direct contrast to our opponents, we had to reach the staff and inform them that Banister and his group hadn't restored any teaching positions and had taken most of the after-school and summer jobs for themselves and their cohorts. Educating the staff that budget estimates in June and the number of teaching positions lost to accommodate these cuts were totally different than the "real numbers" made public in August and September was a difficult task. We explained that once the city and the board of education knew the exact amount of money that was being reimbursed from the estimated June cutbacks, teaching positions were automatically restored to the district and ultimately to I.S.24. It was all economics and Banister and his people had no say on how federal and state moneys were disbursed in regards to teaching positions in the city of New York and, more specifically, I.S.24. In essence, what sounded like such a great accomplishment to be lauded turned out to be nothing more than a sham.

We kept hitting on their taking credit for things they had nothing to do with, as well as their easy programs, inaccessibility to all staff members, and their ever-present arrogance. Our relentless pressure in educating the staff in regards to the aforementioned was beginning to pay off. We were beginning to wipe the smirks off our opponents' faces, and it felt so good.

As days passed and the election drew closer, Banister and his people began to sense that our slogan, "It's time for a change," which they originally demeaned and called "corny," was falling on receptive ears. Banister was quick to realize that I had never alienated members of our faculty and, therefore, most were willing to listen to the message I was trying to impart. The fact that numerous members on my slate of candidates were either friendly to, or part of, the various disenfranchised groups that Banister had offended over the years further enhanced our ability to disseminate our ideas.

Sensing that his campaign was in some trouble, Banister did a complete 180-degree turn and started talking to all of the "peasants" he had snubbed during the year. The fact that this annual con job had lost its effectiveness became ever more apparent as the day of the election drew nearer. Veterans of this annual "I'm a good guy" routine were sick of this phony display of caring and expressed this fact to me

We, in turn, just kept hitting away at our opponents' record and the fallacies they constantly tried to perpetuate. There was no doubt in anyone's mind that the war was beginning to heat up. No one realized that only the surface of all hell breaking loose had been scratched!

Anyone who has ever run for an elected office knows that no matter what is promised or how bad a situation might be, there are those individuals who cannot, or will not, change their eventual vote. In this election, either due to the assumed invincibility of Allan Banister, the fear of retribution if he won, or out of loyalty due to previously received perks, there were some members of our staff who could never be swayed to vote for our slate of candidates. Realizing this, I knew that if we put enough pressure on Banister, he might flinch and be forced into a major blunder, enabling us to win at least a majority of the non-aligned voters.

There were many adjectives used to describe Allan Banister, ranging from arrogant to an outright liar. Yet, never did I hear anyone ever say that he was stupid. As our pressure reached unparalleled heights, Banister finally made the major faux pas we had been looking for. Although not overtly stupid, this unwise action, or in this case, reaction, would and did cost him dearly.

Knowing we had to carry the annex by a 3:1 ratio in order to win this election, I informed Principal Pell that I was going over to their building during lunch the following day in order to discuss my agenda with the staff. This would give them a chance to meet me and learn first hand what I stood for. It also would allow me to get a hands-on pulse of the thoughts and trepidation's of people that comprised the annex staff. Word of my intended visit had been circulated by some of my backers and was slated to be held at 12:30 p.m.

After punching my time card the following morning, I noticed in my mailbox a memo to report to Leonard Pell's office. Upon entering his office, Principal Pell informed me that he had received a directive from the district superintendent's office stating that I was not allowed to go to the annex to have this meeting or to campaign there at a later date. When I expressed to Pell that lunchtime was my time to do with what I wanted, I was told I was wrong. Rethinking my response, I ultimately said, "Fine, I'll go there after school, and nobody can say squat."

Wrong again. Leonard Pell told me, "Sam, if you go over there you'll be arrested for trespassing!" and from the tone of his voice, I knew he wasn't kidding.

"What about Banister's visits over there?" I inquired, now using a totally sarcastic tone of voice.

Pell had an irrefutable answer. "Allan Banister is the chapter chairman and represents the entire staff, so he can go to the annex any time he wants to," Pell replied.

This ill-conceived plan of barring me from going to the annex was just what we needed to give us renewed strength since we were all wearing down. With a couple of well-placed phone calls, the staff of the annex was informed that I wasn't allowed to meet with them either during or after school, and if I tried to do so, I would be arrested.

Now, even the most naive optimist had to concede that Banister and his cohorts were not only in bed with the school administration, but also with the district superintendent. This realization only added to the annex staff's trepidation of being incorporated into the main building. Now, to say the least, a majority of the annex people not only didn't trust Banister, but they were pissed off at him, too!

Realizing that we had just been handed a great opportunity, there was no way I was going to miss out on this chance of an election lifetime. To stick it to our opponents, I immediately typed up a letter informing the faculty in both buildings of what had occurred. Everyone had to know that we were fighting against a stacked deck. If this infringement on my freedom of movement didn't explain it to them, nothing would.

With my completion of this letter, nearly 200 copies were in the process of being placed into the mailboxes of faculty members. Upon seeing this, Leonard Pell ordered us remove every letter.

"You're not allowed to use school resources for the purpose of campaigning!" he explicitly informed me.

Of course Banister was allowed to do this since he was the chapter chairman and therefore could use school resources to inform the faculty about union business, or in this instance, campaign.

Did these fools think we were brainless? Using outside copiers and store-bought paper, we ran off a revised newsletter explaining the annex debacle, as well as the restrictions imposed on me in the main building. We made sure everyone knew that we paid for these letters out of our own pockets since we were not allowed to use school supplies.

Having been denied access to faculty members' mailboxes, by 3:00, our newsletters were being handed out to staff members from both the annex and the main building as they walked to their cars. Thankfully, my opponent and his cronies didn't know anyone who owned the streets! To tell you the truth, I wasn't so sure about that either!

The reaction to our letter was spectacular. The following day, everyone was talking about how my constitutional rights had been violated and that Banister was not only in bed with Pell and his administration, but also the district superintendent and his entourage. When speaking with faculty members, we hinted that our district representative was also part of this concentrated effort to insure our defeat. This entire fiasco by Banister and company was an adrenaline rush for all of my people, and made us work that much harder to secure more votes. There was no doubt that my opponents had miscalculated our reaction and that of the staff, and this just added a few more nails into their political coffin.

We were on a roll. I, taking a cue from past Banister performances, played the role of a wounded soul who had been wronged. The difference between the two of us was, I really had been wronged! I used this entire episode for maximum effect, securing votes for my slate of candidates, as well as for myself.

With two days left before votes were to be cast, our opponents proposed a debate before the entire staff. I guess our tenacity had finally hit home, and this was basically their last chance to remind the membership what they had done for them in the past, as well as stop our now unchecked momentum. Of greater concern was my realization that this was their opportunity to embarrass me in front of the entire staff. They would have their people ask me questions that I couldn't possibly answer, thus casting a cloud over my ability to be a competent chapter chairman.

I must admit that their strategy of trying to make me look incompetent was pretty smart. Yet we weren't too stupid ourselves. We had anticipated such a move after the numerous blunders they were now constantly making. Hopefully this would be another failure on their part. One fact couldn't be denied: non-acceptance would have shown weakness on my part and would have been a political disaster.

In order to respond to my adversaries' challenge, Principal Pell now informed me that I would be allowed to use the rexo machine and school paper. Amazing! Now that they thought they had me, why not let Sam Ross use all of the school resources he needed, thereby negating his claim at not having access to supplies to run his campaign? Well, I wouldn't disappoint them! Every mailbox had a letter inserted into it, expressing my pleasure in participating in this debate, as well as my "amazement" at now being allowed to use school resources. My sarcasm would not go unnoticed.

The day before the scheduled debate, I met with my running mates, as well as with most of the individuals who had attended the initial meeting at my home. Two individuals were not invited, since I was sure at least one or possibly both could be "the rat" that informed Banister of our every move. Phone calls late into the night concluded another hectic day with the following consensus: our opponents would attack my inexperience and extol their knowledge of the union contract and the inner workings of the union itself. They would reaffirm their commitment to the entire staff and emphasize their past successes.

Everyone concurred with my prediction that Banister's people would try to pigeonhole me by having people ask me questions that I couldn't possibly answer since only a chapter chairman would have the information necessary to make such an informed response. Every question would have the same intent: make me appear inept and unqualified to lead I.S.24.

With input from every possible source, I conceded that I couldn't fight the inexperience factor, but I could turn it around by informing everyone of the years of experience many of my running mates had. I would reinforce this with a pledge that I would tap into the vast source of knowledge and experience from numerous members on our staff. I would cement my answer by stating, "With such an array of accessible help, only the best possible decisions would be reached for our entire membership."

All of my people agreed that during the questioning, I would take every opportunity to reiterate that my candidates and I would represent all members of our union to the best of our abilities. I would hammer away at the fact that under my leadership, our union would be inclusive of all members of the I.S.24 staff. I would let everyone know that, although the ultimate decision-making process would be mine and mine alone, I would listen to anyone's point of view in order to successfully represent our chapter. I would emphasize as often as possible that under my leadership, such words as "we" and "all" would define what the chapter of I.S.24 was all about.

I would further make it clear to one and all that Sam Ross would only represent teachers, paraprofessionals, and secretaries, and not be in bed with the school administration or those at the district office. There would be no more backstabbing, unfair appointments, or short teaching programs. I would teach a full program just like the majority of individuals I would represent and would remain "in the trenches" to share the emotional ups and downs, as well as the dangers my fellow members encountered, on a daily basis. Finally, I would echo our theme that "it was time for a change," and hopefully the membership would give me and my running mates the opportunity to implement the changes so many in our chapter were desirous of.

The next day, after the dismissal of the entire student body and with the arrival of union members from the annex, the debate commenced. After opening remarks, mine short, concise, and to the point, the question and answer period began. Since I had no previous record to defend, try as they might, my opponents couldn't find an opening to make me feel and sound like an incompetent. As expected, they asked questions I couldn't possibly answer, just as we had predicted they would. I assured the staff that, once in office, I would have access to the necessary information that would allow me to give them forthright answers. I hammered away at the fact that I would also rely heavily on the experience of those members on my slate of candidates, as well as those on staff at I.S.24. I made sure to emphasize that there was no way that my ego would deter me from seeking assistance from anyone who could help me.

Since two could play the same game, I had my people ask Banister some poignant questions, forcing him to defend many of his actions. There were questions about unfair programming, after-school jobs, summer jobs, his inaccessibility to all staff members, his relationship with the administration and the district superintendent, etc. Everyone knew that Banister was not being set up since these questions had been posed to him on numerous occasions during the campaign. The only difference was, now he had to answer them in front of the entire membership.

Never in my preparation for this debate did I doubt that Banister was an accomplished speaker. Years of experience and leadership had refined his oratory abilities, and, to say the least, he was sharp! As the questioning continued, for the first time, many of us noticed some cracks in his debating ability. Although I believe that he still felt he could win this debate, as well as the election, his posture, temperament, and overall appearance now portrayed an individual who had finally come to the realization that this election was not as easy as he thought it would be. For the first time that I could ever recall, there seemed to be hesitancy in his response to questions asked by aligned and non-aligned members of our union. It was Banister who now seemed uncomfortable and over-rehearsed, rather than Sam Ross, the inexperienced newcomer to politics.

My ability to keep my composure and respond to general questions with informative and concise answers was an asset of mine that my opponents severely misjudged. Now for the first time, I truly believed that Banister could be beaten. Unless a travesty of major proportion occurred in the next 18 hours, I sensed that some of the fence sitters, now feeling less threatened, could and would vote for our slate of candidates. It was so great to truly believe that we could win this war. Undoubtedly, Banister's call for a debate and all he hoped to achieve from this face-to-face confrontation had blown up in his own face. I loved it!

The day of reckoning had finally arrived, and I was totally spent. The previous evening, as now seemed to be the norm, had me spending innumerable hours on the phone, making sure that those who had pledged their vote for our slate were still on board. I also tried to get the votes of those that I felt were still uncommitted. Of course, anyone could have said they'd vote for us and go the other way. I wasn't so gullible as not to realize that this could and ultimately did occur.

When I punched my time card the morning of the election, the first order of business was to find out who had called in sick. We couldn't afford to lose a single vote. If necessary, one of us would pick this individual up, bring him in to vote, and take him back home. I was now so obsessed with beating Banister that I probably would have sent an ambulance if it were necessary to secure another vote. With a little persuasion, two ill faculty members came in to cast their votes for my running mates and me. With this situation resolved, it was time to cast my vote and move onto other matters.

The entire day proved to be a study in the American political process. Everyone involved in this election tried to secure that last-second vote that could mean the difference between victory and defeat. At times it seemed that "no stone would remain unturned." By day's end, every one of my people were mentally and physically beaten into submission. Not only was I a member of the exhausted club, but my stomach ulcer was causing me some serious misery. Finally, with the dismissal of my homeroom class, I began what seemed to be an endless trek to where the ballots would be counted. I guess it truly was a long walk since with every step I took, I kept rehashing everything we had done to try to win this election.

As I entered the room where our fate would be determined, there must have been 30-40 people waiting for the tabulation of votes to begin. In past years, if 15-20 people were present, it would have been considered a sellout. Right behind me came the sealed box, containing ballots from the annex. Not being melodramatic, the tension was unbelievable as they began the count. Us, them, them, us, and so it went. With so much on the line, every time my name was called you could hear some sound emanating from the audience. With about 65% of the votes tabulated, Banister was ahead by about six or seven votes, but they still hadn't counted any votes from the annex.

When the ballot box from the annex was finally opened, my heart was pounding a mile a minute because I knew that this would be the moment of truth. With many onlookers clapping with each successive ballot, we edged closer and closer, eventually pulling even. Finally, in what seemed like a surge from heaven, we shot into the lead. With a six-vote advantage and with only a few votes left to count, Banister stood up and stormed out of the room. Knowing that there was no way my lead could be overcome, a number of my backers began to celebrate. We'd beaten the son of a bitch by a total of four votes.

Talk about incredible accomplishments, our victory was one for the books. One of my tireless backers, out of sheer joy, lit up a victory cigar as everyone started congratulating one another. The other side sat stunned! When they got up to leave, a select few had the decency to offer congratulations. Most walked out in utter disbelief. I was so overcome with exhaustion that I didn't have the energy to revel in our victory. The fact that two candidates on my slate had lost also took some starch out of my happy, yet muted, demeanor.

After calling Dianah with my good news, and thanking everyone for their Herculean effort, my main goal was to get home, be with my wife, and relax! As I drove home, nothing could stop me from rehashing the entire campaign. When I finally parked my car, there was my wife, waiting to give me a gigantic hug and kiss. Both felt so good. This entire experience had been so hard on Dianah as evidenced by the tears streaming down her cheeks. We both hoped some semblance of order would return to our family life. Little did either of us realize that not only was this combative election not over, but in reality, it had not yet begun.

Driving to work the next day was a pleasure. Just knowing that I didn't have to campaign was so liberating. Thursday night had been a joyous nightmare. The phone didn't stop ringing as congratulations poured in. You would have thought I had been elected mayor of New York City.

As I approached I.S.24 the following morning, although quite proud of myself and those that had worked so hard to secure our victory, I humbly entered the main office to punch my time card. Before I knew it, I was receiving congratulations from the main office staff. Even Principal Pell came out of his office to wish me well. He expressed his hope that we could work in a friendly yet professional manner when I officially took office in September.

As the day progressed, from the way I was being lauded, you'd have thought 90% of the staff had cast their votes for me, which in reality was total nonsense. One fact stood out and would remain a constant for the next two years: My opponents looked upon me as a pariah. When I approached Banister to offer some consolation and talk about reconciliation, he wouldn't even acknowledge my presence. If looks could kill, I would be a candidate for an autopsy at the city morgue. Thankfully, the day passed in a peaceful fashion, and it was "weekend time."

What a pleasure! My first days of rest and relaxation in what seemed like ages. This is not to say that I didn't think of the new responsibilities I would be assuming, but at least for these few days I could be with Dianah without any distractions. I can't remember if we did anything spectacular that weekend except to go to the pool club, but the tranquility I experienced was well appreciated. With less than ten days left on the school calendar, I drove to school that Monday extremely upbeat and somewhat rejuvenated. Too bad those feelings would not last long.

"Monday, Monday" was a great song by the Mamas and the Papas in the '60s. Its primary message was that you should not trust this day of the week. Years later, I would come to realize that no truer words had ever been written. When I reached school that Monday, never did I anticipate that events would unfold, forever making me weary of this day. Decades later, I can tell the reader, without hesitancy, that this day of the week still scares the hell out of me!

With the hope of a return to normalcy, I punched my time card Monday morning and within moments, was chatting with some friends. It didn't take but five minutes for Leonard Pell to appear and hand me a sealed letter, with the U.F.T. logo on the envelope. Figuring it was congratulatory in nature, I enthusiastically opened it. As I read the letter's contents, utter disbelief, inconceivability, and finally, outrage replaced my optimism. I was so incensed that I was ready to put my fist through the nearest wall. My first non-violent thought was *Well, I'll be a son of a bitch! Those mother fuckers.*

Emanating from the U.F.T. Brooklyn Borough Representatives Office, this letter informed me that the election of the previous week was ruled null and void! It further stated that the ballot box, which had been brought over from the annex, had been tampered with. Although they were not personally accusing me of complicity in this deceitful act, it had been determined that a new election was going to be held in one week.

Dumbfounded, I left the main office to inform those who had worked so hard for our victory about this new turn of events. While walking through the hallway, I happened to pass a member of the opposition. The smirk on that bastard's face let me know immediately who was responsible for this travesty and that my opponent already knew the contents of this letter. As powerful as Banister was, I realized he couldn't have pulled off something of such magnitude by himself. No, this had to have been orchestrated by someone who wielded a great deal of power and was part of our union hierarchy. In my mind, only one person could have conceived of and brought to fruition such a heinous plan: our district representative himself, Mario Danzio.

Word about this insidious robbery spread throughout the building like a gas-fueled fire. Nobody, except my well-connected enemies, could believe what had happened. After I called Dianah, my adrenal gland must have reached the overdrive mode. I felt as if every blood cell in my body was on fire. They wanted a war? I'd give them a war! All bets were off. No more Mr. Nice Guy. This was going to be a fight to the death, and one fact would not be in doubt: I'd be standing when it was over!

In no time at all, our political machine was up and running, both in the main building and the annex. Using our own paper, we let everyone know what had just occurred. Newsletters would be issued on a daily basis. This time, there would be no moral boundaries as far as I was concerned. I immediately let everyone know who I believed was responsible for this brazen act of sabotage. I tore into my opponent's relationship with the principal, district superintendent, and of course, our district representative. I informed everyone how for years, our chapter chairman, Allan Banister, had been stealing school supplies to stock his own business. I made it clear to everyone how Banister, Pell, Danzio, and our alcoholic district superintendent were screwing us. Any disparaging information that was withheld during the first campaign was now going to be aired. This time, neither side would take prisoners!

To realize to what lengths my opponents were willing to go to secure Banister's reelection only requires knowledge of the following clandestine occurrence. I would eventually learn that our district representative, Mario Danzio, had made numerous calls to members of our staff from Leonard Pell's basement. Using threats and other means of coercion, Danzio, Banister, Pell, and Rodgers employed whatever tactics they felt would insure a victory this time around.

What was so sickening about this entire affair was the fact that here was our chapter chairman and district representative, whose responsibilities included the protection of union members, aligned with the district superintendent and our principal, or those they were supposed to protect us from. The ultimate disgrace was their use of the basement of Leonard Pell's house to threaten and badger union members in order to secure Banister's reelection. This entire scenario was downright despicable and repulsive!

As the date of the second election drew closer, stress-related outbursts by members of the I.S.24 staff increased in frequency. Even our student population knew something was up. A number of my kids, free of charge, offered to "kick the shit" out of my opponents, even though they had no idea who they were or what they represented. They were just pissed off because I was, and they didn't like it when I was upset.

Meanwhile, with tension reaching once considered unattainable heights, my opponents were really flexing their political muscle. Teachers and paraprofessionals were threatened with the loss of their jobs if they didn't vote the "right way." Eighteen paraprofessionals who eventually voted for me would lose their jobs, although this erroneously was blamed totally on budget cuts. Those with after-school or summer jobs were threatened with being replaced if they didn't vote the party line. Intimidating phone calls in the middle of the night culminated with a threat on my life by a caller claiming to be a member of the Black Panther Party. Although I knew that this threat by the so-called Black Panther Party was nothing more than a load of fabricated horseshit, the intent had great significance. Without sounding paranoid, the possibility of an accident in school was quite plausible. When I wasn't teaching a class, my back was now being watched at all times.

To say that the threats of violence, firings, and blackmail had gotten out of hand would be an understatement. At times I felt that I was the President of the United States being protected by the Secret Service. At home, none of my family or friends could believe the lunacy I described to them. Any thought of ever going into local or national politics was a dead issue after having been a participant in this disgraceful and despicable escapade. Anyone desirous of helping the public good could have it as far as I was concerned. I would never put my family, friends, or myself through something like this again!

I'm pretty sure I said this before, but finally, after another week of outright barbarism and loathsome behavior on the part of my opponent and his people, election day was upon us. After making sure that no one from our camp was out sick, all of us vigorously campaigned until the last possible moment. The Brooklyn Borough Representative in person monitored the elective process in the annex.

To think that this local election was so hotly contested that the Brooklyn Borough Representative, the highest-ranking member of our union in Brooklyn, was brought in to monitor its final chapter was mind boggling! This election had sent shock waves up our union's entire organizational ladder, much to the chagrin of our union hierarchy. Our borough representative personally hand-delivered the ballot box from the annex to the main building, where its contents would be counted. She had watched that ballot box the entire day, thus insuring its legitimacy. No one could claim that this box had been compromised, unless she did it herself. I wouldn't doubt it!

When I finally entered the room where the ballots were to be counted, I couldn't believe my eyes. There had to be between 50-60 people present at the minimum. Tension permeated the entire room. With the Brooklyn Borough Representative reading out loud the results of each ballot and her assistant keeping a running tabulation on the blackboard, just as in the previous election, Banister took a small lead. With about 25 votes left to count, we finally pulled even. Then, as if a huge weight was lifted from my shoulders, I heard my name repeated about seven times in a row. Within a minute, it was all over.

We had done it! We had beaten them again, and by them I mean all of them, from Danzio down to Banister, back up to Charles Rodgers, the district superintendent, and of course, Leonard Pell. Sure, they had swayed some voters, especially from the annex. We, on the other hand, had convinced some teachers from the main building to switch to our side due to our agenda and the low-life tactics employed by our foes. I guess Banister and company never fully realized that threats and intimidation could only go so far. Without a doubt, there were people out there with morals who had finally gotten tired of the despicable tactics employed by Banister and his people. The resulting backlash added the crucial votes necessary to pull off another upset of prodigious proportions.

The irony of this entire study in power politics was the irrefutable fact that we had beaten our opponent again by the same number of votes—four. They had brought out the big guns and had used every conceivable tactic to try to steal this election, and they had lost by the same number of votes. It felt so good! This time, unlike the previous election, I participated in the victory celebration. I had no reservation in showing my satisfaction that we had beaten them, all of them, by four votes again! It was such a great feeling. Sadly, as before, two of my running mates had tasted defeat. Calls home to our wives, further participation in our victory celebration, and soon Jerry and I were on our way home. Back to the world of sanity, caring, and love—back with our families.

As I neared the time clock the following morning, I remember thinking *Thank G-d in a couple of days we'll all be on summer vacation.* Leonard Pell,who had come out of his office to congratulate me on my victory, interrupted my trend of thought. I'm sure his congratulations came from the bottom of his heart (yeah right!). Out of nowhere, Pell informed me that there

SAM ROSS

was a local school board meeting at 3:30 and that it would be a good experience for me to attend and hopefully meet the school board members. As an aside, he mentioned that if I had the opportunity to speak, he would appreciate it if I'd put in a request for a school nurse.

The school day itself was great. Congratulations on our victory were continuous throughout the day. Many of my colleagues were basking in our victory. The other side, well, what could I say? I knew it would take time to heal the wounds inflicted by such hard-fought elections. Maybe the summer vacation would bring some serenity to everyone's life, and we could begin the next year with more dignity and less hostility.

At 3:00 I punched my time card and went to the local school board meeting, although in an unofficial capacity, since my term didn't officially start until September of the new school year. Rules of parliamentary procedure dictated how the meeting was conducted. After approximately one hour devoted to reading the minutes of the last meeting and discussing old business, it was time for new business. Taking a deep breath, I raised my hand, hoping to be recognized so I could alert the board of our need for a full-time school nurse.

Within minutes I was cognizant of the fact that everyone was being recognized except yours truly. Then, abruptly, the meeting was adjourned, and I was livid! Just as I was saying to a college buddy, whom I had met at the meeting, "What the hell is going on here?" in an outraged tone of voice, the district superintendent just happened to be walking by me.

All of a sudden he turned and said, "Did you say 'Fuck you' to me?" all the while looking at my face.

"What did you say?" I asked him, totally caught off guard.

"You said, 'Fuck you' to me," he replied.

As I tried to respond, he angrily walked away. It almost appeared that steam was coming out of his head. All I could think to myself was, *What an asshole this jerk is!*

That night I had little sleep. I really knew what had happened but tried substituting other logical reasons for this school board disaster. When I punched in the next morning, I looked in my mailbox to see if I had received any messages. There it was, a letter in a sealed envelope from the district superintendent's office. In essence it read:

Sir:

Your behavior at yesterday's school board meeting was the most unprofessional I have ever witnessed. Although you are the chapter chairman elect of your school, I am letting you know right now that I will never deal with you in any way, shape, or form.

Charles Rodgers
District Superintendent

My initial thought was, *He has to be kidding me!* Imagine, all I had done was attend a school board meeting in the hopes of meeting its members and trying to get our school some nursing assistance, and now the head of the entire district was my enemy. I wondered if my calling him an alcoholic during the campaign had anything to do with his emotional outburst. The more I thought about, *I'll never deal with you in any way, shape or form,* the more incensed I became. Knowing that this letter was from a verified lowlife did not make matters any better. I innately knew that I would use this entire incident as an asset when dealing with our union members and the administration of I.S.24. This letter would become my "red badge of courage" and I would use it to show one and all, the collusion that existed between those forces aligned against me.

As my rage ebbed, certain realities came into focus. I would make a copy of this letter available to every union member in our school. I would refer to this letter whenever requests were denied for more security personnel, a nurse, or anything that would improve our existence at I.S.24. I would accept what was now impossible to deny; Leonard Pell had not only set me up, but he was a primary participant in this cabal. Only a blind fool could refute this fact! How could Charles Rodgers, who didn't know me from a hole in the wall, manage to know that I, Sam Ross, chapter chairman elect of I.S.24, was even at this meeting? There was no way he could determine that I was in attendance unless someone had sent me there, thus enabling him to participate in a farce that would result in this ludicrous letter being placed in my mailbox.

In hindsight, there was not a shadow of a doubt that those involved in this plot had only one goal in mind: to show me that they would make my tenure as chapter chairman a living hell! Meanwhile, for someone who prided himself in having a great deal of common sense, I had fallen for this nurse routine hook line and sinker! From this indiscretion, I would add two more additions to the Sam Ross School of Thought: Never drop one's guard when dealing with any administrator, and make retribution for deceit as painful as possible!

There was not a shadow of a doubt in my mind that I would pay Leonard Pell back for setting me up. What was great was the fact that I had the entire summer to prepare for Pell's comeuppance. Undoubtedly, he would learn to respect me, and the office I would hold, or I would make his life at least as miserable as my vanquished foes were intent on making mine. I would never let him forget that he represented the school administration or what my attitude was towards these people.

Finally, almost begrudgingly, the last day of the school year was upon us. Before any of us realized it, it was time to hand out report cards and escort our students out of the building. Saying goodbye to my kids was always something special and, in many cases, extremely sad. As I had done in previous years, I remained outside the school building to sign as many yearbooks as possible. It was my pleasure to do so, especially since I didn't have to campaign anymore.

Soon it was time to go upstairs and finish packing up any items that I wanted to take home for the summer. This task was interrupted when I went out to lunch with some good friends. After lunch, it was back to packing and then spending the rest of the day saying my goodbyes, in my case to friends and foes alike. Unfortunately, some members of the opposition would not even accept my wishes for a healthy and happy summer. It was apparent that I would have to resign myself to the deep-seated hatred that would exist at I.S.24 for years to come.

Finally, our checks arrived from the district office and were handed out. As I approached our school's infamous time clock, I remember thanking G-d for His help in letting me survive another year of chaos in such a dysfunctional environment. In direct contrast to previous years, I experienced emptiness, void of celebration or euphoria. Where, as in the past, our summer vacation was preceded by a staff party of huge proportions, now, there was none. The battle we had endured had split our faculty down the middle, thereby negating festivities which most of us had previously participated in. With the scars of battle still raw, it was best to just punch out and go home. This is exactly what I did.

CHAPTER THIRTEEN

I Never Conceived of the Possibility...

Summer couldn't have come at a more opportune time. All of us were physically and emotionally spent. Just the stress inherent in teaching in such a volatile atmosphere was enough to sap the strength of the healthiest of individuals. Physically, my gas gauge was on empty. Emotionally, I was crippled. Sure, I had experienced these feelings when other school years had ended, but this time it was different. The "war" in our school had exacted a tremendous toll on all of its active participants. All any of us wanted was some peace and quiet.

That summer, again with a surprise monetary gift from Dianah's aunt and uncle, we joined the pool club and thoroughly enjoyed ourselves. Just relaxing in the sun with Dianah and a group of friends was so pleasurable. Playing cards and doing well in the stock market also added to the joy of these precious few months. Unfortunately, in contrast to previous summers where I never thought about school, no less our union, this summer, both demanded my serious attention.

After Banister had again tasted defeat, before leaving the room where the ballots had been counted, he passed me the *U.F.T. Chapter Chairman Handbook*. Having seen this red book in his possession on numerous occasions, I was never fully cognizant of the valuable information contained therein. I was astonished by its contents. There it was, laid out in front of me, 90% of the information needed to be a successful chapter chairman. Undoubtedly, the book didn't give me the personality or oratory ability needed to be a great leader, nor did it outline the steps necessary to gain the respect of my colleagues; but everything else I needed to know to be a successful chapter chairman was there in black and white.

No wonder Banister had been so knowledgeable, if not brilliant, at this job. With this book now in my possession, I knew that I could be as good, if not better, than Banister in my dealings with the staff, the school's administration, and those individuals at the district office. Thankfully, I'd never need this or any other book to give me the personality and oratory ability that this job demanded of its occupant. I already had both and would put them to good use. What would eventually separate me from Banister, thus allowing me to do what I considered a better job, was the fact that I had better people skills. I could, and did, feel comfortable with any person or group of people, whereas Banister could never make this claim, as evidenced by his nasty attitude and demeanor towards various people or factions at I.S.24.

With what free time I had during the summer months, I gorged my brain cells on the wealth of information provided in this handbook. I studied this book with equal if not greater zeal than any required text during my college career. There was no way that I would be perceived as being an incompetent come September. I envisioned how impressed those in our chapter would be at the knowledge and professionalism I'd exhibit during my first chapter meeting.

Adding further impetus to my desire to be all knowing was my inability to get the district representative to return any of the numerous phone calls that I had made to his office. Although I was not happy with being snubbed by this individual, I knew that come September he would have to deal with me whether he liked it or not. Until then, I would study and learn everything this book had to offer. When we would finally meet, even "The Great One" would be impressed with my knowledge of union protocol, rules and regulations, and contractual agreements.

When I had decided to run for chapter chairman, I never conceived of the possibility that, if I won, my initial responsibility would be to make sure that all of our chapter's members would be prepared to pound the pavement. Although rumors of a possible strike had been rampant during the final months of the school year, this was considered just the normal prelude to summer negotiations. On the whole, most of us were not overly concerned even with the excessive posturing emanating from both camps. We still believed that, in the end, a settlement would be reached, and no matter how small our gains, schools would open on time. Were we wrong!

With the school year fast approaching, most of the citizens of New York City had no idea that our city was now being viewed as a financial disaster by one of its leading and most powerful tenants: Wall Street. Municipal bonds, which in the past had an excellent rating and rate of return, had now fallen out of favor on "the street" and were considered by many to be a liability. This fall from grace was mainly due to the financial irresponsibility of the city's previous mayor, John Lindsey, and his inept administration. Mismanagement and incompetence had relegated the once proud and great New York City to be financially viewed as second rate and on the verge of insolvency.

City and state leaders, hoping to regain financial respectability, requested and ultimately demanded that the United Federation of Teachers, along with other municipal unions (i.e. police, fire, sanitation, etc.), loan the city enormous sums of moneys from their pension funds to help restore the city's lost financial luster. The influx of these funds would be used to balance the city's books, ultimately restoring it to a solvent state. Luring the financial community to reinvest in our city would be accomplished by streamlining and cost cutting measures. Who or whatever had caused this financial crisis to come to a head was irrelevant at this moment in time. Recriminations would follow after the crisis was resolved, but for now it was necessary to end this situation as expeditiously as possible.

With the city's financial woes as a backdrop, negotiations between New York city and the U.F.T. began in earnest. Where in the past they had been tedious and at times ridiculous as far as offers and counter-offers, this time even the typists were dead serious. City negotiators not only wanted us to save their hides by forking over assets from our pension fund, but they also demanded givebacks as well. As rumors about givebacks circulated to the rank and file, most of us realized that we were in for a major confrontation. They wanted large sums of money, and we, in turn, would be repaid with larger class sizes, cuts in health benefits, less security personnel, fewer paraprofessionals, and layoffs. Ultimately, the number of layoffs of teaching personnel alone would total a staggering 15,000 individuals, or one quarter of our union membership. All would be terminated under the guise of fiscal responsibility. This would constitute an outright massacre! Even the rumors paled in comparison to the ultimate reality.

For so many years, teachers had been treated like second-class citizens. Securing raises and benefits had taken years of painstaking negotiation and Herculean resolve. Now the city wanted to reclaim what had taken us years to attain in one contract negotiation. It was great that city leaders wanted to move towards fiscal responsibility, but at what cost? First the unions should bail the city out, and then they would kick us in the ass to show their appreciation. Whoever was the architect of such an insane plan had to have some loose screws in his head. If they believed that we'd accept their demands without a fight, then the drug epidemic was worse than even I had imagined.

As the dog days of summer wore on, the rift between all of the concerned parties grew further apart. Each passing day saw the gap widen even as the number of days until the beginning of the new school year dwindled. In the past, it seemed that there was always an "eleventh hour settlement." This time, with the city in such dire straight, the eleventh hour never arrived.

When all semblance of reason and sanity had been exhausted, President Al Shanker, after a resounding stride vote by our delegate assembly, announced at 12:01 a.m. that the teachers of New York City were officially on strike. The rank and file was ordered to report to their schools in the morning, but instead of greeting our new students, we would be walking a picket line.

New York's early morning editions, besides special TV news flashes, let their citizens know that their teachers were on strike. With minimal prodding from city hall, the city's daily newspapers vilified us. We were characterized as "bloodsuckers" whose ultimate goal was to bring the city to its knees. It was amazing how these agents of communication had somehow forgotten to inform their readers of the millions of dollars we had loaned the city in the past to avert the possibility of such a crisis. Other unions had also forked over large sums of money for the same purpose. Sadly, our media detractors never made it clear to the public how through mismanagement and, in many instances outright stupidity, the city managers had squandered away those funds and ultimately forced this public confrontation.

Through all of the confusion, innuendo, and accusations, the one fact that couldn't be dismissed was that in the middle of the entire mess would be Sam Ross. Yes, "Mr. As Green As They Come" was expected to be the consummate chapter chairman. I assumed that I would be required to take charge and lead a successful picket line, as well as be responsible for the entire scenario that would unfold at I.S.24. How could I be so lucky!

Upon my arrival at I.S.24 on day one of our strike, before I could step out of my car, a number of frenzied colleagues rushed up to my drivers' window:

"What do we do?" some asked almost in unison.

"Where are our picket signs?" they inquired.

Seriously, how the hell was I supposed to know? This was my first day on the job, and nobody had called me the night before with definitive instructions or for that matter any kind of information. Our district representative had never returned any of my calls during the summer, no less after the strike vote had been taken. I began to truly believe that the son of a bitch was hanging me out to dry! Undoubtedly, this was payback time for defeating his protégé. As I would soon find out, this time, I was being overly neurotic.

Just as Banister and his cohorts were bombarding me with questions to which I had no answers, a procession of cars pulled up in front of our building, and their occupants began handing out picket signs. You can't imagine what a welcome sight this was. Included in this group of lifesavers was one of Danzio's trusted lieutenants who handed me a note from "His Holiness" himself.

Danzio sent me instructions detailing my responsibilities for the longevity of the strike. Besides my supervision of picketing and other such related matters, I was given a phone number which I was expected to call every fifteen to twenty minutes, keeping him informed of everything that was occurring in and around our school. Any signs of violence, intimidation by school administrators, or trouble with residents of the community would be met with an appropriate response. I was duly informed that there were at least four carloads of union members equipped with baseball bats and that they could reach me in a matter of minutes if their help was requested. Guess who would have the authority to make such an appeal: me!

The reality of this entire situation was quite clear. Not only did Danzio now recognize Sam Ross as the duly elected chapter chairman of I.S.24, but he also realized that he needed my help in carrying out the demands of our union's leadership. What a turn of events!

The atmosphere in New York City with its residents finally realizing the gravity of the situation ranged from gloom and doom from the "haves," to who cares from the "have nots." Prior to our being forced to go out on strike, our union leaders realized that there had to be adjustments made to what had been our normal demands in past negotiations. When these negotiations began, we didn't push for large pay raises, increased medical coverage, etc. Rather, our efforts were directed towards reduction in class size, safer working conditions, increases in the numbers of paraprofessionals, security personnel, and any changes that we believed were beneficial towards creating an atmosphere conducive to improved learning in all of our city's public schools. Unfortunately, our requests fell on deaf ears.

If our union had made one mistake, it had been their inability to inform the residents of N.Y.C. what our demands were. Heaven forbid the news media would have provided the public with this information, but no one was shocked by their omission. Until we were able to inform the populace that a substantial portion of our contract demands entailed improving the educational environment of our students, the majority of citizens, especially those working parents who were worried about their children running the streets unsupervised, were not receptive to our being out on strike.

Mario and other U.F.T. leaders feared there might be violence since New Yorkers in general, and our community residents in particular, were tired of recent sick-outs and other interruptions in city services. Police, fire, and other municipal unions whose contracts would be up for renegotiations in the near future, often used these methods as negotiating tools. Our walking the picket line just accentuated the irritability felt by the populace.

President Ford's ill-conceived remark telling New Yorkers to "Drop Dead" in response to city and state leaders requests for financial aid only added to the tension that filled the air. There was no doubt in the minds of our union leadership that it would be less dangerous for our citizens to take out their frustrations on a picket line of teachers rather than those consisting of police, fire, or sanitation workers to name a few. In plain English, it would be much easier to kick our asses than those of the aforementioned groups. There was no doubt in my mind that this assessment was dead on the money!

Every 15 minutes, like clockwork, I made my call to Mario and relayed any information that I felt would be useful. Although I never spoke directly to him, my calls and ensuing conversations were with one of his trusted lieutenants, or so I was told. At a later date, I discovered that either Banister, or one of his sympathizers, had gotten to this trusted piece of shit who in turn lied to Danzio when he asked if I was reporting in. Considering there was the distinct possibility that we could be caught in the middle of a damn riot, this cloak and dagger horseshit perpetuated by my opposition not only exposed their immaturity, but also the fact that they were dangerous bastards, too!

Finally, after five days of round-the-clock negotiations and some serious pavement pounding on the part of our union membership, an agreement was hammered out. Unfortunately, our heads were used as the hammer. With our leadership and delegate assembly assuring us that this was the best contract we could possibly hope for, the membership complied with their recommendation and painfully ratified the agreement. We had taken a beating. As already stated, we would eventually lose one quarter of our membership. The optimists took solace in the fact that there had been some gains. The realists…we knew we had been nearly destroyed.

In selling the contract to its members, the leadership of the U.F.T. tried valiantly to appear upbeat. We had "won" ten- and fifteen-year longevity salary increases and a deferred pay raise. I'm sure some other gains were secured, but since I can't remember any, I'm positive that they weren't, shall we say, overwhelming. On the opposite end of the spectrum, what we lost was not difficult to remember or easy to forget. Three hundred seventy million dollars, a staggering sum for its time, was taken from our coffers with $150 million used towards purchasing emergency issued municipal bonds, which helped the city avoid default. Other moneys were used in ways to supposedly help our city regain some of its former financial stature. Even a conservative money market account or the purchase of T-bills would have offered a far greater yield. But no, we had to use the "correct" financial avenue of investment so our city could regain its former financial luster. Of course, anyone with the most basic financial background knew that this would not be the case. In reality, it took many years for the city to get investors to regain some confidence in our financial abilities. For the city's teachers, the wait was equally as long and more painful.

Both individually and as a union, the teachers of New York City had gone the extra mile to help the city with its financial woes. Another reward for our generosity was the requirement that teachers, who were teaching out of license, now had to take re-certification exams to get licensed in the subjects they were now teaching. Thousands upon thousands of teachers were in this position. What would add further insult to injury was our leadership being sold a "bill of goods" by city and state officials that these exams would be a mere formality. For a mere formality, the exams were killers! I believe that close to 75% of those who took the science re-certification exams, failed. Thankfully, I wasn't one of these unfortunates. Those that failed were summarily dismissed. Most would not try to return.

Those of us who passed these re-certification exams were now forced to go back to night school and earn the credits necessary to validate our newly issued temporary licenses. All were expected to fulfill this obligation within a two-year period or be terminated. This added further misery to our already terrible lot. The ultimate disgrace was the fact that we had to pay for each credit we took, further lowering our net earnings. This unexpected cost forced many teachers to take other jobs so that they could supplement their salaries. Their constant absence from their homes added further pressure on marriages, and some never recovered.

Just the re-certification disaster alone let most of us know we had taken a beating. Any fool who, through rose-covered glasses, believed we had won left me to wonder what ingredients they believed were necessary to declare a major defeat. The only consolation of this entire travesty that helped temper the sting of our defeat was the gains that were secured for the city's student population: GOTCHA! Any requests that would have resulted in better student performance, such as more security guards and paraprofessionals, lower class size, and so many other important issues, were never really addressed. Important reforms regarding our students were stonewalled from the onset of negotiations. Our negotiators tried valiantly to achieve a few successes in this arena, but ultimately, they didn't have a shot in hell. Money was the focal point of this entire negotiation, and since the city didn't have any—"Sorry, kids!"

Throughout this entire horror show, our union's leadership kept insisting that there was money to be had. City and state leaders contended there was none. When the truth surfaced, the results were disastrous. Our leaders had been wrong, and their membership would pay dearly for their miscalculations.

The finality of our "bloodletting" occurred when the city invoked something called the Taylor Law. Past negotiations had seen the U.F.T. and other municipal unions threatened with this law, but ultimate enactment had never materialized. This time, we weren't so lucky.

The Taylor law basically stipulated that any strike by a municipal union was illegal. As a penalty for such an illegal action, the law called for participants to be assessed a loss of two days' pay for every day on strike. Since we were out for a week, we would be penalized two weeks' pay. The money would be deducted from our bi-monthly checks over a specified period of time. The bottom line of this entire fiasco was simple: You didn't have to be a genius to realize that the city had us by our throats the entire time, and our leadership had failed to see the handwriting on the wall. The longer we were on strike, the greater the financial penalty. Yes, we would learn from our mistakes, and this knowledge would be invaluable in future contract negotiations, but that wouldn't save us this time. The rout was now complete.

Unbeknownst to most of the union's membership, myself included, there was a major positive to this near total debacle. When the smoke had cleared and the rhetoric had been muted, it became public that there had been a concerted effort by numerous city and state power brokers to weaken and finally destroy the United Federation of Teachers as its members knew it to exist. Only through the astute leadership of Al Shanker, in conjunction with help from other municipal union leaders, were these plans thwarted. Although seriously wounded, our union would remain a viable entity. Eventually, we would resurface stronger than ever. Shanker had brought us needed time and, I'm proud to say, not a second was wasted.

The tremendous gains made over the past 28 years by teachers, paraprofessionals, retirees, etc. are a byproduct of this 1975 confrontation. So many people endured tremendous hardship, and many, unfortunately, lost their jobs as well as their dignity. Ultimately, we grew stronger to achieve the status we now enjoy. Hopefully the new generation of teachers in New York City is appreciative of the sacrifices we made during such a trying period in our union's history.

On a more personal note, some basic observations and conclusions could be derived from this unexpected experience, which marked the beginning of my tenure as Chapter Chairman of I.S.24:

1. We had been on strike, and I, Sam Ross, had been successful in performing the duties required of me as a chapter chairman, at least in the eyes of a majority of the staff of I.S.24.

2. We had basically gained nothing for our students or ourselves. Unfortunately, a few of my colleagues and members of the community would take their frustrations out on me.

3. I was incessantly pigeonholed by my adversaries and realized that this behavior would never stop as long as I was chapter chairman of I.S.24.

4. Danzio finally recognized me as chapter chairman of I.S.24. Unfortunately, through the lies and deceit of one of his trusted lieutenants, I had managed to piss him off since he believed that I hadn't called in every 15-20 minutes as requested. Although he would eventually learn the truth, he would still throw this purported failure in my face whenever the mood suited him.

5. Adding to this overview was the fact that I had managed to secure the everlasting hatred of a vindictive and extremely dangerous district superintendent some three months earlier.

In all honesty, I can sarcastically state that I was pretty impressed with my initial foray into school and district politics. I had managed to alienate the two most powerful people in our entire district: the district superintendent and my district representative. All in all, it had been quite an inauspicious start to the chapter chairmanship of one Sam Ross of I.S.24. Hopefully it wouldn't get any worse.

CHAPTER FOURTEEN

My Stewardship

Section 1: Getting to Know You, or Is it Getting to Know Me?

Our first days back on the job were used to jumpstart those processes which had been derailed by our necessary but untimely strike. Our students would not start the school year for a number of days, allowing us the time necessary to get our programs ready and the wheels of education back on track. The many hours spent during the summer studying the chapter chairman handbook were immediately put to use when I informed Leonard Pell of my desire, and contract right, to have our first union meeting on this, our first day back. Pell had no option but to agree to my request.

To say I was not apprehensive in anticipation of my first official meeting with the entire staff would be an outright lie. The realization that the meeting would not last for more than an hour was comforting. The purpose of the meeting would be multifarious in nature. I would have the opportunity to formally welcome the staff back from summer vacation, as well as officially welcome the teachers from the annex to their new home. I also hoped to inform our membership of my agenda for the year, as well as reiterate that I would be available day or night to help with any problems that might arise. Finally, there was the issue of the strike. I knew something had to be said, but I'd have to play it by ear since I was void of all of the facts of the settlement.

With everyone seated, I began what I hoped would be the first of many successful meetings. It didn't take but a few minutes before a member of the opposition interrupted me.

"How are we going to get back the teaching positions we lost due to cuts in the budget?" he asked in a snide tone of voice.

This was followed in rapid succession with, "When is our district representative going to come to our school and explain the new contract?" asked another member of Banister's inner circle.

"Why don't we have our programs yet?" inquired a non-aligned staff member.

"What about class size?" asked another faculty member.

We had been back on the job for a couple of hours and no one, not even Leonard Pell, knew the answer to most of these questions. My adversaries couldn't have cared less. All they wanted was for me to look bad, and they would use any avenue available to achieve this goal.

Although seething inside from this unabashed verbal assault, I still was able to present to our membership an outward appearance of poise and confidence. Under the guise of this illusion, I informed everyone in a strong steady tone of voice, "I will have the answers to these, and other questions, as soon as possible."

I let it be known that I had asked Leonard Pell and Mario Danzio these same questions, and their response basically was that they would have to get back to me. I then made it clear to our members how disappointed I was with their lack of knowledge regarding these matters.

"As soon as they get their act together and have the answers I need, I will convene another meeting and pass on the information that they should have already gotten!" I promised our membership in an annoyed tone.

In essence, what I had done was turn around my opposition's verbal assault and place it squarely on the shoulders of those who had supported their candidacy. I always knew that the verbal harassment directed at me by Banister and his crew would never stop. What I had to do was deflect their incessant criticism in such a way as to allow the rest of the membership to see what a bunch of low-lifes they were. I knew that as long as I kept my cool and exuded an air of confidence, everyone would see that their true goal was to wrestle back the power they had lost. I, through diligent work, would make sure that this would never happen.

When the meeting was over, I conferred with a number of my people and let them know that my first order of business would be to have a "sit down" with Leonard Pell. In no uncertain terms, I would let him know with whom he was now dealing. I would make sure that he would understand that I intended to be the chapter chairman of I.S. 24 for many years and he'd better get used to the idea!

When I eventually entered our principal's sanctuary, much to my surprise and Pell's dismay, there, sitting in a seat with his feet up on the conference table, was my defeated adversary, Banister. It seemed to me that the old birds of a feather were still flocking together. This was going to end right now!

"Mr. Pell, could you tell my colleague to leave the room so we can privately discuss a number of important school matters?" I requested in a forceful yet respectful tone of voice.

With an indiscrete nod from Pell, Banister rose and left the office with his usual smart-ass smirk. As I sat down in the seat that Banister had just vacated, one thought traipsed through my mind: *When I'm done, I'll wipe the smirk off both of your faces!*

Pell began our meeting as if what had just occurred meant absolutely nothing. With his discernible two-faced personality in overdrive, he, in essence, expressed his hope that we could work together for the betterment of our staff and students. I basically informed our principal that I was totally receptive to such an arrangement as long as everything was done by the rules and regulations called for in our contract. I made it clear that nepotism of any kind would not be accepted and that collusion with the district superintendent or my district representative would be vigorously frowned upon. Furthermore, I made it perfectly clear that our relationship would be strictly professional and that this would also apply to the rest of his administrators. Of course if Pell or any of his administrators decided to play by another set of rules, the repercussions would be fast and decisive.

In order to impress Pell with my professional ethic, as well as my knowledge of the union contract, I inquired if he'd supply me with a list of the number of classes at I.S.24, as well as the number of students enrolled in each class. This request was within the parameter of my job as chapter chairman. When Pell presented me the list, in the most professional vocal tone possible, I told him, "Principal Pell, I want you to know that I am now verbally filing 80 first step class size grievances against you!" all the while showing no emotion.

This first step grievance procedure meant that there were classes with too large a student population, therefore representing a violation of our collective bargaining agreement.

"You have three days to make the necessary changes!"I continued.

Pell knew he had three days to rectify this problem. I just wanted him to know that I also knew this contractual obligation. The changes in class size that I basically demanded were nearly impossible to accomplish in such a short period of time. To make Pell even more miserable, I warned him, "If these changes are not in effect three days from now, I will file 80 second step grievances!" thereby applying even greater pressure on him to comply since this step in the grievance procedure was written rather than oral.

Pell was never good at masking his emotions, and you could see his jaw drop when I informed him of my intentions. Sensing a less confident individual as exhibited not only by the change in his facial expression but also in the tone of his voice, I decided to lower the boom on him. I knew for a fact that he didn't like confrontation, and now he would painfully learn to never consider trying to set me up again! I had promised myself that I'd pay him back for that school board nurse debacle, and payback time had arrived!

To understand what would happen next, a little background information is necessary. During our summer vacation, our school, like all others in the city, had people working on setting up both teacher and student programs for the upcoming year. At I.S.24, only two people, besides one or two A.P.s, had the qualifications necessary to carry out this task. Since both of these programmers were part of my adversaries' contingent of friends, it didn't take the wisdom of a King Solomon to assume that those individuals who voted for me in the past elections had been paid back with the most undesirable programs possible. Conversely, their friends and those that they believe had voted for them received the best programs. With my acquisition of some inside information, I believed it was time to confront Leonard Pell with my findings.

With a facial expression and vocal tone representative of the seriousness of the matter, I informed Pell of my displeasure with the soon-to-be-distributed programs. I inferred that he knew about the biased programming that had taken place during the summer, as well as the fact that he did nothing to stop this travesty. Obviously shocked by my allegation and pleading total innocence of any wrongdoing, Pell went so far as to express reservation about my insinuation.

Using his skepticism, I was able to goad Leonard Pell into showing me everyone's programs. Inwardly praying that I was correct in my suspicions and that the copies of the programs that I had acquired were real, I proceeded to separate the entire pile of programs into two stacks: those who I believe had voted for Banister and those who voted for Sam Ross. As we went over each program, it became quite evident that my accusations were right on the money. Those who had voted for Sam Ross, and his slate of candidates, had gotten the royal screwing!

Being the so-called consummate diplomat, Pell expressed utter disbelief at what was now irrefutable evidence. He then made the first of many miscalculations when, with utter gall, he offered to switch programs.

"I'll give all of the good programs to your people and the lousy ones to Banister's," Pell said in a conciliatory tone.

Again, with a fabricated look of shock, I remember saying to Pell, "Are you kidding me? I ran for the office of chapter chairman to represent everyone, not a select group of people!"

It was at this juncture that the window of opportunity I had been looking and preparing for had finally arrived. I stated, "Leonard, if you don't reprogram this entire school, I promise you that I will file grievances against every teaching program issued at I.S.24."

Payback time was here and now he'd pay for his deceit, lies and for the school board double cross.

I really thought that Leonard Pell was going to need an ambulance as the color drained from his face. In deep shock, his only response was, "Sam, it will take two weeks to reprogram the school. Your teachers will have to stay with their official class the entire day. Everyone will hate you!" he said, pleading for me to reconsider my threat.

I remember looking at Leonard Pell in a nonchalant manner. Without giving him any inkling that I knew he was right, I responded, "Who cares!" in an aloof, non-caring retort.

I remember thinking, *Yes, the entire staff might hate me when they find out about the reprogramming, but once I call a meeting and inform everyone what occurred during the summer, they will hate Pell and the programmers for trying to pull this type of bullshit!*

You can't imagine my sense of elation when it appeared that Leonard Pell might need the nurse he had sent me to secure at that local school board meeting some three months earlier.

Later that afternoon, after explaining to my executive committee what had occurred, notification of a second union meeting in less than 24 hours was made over the school's public address system. With members of my coalition spreading word about the programming farce, I knew the turnout would be close to 100%. If all went well, this meeting would be a tremendous boost towards the staff's recognition of my leadership qualities, as well as a forum to admonish my opponents for their disruptive vendetta against me. Figuring on being bombarded with legitimate questions, as well as those of the pigeonhole variety, I knew that I had to accomplish five goals amid all the noise and confusion that would characterize this chapter meeting.

1. Tell the entire staff the truth about why the school had to be reprogrammed and to discuss what I had discovered about the original programs.

2. Stop any rumors my adversaries were so adept at initiating. With the truth out in the open, what could they lie about?

3. Show the staff in no uncertain terms that I was on the job and capably representing them.

4. Eliminate the fear that many of my colleagues had in regards to being overly burdened with lousy programs or suffering other repercussions for supporting my candidacy.

5. Remind everyone that they would be treated fairly and represented in a diligent manner regardless of their affiliation. Everyone would be equal. All would share in the wealth if there was any to be had. Our school's chapter would be everyone's chapter, united and fighting for the betterment of all of its members!

The meeting commenced as expected. It proceeded as if it had been scripted at an earlier date, and I was allowed to read the reviews before the event had even unfolded. As would be the norm, my opponents started sniping right from the outset. Thanks to the dissemination of information before the meeting, most of the staff realized that they were trying to cover their own butts. No matter how hard they tried to imply that I had ulterior motives by forcing the school to be reprogrammed, nothing worked. My teaching a full program with an official class let everyone realize that I was in the same boat as they were. Even Banister would have to relieve teachers by covering some of their classes.

There was no doubt in anyone's mind that the next two weeks would be a horror, but at least we'd all share in the misery! There was no way that I would try to make our impending anguish easier to accept. I wanted everyone to always remember those who caused this pain. This memory would hopefully keep them from ever regaining power at I.S.24.

With the majority of the membership accepting my explanation as to why I had insisted that Pell reprogram the school, it was later disclosed to me that many of my colleagues also realized that our chapter was headed down a new path. No longer would it be business as usual or one individual being treated better or worse than another. Finally, there would be equality for all.

This new approach was a difficult concept for many members to adjust to, especially since so many had been screwed for so many years. Old habits are hard to break, and this meeting let our membership see first hand that a new era, under the leadership of Sam Ross, was underway, and no one could stop the changes that I proposed from being implemented.

Just as this chapter meeting would result in a new mind set on the part of our union membership, so too did I foresee a change in Principal Leonard Pell's outlook on life at I.S.24. Undoubtedly, the man had received an eye-opening revelation when he discovered that I couldn't be bought off, as had been the norm during the previous chairman's tenure. Being a man of my word, I also kept the promise I had made to myself to pay Pell back for his nurse school board indiscretion. As I prepared to leave his office after our "Getting to know you" meeting had ended, the dazed look on Pell's face and his slumped seating posture led to one undeniable conclusion: I had not only gotten his attention but also his respect. Inherent in this entire episode was one irrefutable fact: former Chapter Chairman Allan Banister was exactly that—former. There was no doubt that the past 24 hours had been a great day for me in my position of leadership. Hopefully, there would be many others in the foreseeable future!

Section 2: The Magical Molotov Cocktail

The study of human nature usually allows the observer to formulate theories, which, when tested over a period of time, may prove to be correct. Even as a youth, I often observed how individuals, when put in situations of duress, reacted more often than not in such a way as to make a stressful situation even more complicated. To this day, I have no idea if Pell, Danzio, or Charles Rodgers, either individually, collectively, or in some combination, had conceived of and carried out an action which was a direct result of the programming confrontation I had with Leonard Pell the previous day. Never did I expect to learn the following morning that "someone" had firebombed the programming room during the previous evening.

I remember standing at the time clock in a semi-state of shock as I processed what had just been revealed to me. Imagine, every piece of paper regarding teacher and student programs was now nothing more than useless ash. Undoubtedly, somebody, or all of my antagonists, felt that they had to erase any trace of the biased programming that had taken place during the summer. The possibility that I might expose this entire debacle to the higher ups at the board of education or possibly the news media led to one inescapable conclusion: My programming allegations had caused such fear, only a charred room that once housed our now cremated school programs now remained.

Final analysis of this entire mess led to some cruel realities. I had opened up a can of worms, and the reaction of the fish to my alluring bait was so drastic that under the right set of conditions, someone could have been seriously injured or possibly a life could have been lost. Also noted was the fact that, when put in a situation of duress, intelligent people had taken an extremely stupid approach towards eradicating a potential disaster by creating one of even greater proportions.

Leonard Pell, who in my mind was a definite participant in this act of arson, was given the unenviable task of explaining or theorizing how this felony was perpetuated. For such an educated man, his take on this event was so pathetic that the most a-political person could only conclude that he was full of shit.

Trying to convince members of the staff that someone, most likely a student, had thrown a Molotov cocktail through a wire-reinforced window was asinine in its own right. Further elaboration that after the bomb broke the window, it managed to roll down a hallway, make a right turn…utterly preposterous!

Throughout this entire charade, I was continually entertained, yet mystified, by my opponents' thought processes. How stupid were these so-called political savvy individuals? The first thought to enter my mind was: *Was I held in such low intellectual esteem, although having won two elections, that they'd believe I'd buy into this contrived fairy tale?* Moreover, hadn't any of these geniuses considered the possibility that I had secured a copy of these now defunct programs since I had dared challenge the integrity of the programmers and the veracity of Leonard Pell the previous day?

Needless to say, fear, arrogance, and outright lunacy had joined hands and allowed my enemies to take this drastic action. Unfortunately for them, I did have a copy of these prejudiced programs, and knowing my bitter foes, I believed that sometime in the foreseeable future I would need these little gems for leverage in some type of situation. Fortunately for all concerned, I never had to use these "beauties."

As I stated earlier, I was a quick learner. My adversaries had inadvertently taught me one undeniable fact: To survive in district 16, you had to know how to play the game of "power politics." Saving my copies of these rigged programs, at the least, allowed me to sit at the table and ante up.

Our two-week babysitting diversion gave me the opportunity to immerse myself in union business and to take stock of what had occurred in the short duration of my chairmanship. Without self-aggrandizement, I was extremely proud of what I had been able to accomplish, considering the vicious attacks and never-ending harassment of my detractors.

On the negative side, the ominous results were as follows:

1. I had a district superintendent who wouldn't deal with me in any way, shape or form.

2. I had our district representative use every conceivable method to destroy me, without even trying to meet with me so we could iron out our differences.

3. I would have enemies trying to sabotage my every attempt at improving our existence at I.S.24, in their hopes of regaining the power that I had succeeded in depriving them of.

4. Between teaching, parenting, holding the office of chapter chairman, and going to night school for my science license, my life as I once knew it, would never be the same.

On a more positive note, the following accomplishments had been realized:

1. Leonard Pell quickly learned that he had grossly miscalculated my abilities to lead our chapter and to hold my own in the political arena.

2. When the new programs were issued, all concerned realized that they and the rest of the staff had been treated fairly and that I couldn't be bought off.

3. I had quickly gained the respect of most of our school's union members, Leonard Pell, and, hopefully, my district representative.

4. No matter what means my enemies used to undermine and ultimately try to destroy me, I was still standing and stronger than ever before.

5. As with a double-edged sword, the district superintendent had stated he wouldn't deal with me in any way, shape, or form... thank you, G-d!

All in all, not bad for an individual who was considered a flyweight in the political arena. Miraculous could best describe the fact that I, Sam Ross, was able to unseat what had been considered to be an undefeatable chapter chairman. Yes, there was a lot I had to be thankful for. Hard work, guts, good friends, and a strong constitution had taken me to a higher level in such a short time span. Without sounding too egotistical, my only thought on this matter was: *Not too bad for a street kid from the Bronx and the East New York section of Brooklyn!*

Section 3: I Get to Know the Real Mario

With the issuance of the new programs, the school year proceeded at a blistering pace. A full teaching program and the added responsibilities of being chapter chairman made the year the most complex, yet enjoyable, I had experienced at I.S.24. The ultimate coup was Danzio, my district representative, finally recognizing the fact that I wasn't a revolutionary intent on causing all kinds of havoc. With this realization, there developed between us a sense of mutual respect and, in some instances, admiration. As our association matured, we both became cognizant of the fact that our constant interaction had laid the groundwork towards the ultimate loyalty each of us demanded.

In my life, I have known many characters, but our district representative took first place hands down. Funny, intense, powerful, compassionate, devious, brilliant, and extremely loyal only scratch the surface when describing this complicated man. To watch people shake in their pants/skirts, when he went off on one of his patented rampages was a sight to behold. Oscar winners couldn't compete when Mario went into one of his legendary tirades. This extraordinary man, so complicated yet so simple, was remarkable in every sense of the word!

It was midway through the school year that Mario called a meeting which every chapter chairperson in the district was mandated to attend. Except for death, no excuse for being a no-show would be tolerated. In a matter of minutes, Mario was screaming, cursing, and calling people all kinds of names, some of which I hadn't heard in years. Before you knew what was occurring, Mario had a female chapter chairperson in tears. As far as I could discern, something had happened at her school, and she had not handled the situation correctly.

Before you could blink, Danzio's tirade soon incorporated every elementary school chapter chairperson, most of who just happened to be female. In what seemed like seconds, these individuals were verbally stripped of their dignity and relegated to crying like a bunch of five-year-olds. It was like being at a funeral, that's how freely the tears were flowing. In the middle of his adjective-filled tirade, Mario turned his head towards me, gave this impish smile, followed by a partially concealed wink, and went back to his verbal barrage.

I must implore the reader not to misconstrue Mario's verbal tongue lashing as being anti-woman. Mario was far from being a male chauvinist pig. He didn't detest women, he detested stupidity. He believed that all of the chapter chair people were representative of his leadership, thus any foul ups were taken as a personal affront. Mario believed that after a verbal altercation with him, any dispute between a chapter chairman and, say, a principal, was nothing more than child's play. Mario demanded the best from his people, and under his tutelage, you were expected to be the cream of the crop. Those that didn't fall into this category were useless and were treated as such. Time could not, and would not, be wasted on those that failed to represent their constituents with "Marionesque" ability and efficiency. You either rose to the occasion or fell by the wayside.

The more I got to know and understand Mario, the more I realized that he had to be one of the best, if not the best, district representatives in the entire city. This man touched so many lives, with a majority being in a positive manner. Whether he liked or detested you, every moment spent with this man was a learning experience. What some people in our union couldn't understand was, whether or not he was giving an impassioned speech to motivate people, or one of his famous tongue lashings to accomplish the same, each experience had a purpose—to teach and make you a better chapter chairman or union member. You might not know it at the time, but somewhere down the line you would finally realize this.

Hopefully, at a much later date, if anyone is asked to give a eulogy at his funeral, I sincerely pray that it would go something like this:

"Here lies the body of a man whose life work will always be remembered in the annals of our union's history. Word has it that, when rushed to the hospital with a possible heart attack, doctors found five blocked arteries. When trying to open these blockages, all were shocked to find that a copy of the teachers' contract, which somehow had managed to make its way into his circulatory system, was at the root of the blockage.

"Never was there any doubt that the union superseded family, friends, and at times, life itself. Upon entering heaven, Mario's first question to G-d was, 'Are you a union member?' Appraised of the fact that he wasn't, Mario took out a U.F.T. membership card and said, 'If you don't fill this out, I'll get Satan to join up!'"

Section 4: The Year in Review

Although there were many internal and external conflicts during my initial year as chapter chairman, other than bouts of severe exhaustion, I did manage to get through the year relatively unscathed. My former opponent and his loyal inner circle never stopped trying to undermine my leadership abilities, but as the year progressed, their vocal outcries fell on deaf ears. With fair programming, the promise of an equal distribution of after-school and summer jobs, and my availability to anyone needing my assistance, respect for the job I was doing soared. The fact that my executive committee, including two of Banister's own people, contributed to my success cannot be overlooked. In essence, my success could be attributed to a group effort, something which had not been seen at I.S.24 for many years. Yes, the school atmosphere had improved. Surely, further work needed to be done!

Not being a self-absorbed egotist, I'm positive that I offended staff members either with a decision I made or through my use of reprehensible language. Sadly, I must confess, there were times when only through my use of vulgarities was I able to incite a union member or at times the entire chapter to respond to a situation in an appropriate manner. Yes, I made mistakes. Everyone makes them. What was important was the fact that my mistakes were due to inexperience or an error in judgement, rather than out of vindictiveness or retribution, which had been a hallmark sign of the Banister years. Although my opponents were treated with equality and with the same respect I bestowed on my most ardent supporters, some could never reciprocate.

With the end of the school year fast approaching, it was with a sense of pride and humility that I accepted the honor of having my name placed in nomination for the office of chapter chairman for the upcoming school year. Again, through hard work and perseverance, we were able to win another election. In contrast to our initial victories, this time we decimated Banister's slate of candidates.

Their sacrificial lamb for chapter chairman received fewer than 30 votes out of more than 100 cast. Only Mike from Banister's group won a spot on the executive committee. This was fine with me because, much to his credit and sense of morality, the union and its importance came first. The man cared, and that was all I could ask of anyone.

In retrospect, I felt for the first time since my appointment to I.S.24, our union was less fragmented. I, as well as most members of our chapter, knew that Banister would never accept Sam Ross or any other individual sitting on the throne he had once occupied. The difference from the previous year was that this time no one, except the remnants of his inner circle, cared.

As had been the case since the inception of my teaching career, the school year had exacted its pound of flesh from my being. I was mentally and physically exhausted. Summer vacation never looked better. Just knowing I could look forward to the next school year with a sense of confidence and pride, due to my successes as both a teacher and a chapter chairman, was so important to my overall sense of being. An enjoyable summer was on the horizon, and I would make the most of it.

Section 5: I Was Touched by the Standing Ovation…and Humbled by the Tears

My second year as chapter chairman proceeded with the pitfalls inherent in the job. Staying on top of union business as well as teaching a full program continued to occupy a major portion of my teaching and "leisure" time. Closer contact with Mario and his antics helped make the job of being chapter chairman more enjoyable than the previous year. Life would have been considered pretty good except, for some reason, this was not meant to be.

Twenty-four diarrhea diapers and numerous episodes of projectile vomiting in the span of 24 hours, and still our doctor had no answers. Our three-month-old son was so sick that he just cried, cried, and cried some more. Then there was the medication, then different medications, along with Similac, Prosobee, Enfamil, etc. Nothing worked! Day after day, week after week, I walked the floors with my child.

One to three hours of sleep became the norm, rather than the exception. Dianah and I were both teetering on the brink of total exhaustion. I would put in a full day of teaching and dealing with union matters, come home, help Dianah out, eat dinner, and then go to school four nights a week to get the necessary credits to validate my new science license. After class, I would drive home, take the baby from Dianah and go back to walking the floors. We now had a routine that felt more like a prison sentence.

Finally, the results of all of the tests we had subjected our child to were in, and Dr. Cooke's office called for us to come over. Dr. Cooke, ashen faced and with tears in his eyes, barely could utter what had to be said, but when he did, I felt that my entire life force had been sucked from my body. Our child would never live past the age of seven. A sweat test had confirmed what Dr. Cooke had suspected all along; our baby was diagnosed with cystic fibrosis; life expectancy was seven years at best. Our son had been sentenced to death! A maximum life span of six years and nine months was the most we could hope for. There was no chance for clemency, no avenue for appeals, nothing to do except walk the floors and prepare for the inevitable.

Twenty-eight years later, I still have no idea how we made it home. I remember driving as if I were in a trance. To say we were devastated would be a monumental understatement. I knew I had to remain strong for Dianah, my son, and for so many other family members and close friends. When I was alone, I cried bitterly and what seemed endlessly. Why us? We had never hurt others. If anything, we were too nice to people. I always believed that G-d only gave you what you could handle…but not this. How do you handle the eminent death of your child?

A week or so later, we received a call from Dr. Cooke telling us to take our child to the Long Island College Hospital in Brooklyn. He explained that the sweat test was considered by some doctors to be antiquated and that this hospital was using what they considered a more definitive test. A quick call and we were to report to the outpatient area at 6:30 a.m. the next morning.

With all of the craziness that I'd experienced in my life, time never moved slower than it did waiting for my son's test results to be calibrated. We were told it would take some time, but never did I expect to be sitting on pins and needles for such an extended period. Finally, the call, which had consumed our every waking moment, came: "Results negative for cystic fibrosis." When Dianah and I hung up our phones, we just held on to each other and cried. G-d had spared our child, and modern medicine had confirmed it.

A couple of telephone calls to family and friends precipitated a deluge of calls from well-wishers. We were so caught up in our good news that we failed to realize just how sick our child still was. A return call to Dr. Cooke mildly tempered our jubilation. Our son was highly allergic to many foods. We would restart the process of introducing one food at a time, and eliminate any item causing an adverse reaction.

We must have tried every baby formula known to mankind. Concoctions were practically invented until we found something that wouldn't make our infant sick. Still, my nights were endless as I continued to walk the floors getting little or no sleep. Finally, morning would arrive, and there would be Dianah measuring out the proper amounts of whatever our son could possibly eat and drink. Then, as if on cue, the endless diarrhea diapers and episodes of vomiting resumed, and we were practically back to square one. Through it all, we thanked G-d for being so good to us because we knew our child would live.

In contrast to previous years, by the time March arrived, I was totally exhausted. The simplest task required a superhuman effort on my part. Undoubtedly, the mental and physical stress from my son's illness played a major role in my being fatigued. Nonetheless, I sensed that another factor, far greater than walking the floors, was contributing to my state of weariness. One evening, I fell asleep and awoke 14 hours later. Having never been a great sleeper, once the shock of how many hours I'd slept had worn off, I knew something was terribly wrong. As I tried to stand up, my last memory was that of the floor lifting up and hitting me in the face. I'd passed out.

When I came to, a shook-up Dianah rushed me to our family physician's office. Besides suffering from complete exhaustion and dehydration, I was diagnosed with having hypoglycemia, i.e. low blood sugar. With my blood sugar count registering a paltry 32, which was dangerously low, Dr. Wilkens informed me that I had to change my lifestyle, as well as be on a special diet for the rest of my life.

No matter how much I tried to find ulterior causation, the fact remained that being a chapter chairman had imposed tremendous demands on my life. There was no getting around the fact that this was one of the changes I'd have to address. I had put my heart and soul into trying to be the best chapter chairman in the entire city. I had overcome immeasurable adversity to win the office that I held so dearly, but one fact would never change as far as I was concerned: My family was the most important entity in my life! There was no doubt in my mind that they needed a healthy me. Therefore, the decision I had to make was one of the easiest I've ever made in my life. I would resign.

Later that evening, I called Mario to inform him of what had transpired over the past 24 hours and that I would be resigning as Chapter Chairman of I.S.24, immediately. Mario was caught completely off guard, as attested to by the silence on his end of the line. Then he finally spoke.

"Sam, please hang on until the end of the school year or at least until a suitable replacement can be found to finish up the year and run for the office," Mario pleaded. "Let your vice chapter chairman and other office holders do all of the leg work until we see if you're feeling better," Danzio continued.

"You have all summer to get better, Sam. Don't do this to me!" was Mario's last attempt at changing my mind.

Mario had always been a great negotiator, but this was one of the few times I ever heard him pleading with someone. As stated earlier, I really had gotten to like this man and the loyalty he exhibited to his people. I'd practically forgiven him for his role in the Banister wars. He would do anything and everything possible to protect and defend those who were loyal to him, and I couldn't fault him for this. Now he would have to understand that I, too, had loyalty and it was to my family. They took precedence over anyone or anything and this included my being chapter chairman of I.S.24.

During the past 19 months, I had witnessed Mario charm the hell out of his most vocal detractors. Try as he might, he finally realized that there was nothing he could do or say that would change the decision I had already made. As far as finding a "suitable replacement," he should have known that everything I did was on the up and up, and there would be no "suitable" anything. By law, the vice chapter chairman would assume the leadership role of the chapter, and that was the way it was going to be.

After finishing my conversation with Danzio, I called my vice chapter chairman to let him know that after an emergency union meeting the next morning, he would assume the union leadership of our chapter. Bill Brandeis was totally shocked when I told him of my eminent resignation. Billy and I had been close friends for a number of years, and he knew what had been going on with our child, as well as how lousy I had been feeling. Even with this knowledge, Billy could never have anticipated that I would resign from a job that I loved and that so many had fought so vigorously to acquire. To tell you the truth, I'm not sure who I had shocked more, Mario or Billy.

During our conversation, I told Billy that I would assist him when and if he needed my help. I let him know that he was up to the task of being an excellent chapter chairman, especially since he was liked and respected by most members on our staff. As far as Banister's group was concerned, I told him to ignore their stupidity and focus on the way the rest of the union membership perceived him. When our conversation was over, I wished Billy the best of luck. Almost immediately I thought: *Billy isn't going to sleep well tonight!*

To say the least, it had been one hell of a day. When I lay down in bed, I must have immediately fallen asleep. As if scripted for a movie, my son, for one of the few times, let me sleep through the night. If I didn't know better, I would have bet my life that this was his present to me for my decision to resign.

When I arrived at I.S.24 the next morning, with Leonard Pell's consent, it was announced on the loud speaker that there would be an emergency U.F.T. meeting in the library. Addressing the chapter from behind the now very familiar podium, was without a doubt the most gut-wrenching oration I had ever given. Only a eulogy at my father's funeral some seven years later proved to be more difficult. Using every trick I had learned in regards to the art of public speaking, I managed to keep my composure as I informed the membership of my condition, our son's illness and our doctor's recommendation. I thanked everyone for their support as well as the honor that they had bestowed upon me by allowing me to represent them for the greater part of the past two years.

Fighting back every instinct not to make this into a soap opera tear-jerker, after introducing my legitimate successor, I walked over to a vacant seat and watched as Bill Brandeis took over the reigns of leadership. As I scanned those in attendance, I was deeply touched by the onset of a standing ovation the membership was bestowing on me. I was extremely humbled by the tears being shed by many of my colleagues. I remember thinking how this gesture almost made all of the misery and insanity that I had endured the past two years worth the physical and mental abuse my body had been subjected to.

When the meeting was over, many of my colleagues came up to me to offer heartfelt wishes. Even Banister, who had not said one word to me in almost two years, wished me a speedy recovery. To say the least, I was taken aback by his offering. I was overwhelmed with this entire experience, as well as the finality of the long arduous journey that started almost two years earlier. Fighting off numerous emotions, I left the library and went to my room to enjoy the weight that had been lifted from my shoulders.

For whatever reason, which I can't recall, the next day I was at the district office. Upon entering the building, many acquaintances that I had made during the past two years came over to offer their support. After all I had experienced during my stewardship, I still was impressed by how fast news traveled throughout the district. Then, in utter disbelief, the district superintendent came out of his office to wish me the best, and stated, "If you need anything, please let me know," exhibiting warmth I didn't know he had in his cold-blooded veins.

Having sat down only moments before his appearance and shocking offer, I stood up and with utter disdain reminded Rodgers of the following.

"You once told me that you would never deal with me in any way, shape, or form. I don't need anything from the likes of you!" With this said, I slowly turned and walked away.

I remember thinking, *The nerve of that son of a bitch!*

Yes, I was sick, but I still had my dignity, something this character was totally void of. Undoubtedly, it would be a cold day in hell before I'd ask that bastard for anything!

Except for a one-minute meeting three years later when he signed my transfer papers, this was the last time we had any contact with each other. I guess it's true that some good does come out of the most difficult of circumstances. Just think, except for Divine intervention, I would never again have to deal with this "distinguished" district superintendent in any way, shape, or form. What a tragedy!

CHAPTER FIFTEEN

Move over! Here I come.

Section 1: Everything Was Fine until Murphy Showed Up

The transition of Sam Ross, teacher/chapter chairman, to Sam Ross, teacher of a seventh grade self-contained class, was an easy if not welcome process. Although the next two years would present new and often chaotic situations, being exclusively back in the classroom was a welcome relief. Relinquishing my duties as chapter chairman also saw my home life undergo a positive metamorphosis. Dianah and I experienced our personal relationship return to the pre-insanity union leadership days. Although far from being cured, our son's health underwent a dramatic reversal. Just knowing he was capable of a normal life expectancy made Dianah and I ecstatic. There was marked improvement in so many aspects of my life. If only I could get my blood sugar to jump on the bandwagon.

Constant fluctuations in my blood sugar, and the resulting effects on my body and overall personality, were so demoralizing that I finally sought out one of the top specialists in this field. Dr. Reed would eventually inform me that I did not have low blood sugar and that the diet my doctor had put me on was basically starving me to death. To this day, I remember his exact words of advice. "Go home and have a bowl of ice cream!" was his first order.

"Tomorrow have a bowl of ice cream and then a bowl of spaghetti," he advised me with a broad smile on his face. "Continue this until you're on a normal diet." And with those words, he went into the next examining room to see his next patient.

Following Dr. Reed's advice, I saw a frail 125-pound skeleton begin to regain his weight and strength. It was like a gift from heaven knowing that I could eat anything I wanted to eat. Undoubtedly there would be setbacks, but they were very infrequent. It was great going into a restaurant and ordering whatever I wanted. When everything was taken into consideration, there was no doubt that we were becoming a family again and our future looked brighter than ever before.

It's so difficult for an adult, or anyone for that matter, to realize they are stupid. I must admit to everyone that I was stupid! Everything was falling into place and was going smoothly. Why didn't I anticipate that "Murphy" was about to jump up and bite me on my ass? Of course, I couldn't have guessed something so drastic would happen, ultimately destroying my newfound contentment, yet I should have known that Murphy was lurking in the shadows just waiting for the opportune moment to totally destroy what looked so promising. Never could I fathom that a colleague of mine, who just so happened to be a close personal friend, would unleash a chain of events that would cause me to suffer a devastating injury. My unfortunate intervention in a fight between a friend and one of my students would culminate in my undergoing two surgeries and spending the rest of my life in severe to unbearable pain and seeing so many hopes and dreams banished from the realm of reality.

The summer of 1979 again saw us as avid participants in our neighborhood pool club. Despite my first ulna nerve operation and rehab, I was enjoying my family as well as my continued good luck at the card tables. Unfortunately, as the summer progressed, each movement of my left arm caused the pain from my surgically repaired ulna nerve to reach new levels of discomfort. The psychological scars, which I had unknowingly suffered from this debilitating injury, continued their unimpeded trek towards my conscious awareness with each passing day. Four days before the start of the new school year, severe pain clashed with a confused mental state, and the result was utter chaos.

Late that Thursday morning, I was sitting on the lower steps outside of our apartment when four men got out of a van and started towards me. Each was in possession of a butcher knife, and the look on each of their faces was that of outright hatred! Quickly I arose and, taking three steps at a time, climbed a flight of stairs to warn my family and secure any possible weapon. As I neared the top steps, I noticed that the knife wielders were in reality a husband, wife, and their two children. Rather than being armed with knives, they were only carrying presents for whomever they were visiting. In that split second of reality, I knew what had to be done. Dejectedly, I walked into our apartment, picked up my telephone, and dialed a friend who worked at the New York City Board of Education.

Section 2: Howie to the Rescue: Goodbye I.S.24

Howard Trent and I had met while we were both in college. What I think we both liked about each other was the fact that we were both perceived as being off the walls. What some considered crazy was nothing more than two exuberant teenagers who liked to have fun. The reality of being in college didn't mean you had to surrender your sense of humor, and neither of us did. Our friendship continued through graduate school and definitely was cemented when we were tossed out of a couple of lecture halls for laughing and fooling around.

Our paths crossed again when I found out that Howie was teaching in the same district that I had been assigned to. By the time I became chapter chairman, Howie was Mario's right hand man, and it would be Howie's behind-the-scene assistance that stopped Mario from trying to totally incinerate me. A few years later, I learned that Howie had left our district and was now working at the board of education. When Howard Trent's phone rang at the board of ed., it was Sam Ross on the other end of the line.

Howie had heard through the grapevine that I had been severely injured after being stabbed by a student during an altercation. Although the story related to him was incorrect, the extent of the injury wasn't. When I explained to Howie that I wanted to transfer out of I.S.24, he told me to get down to his office ASAP.

When I arrived at the board of education and walked into Howie's office, we exchanged heartfelt pleasantries. We really had experienced some good times together, and it was great to see an old friend. Of course, the reason for this reunion could have been under more favorable circumstances. When I reiterated to Howie that I had to get out of Bed-Sty, his reaction was, "Ah, shit, Sam! If you only would have called me yesterday! We had three science openings in the neighborhood you live in and I had to scrounge around to get people to fill them," he continued, more disgusted than anything else.

As my heart sank, Howie asked me with some signs of trepidation, " Sam, would you be willing to teach in the East New York section of Brooklyn?"

Just as I was about to reply, Howie interrupted me and said, " I can have you transferred to I.S.302, which is right near where you used to live."

I jumped at his offer! I had grown up in East New York, and I.S.302 was only five minutes from where I now lived. Then Howie told me, "Sam, there's only one problem. I only have a 7th grade math position open. Is that okay with you?"

I knew that this offer was a G-dsend in disguise. My inability to properly use my operated left arm had realistically ruled out my accepting any of the three science positions if they had still been available. When confronted with the reality that dropping a math book was a hell of a lot safer than a bottle of sulfuric acid, I knew that math would be fine.

Howie and I began to reminisce about our history and we started laughing at all of the crazy things we had done together. I must admit, I couldn't remember when I had laughed so hard. It seemed that most of my happiness had disappeared due to the severity of the pain I now experienced on a daily basis. After rehashing old times, it was time to say goodbye. Shaking hands and thanking my friend for all he had done for me, I headed to the elevators. Little did I know at that moment that this would be the last time we would ever see each other again.

How ironic this entire adventure had been. My professional career had started with my walking up to New Lots Avenue in the East New York section of Brooklyn to catch a bus. Now, ten years later, I was back with an abundance of experience and a severely damaged limb. My career had come full circle.

Words could not express the exhilaration I felt, knowing I was finally free. Ten years at I.S.24 had come to a screeching halt. I could breathe again. Hopefully, I would never again envision a car parking in front of my house and its occupants getting out with knives in their hands, desirous of ending my life. No matter where I was going, it had to be a far cry from where I had been!

My life would now begin a new chapter; one which I hoped would reinvigorate the optimism I once held. Hopefully I would now find the real Sam Ross, who had lost both focus and direction in all aspects of his life the moment he felt that initial twinge of pain in his elbow. I really had liked the old Sam Ross. Quite possibly, this new job would allow him to return from where he had been exiled for the better part of six months.

As I revealed in the prologue, I had grown up in the East New York section of Brooklyn, and the neighborhood I would return to ten years removed was a far cry from the one I had left. Urban sprawl had exacted its toll, but nonetheless, it still was home to me. There were so many changes, yet some things hadn't changed at all. I knew most members on the local school board and numerous teachers in the district. My in-laws had been involved in local politics for many years and knew many influential people, including the district superintendent. Not that I needed their help, but it was nice to know that I had some powerful people watching my back.

The first day of the 1979-80 school year had me returning to I.S.24. I had been informed by the principal of my new school that I had to go back to I.S.24 and have Principal Pell and the district superintendent sign a letter of consent, which would make my transfer complete. On a more positive note, this visit would give me the opportunity to say goodbye to so many good friends, allies, and other members of the staff. The mid-morning ride would be the calmest I'd taken to I.S.24 in a long time.

Upon my arrival, I went to Leonard Pell's office to inform him that I had transferred to a new school. The look on his face was one of disbelief, if not utter shock, when I handed him my transfer papers. For a few moments, Pell couldn't even speak. When he finally was able to verbalize his thoughts, he tried every means possible to get me to change my mind. Finally, realizing that he was beating a dead horse, Pell wished me the best of luck and signed the letter of consent.

As I left Pell's office, I reflected on all that we had been through. As stated earlier, Leonard Pell was not a bad guy. Like many before him, he was just stuck in a lousy, no-win situation. This man had been promised so much by his superiors, but when the smoke had cleared and the supply caravans had dissipated, little help was rendered. I always wondered if things would have been different if he had shown a greater amount of courage when fighting for what he believed in.

When I entered my classroom, so many thoughts and memories raced through my mind. So many great experiences were contained within these walls, along with so much heartache. As I began to pack up a couple of cartons of personal effects, my room began to resemble Grand Central Station. Word of my transfer must have spread through the building like an epidemic, and numerous colleagues came by to wish me the best of luck. Plenty of hugs, kisses, and tears were shed, and this seemed representative of the history of every classroom in I.S.24. After placing the last of my belongings in my car, I went back inside for what, hopefully, would be my last tour of a building that had been such a huge part of my life for the past ten years. I tried to say goodbye to as many people as possible because, I hoped, when I walked out of the front doors it would be for the last time. Except for a brief visit years later, after some final goodbyes, I walked through these doors and never looked back!

Section 3: Here I Am

Few teachers can have the distinction of stating that the school they work in is located under a parking garage. When I first reported to I.S.302, the exterior beauty of the building blew me away. How could I possibly foresee that I would never get a chance to teach in this state of the art facility? After meeting my new boss, Harold Sanger, I was informed that I would be teaching seventh grade math in the annex. Did he say annex? After learning that this annex was situated under a parking garage, I was introduced to Victor Rawlings who was the AP in charge of this "building." A handshake, an inanimate nod, and absolutely no eye contact gave me an immediate feeling of, "Uh-oh, here we go again!"

Until my program was finalized, I was given the opportunity to explore my new environment. It was so weird walking down steps into an underground school, but that's exactly the way it was. With simple directions, I managed not to get lost in my quest to find the teachers' room. When I entered this future sanctuary, I thought I'd have one of Fred Sanford's infamous "heart attacks." I was spellbound, in total shock, mesmerized, and totally speechless.

My immediate thought after my bugged-out eyes had returned to their sockets was, *Holy Shit!* Either I had died and gone to "the big school in the sky" or this was the school equivalent of the Garden of Eden. All I could repeatedly say to myself was *Look at this!* There were couches, chairs, a huge table to eat at, a refrigerator, a stove, sink, a coffee maker, a soda and sandwich machine, a microwave, and to top it all off, a regulation-sized Ping-Pong table. Even the walls and the floors were spotless! This had to be a mirage!

When I exited the teachers' room, just like on television or in the movies, I pinched myself to see if I had been dreaming. When I realized I hadn't been, I continued to explore my new home away from home, this time with an energized bounce in my step that I hadn't experienced for years!

Scouting around this underground bunker was quite a trip. The place was so clean you could eat off the floor. The cafeteria was in pristine condition. Seriously, this entire place was so antiseptic that an operating room could have been set up and passed all health codes. In a matter of seconds, I found myself looking into a room that even I could figure out had to be the school's supply room. It was huge! Anything and everything you wanted or needed as a teacher was somewhere in this supply depot. While in this total state of euphoria, I had inadvertently made one mistake. What I thought was the supply room for the entire school was in reality just for the annex.

I was dumbfounded! There were more supplies here for one grade than for the three grades we had at I.S.24. Then it hit me; *This undoubtedly was the showcase school for the entire district.* I remember thinking that I had gone from the bottom of the ladder to the top rung, one arm operation removed. Howie Trent had definitely sent me to heaven.

Later in the day, I was given my teaching program.

"My G-d…two SP classes!" I uttered, totally astonished!

I had been given two of the top classes in the grade to teach. Then I noticed that I was also given the two lowest numbered classes. I knew that this was just a way of balancing out my program, but the joke was on them! These two "slow classes" were like the top classes at I.S.24 as far as behavior was concerned. Imagine four classes basically void of behavioral problems—unbelievable! Of course, ten years in the trenches had taught me to never let my guard down, and this lesson would not be forgotten.

Just when I thought my luck had changed, I noticed that there were seven missing teaching periods on my program. I should have known this was too good to be true. I guess it was time for "Murphy's Law" to make its usual appearance and cause the usual carnage. Why did this S.O.B. always show up when things were looking so good? All the misery I'd gone through in the last ten years, wasn't it enough? Hadn't I paid my dues yet?

As I was waiting for the proverbial "shit to hit the fan," I learned that the seven missing periods were like the magnificent maraschino cherry on the top of a chocolate sundae. I had been given seven periods to teach any subject of my choice as long as it met with the approval of Victor Rawlings. This time, instead of pinching myself, I began to wonder if I was an unknowing participant on *Candid Camera.* If Allan Funt had suddenly appeared, I wouldn't have been surprised.

When the appropriate time came, I informed Victor Rawlings that I wanted to teach an animal studies class. Since my earliest recollections, I'd always loved anything associated with the animal kingdom and nature. Now I had the opportunity to pass on the knowledge I had accumulated over the years to my new students. During this time period, I had amassed a huge collection of pictures, slides, and other visual effects. I knew they would keep the interest of most, if not all, of my students. We would discuss all aspects of animal life, including migrations, feeding habits, and of course, sex. I knew beyond a shadow of a doubt that any student that walked through my front door would love this class. Undoubtedly, with my personality and innate ability to put on a show, this would be the most popular class in the school. Without sounding too conceited, I was 100% right. After an 8-10 week period, when a new rotation began, practically every kid in the seventh grade wanted to get into this class.

For the first time in years, I couldn't wait to get to work in the morning. Within 7-10 minutes from leaving my house, I'd be in my classroom. No more of this nonsense of departing an hour and a half early just to get parking near the school. Finally, I didn't have to get neurotic about snow or sleet storms or icy roads. Highways were always cleared off first, and our school was right off the Belt Parkway in Brooklyn. Besides, there were so many other ways to get to my new school that these elements were no longer a significant problem. Imagine 3:00 dismissal and home by 3:10, absolutely incredible!

I must admit that it was very hard to get used to the fact that I could park my car near the school and not have to worry about it being vandalized. This was mostly due to the tremendous amount of security both in and outside the school building. During the short walk to the main entrance, I didn't have to look over my shoulder every couple of steps to make sure someone wasn't getting ready to jump me, a possibility that always existed at I.S.24, no matter how much I was liked. I never could adjust to this security feature at I.S.302 after my stint at I.S.24.

I found it inconceivable that security guards and the police were always in direct contact with each other, working harmoniously. Both patrolled the garage as well as the entire perimeter of the school while it was in session. This entire security operation was unbelievable! I was always cognizant of the fact that nothing was 100% safe, but this was as close as it could get. Anyone who knew me could see the change in my demeanor; I was happy!

As in years past, all of my new students were honored with my infamous "opening day" speech. Even those kids in my bottom two classes couldn't believe what they were hearing. Although this wasn't Bedford Styvesant, this was still a tough inner city school, so my rationale was "Why change now?" When I delivered my "pet speech," you could have heard a feather hit the ground, that's how shocked my kids were. Of greater importance was the fact that many of my new students, although definitely feeling threatened, also felt that they now had a teacher who cared. When classes let out at 3:00, quite a few rushed up to me to tell me how cool and crazy I was and how happy they were to be in my class. I told every one of them if they lived up to our agreement, we would have a ball. None of us would be disappointed!

Every day teaching at I.S.302 was such a great experience. The days literally flew by. I never looked at my watch to see how much time was left in a period, no less in the school day. Although my students and I were enjoying ourselves, I did notice something bizarre happening each and every day. I became aware of the fact that, while I was in the process of teaching, more often than not a female teacher would peer into my room to see what was going on. Since I wore my wedding band and wasn't a Georgio Armani male model, I couldn't figure out what was luring these women to my room when classes were in session.

After a while, this behavior was beginning to annoy me, but I didn't want to ask any of these ladies what their problem was. I was having a ball with my students and I just wanted to be left alone! I had no desire to get involved with union business or my coworkers' problems. My goal was to teach to the best of my ability, speak with as few people as possible, and play Ping-Pong in the teachers' lounge. Everything was so calm and serene, and I wanted to keep it that way. A simple hello and goodbye would suffice as far as I was concerned. These 14 or so days of utter bliss had made me realize that my ten years at I.S.24 constituted enough excitement for a career lasting 30 years. If I could, I would have put a flashing neon sign on my door stating, "Thank you for letting me teach, and please leave me alone!"

One afternoon, while enjoying the company of one of my nature studies classes, I noticed a young female teacher staring into my classroom. All of a sudden, she signaled for me to come out into the hallway. I asked my kids to give me a second so I could go outside to talk to her and hopefully find out what this entire mystery was about. This peeking into my room routine had gotten out of hand, and unfortunately for this teacher, she would bare the brunt of my wrath.

Before I had the opportunity to find out what she wanted, she inquired, "How do you control these animals?" in this high-pitched annoying voice.

So this was what this mystery was all about. The more I thought about her stupid question, the more incensed I became. *How do you control these animals?* These so-called "animals" were just a spectacular bunch of students. They were intelligent, well-behaved, inquisitive, etc. They were in essence any teacher's dream class.

Immediately thinking of all of the amenities my new colleagues had and what my people at I.S.24 never enjoyed, my response to her question would be ruthless. "Animals? " I inquired in an annoyed voice. "Are you fucking kidding me?" I continued, getting louder with each word I spoke. "Lady, I spent ten years of my life in a fucking war zone! When you punched your time card in the morning, you wondered if this would be the day your car was stolen, you'd get into a fight, be stabbed, or possibly killed! Don't you realize how great you have it here?"

Then, in almost a knee jerk reaction, I pulled up my left shirtsleeve, which had been covering my hideous, raw-looking, six-inch scar and screamed, "Look at this fucking arm!"

After turning her head away from my grotesque limb, she proceeded to run down the hall with me feigning chase. Yelling at her to "quit," the first thought to enter my deranged mind was, *Wow that was great! Look at her go!*

Talk about being blunt and getting to the heart of the matter. I remember thinking to myself, *You should write a book entitled: The Art of Making Friends* by Sam Ross. To tell you the truth, I didn't give a damn how she felt! These kids were fantastic, and if she couldn't deal with them, then she should get the hell out of teaching and find a new profession.

My goal teaching at I.S.302 was to enjoy the peace and quiet of this new school. Somehow, I knew this incident with this immature, self-centered brat would be the catalyst necessary to unleash a chain of events forever destroying the inner peace I had finally found. Everything up to this point had been too good to be true. Murphy was due to step up and take center stage as he had so often done in the past. As also was the case, the ramifications of his appearance would not be favorable for Sam Ross.

Section 4: Some Things Never Change…or Do They?

During the first days of a new teacher's orientation, the probationer is usually informed that they will be subjected to two informal and one formal observation during the school year. This, they are told, is mandatory and is part of the collective bargaining agreement between their union and the board of education of New York City. It is further explained to the "prized rookie" that either the chairman of the department they are teaching in, an assistant principal, or even the school principal can, at any time, enter your classroom and casually observe you teaching a lesson. This usually will culminate with your getting a memo from the observer, letting you know what they thought of your lesson, as well as your overall classroom performance.

In direct contrast to this informal observation, there is the formal variety. This consists of both parties agreeing to a specific date and time when the principal, or designated supervisor, will enter your room, usually sit in the back, and take copious notes on your presentation. You will later receive a formal, written report detailing their impression of the lesson you taught, your appearance, classroom management skills, and other aspects inherent in this process. The teacher is then required to make an appointment with the observer to go over this evaluation and, after this conference, is required to sign this report, signifying the conclusion of this process.

It is at this point in time that your formal observation becomes part of your permanent teacher file. This file will follow you throughout your career no matter if you continue to be a teacher, become a guidance counselor, assistant principal, or principal. Every important bit of information about you is contained in your file, and if you are transferred to a different school, it will accompany you. A copy of this file can be requested from another city or state if you decide to move and teach somewhere else.

As I began my third week teaching at I.S.302, I received a memo from Victor Rawlings stating that he wanted to do a formal observation of me teaching one of my classes. He wanted to know which class and period I would feel comfortable with and if the date I chose fit into his schedule. As luck would have it, everything I proposed was agreeable to Rawlings, and we were all set.

What I immediately found peculiar about this entire matter was the fact that a teacher usually had their two informal observations first and towards the end of the year, their formal one. After ten years of enduring this process, I could only conclude that Rawlings was doing this for the expressed purpose of "busting my chops" as he had done to others before me.

I had been warned by a new colleague to expect this request for a formal observation. Rawlings, true to his reputation, did not disappoint. Under the guise of just "doing my job," Rawlings was essentially letting me know that he was the boss and not to forget it! My initial thought was, *Here we go again, another power-hungry Claude Jennings clone.*

The day of my observation arrived, and there was not a trace of nervousness on my part. Since I was a tenured teacher, I knew this observation meant nothing as far as job security was concerned. Even a scathing review meant absolutely zero, since I already had so many positive reports from previous years. The most horrific report would have been construed by anyone reading my file as nothing more than a bad day on my part or, more significantly, a report from an assistant principal with an "axe to grind." Of greater import was the fact that I knew I was an excellent teacher, and since I had about nine positive observations in my file, why get bent over this stupid ploy of Rawlings. Of course, if push came to shove, I had plenty of backup on the district level, as well as the superintendent's friendship. Bottom line, contesting the report and having it expunged would be no problem!

At the specified time we had agreed upon, Rawlings entered my classroom and sat down towards the back of the room. With the sounding of the late bell, he began to take copious notes. I proceeded with my lesson as if no one special was in my room, and to tell the truth, no one was. I taught my lesson as outlined in the lesson plan I had submitted to Rawlings, told a few life-related stories, and cracked my usual amount of insane jokes. There was no way that I would change my teaching technique for Rawlings or anyone else. I had even warned my kids to be themselves and not feel threatened when Rawlings sat down and watched me teach.

When the lesson had ended, Rawlings thanked me for allowing him to be present, as if there was an option, and went out into the hallway to help with the passing of classes. I remember thinking that even he had to be impressed at how I had taken a boring math lesson and energized it with my personality, yet I hadn't forgotten the purpose of Rawlings' request for an early formal observation: to show Sam Ross who was the boss.

I believe it was the next day that I received a typewritten critique of my lesson. Accompanying this review was a memo reminding me to sign it and make an appointment with Rawlings to go over my performance. I knew I had taught a really great lesson, and Rawlings' assessment confirmed my belief. Like any good administrator, he also managed to find three aspects of my overall performance that needed improvement. There had always existed an unwritten code that an observation contain a couple of negatives since there was no such thing as "the perfect lesson." Being a stickler for regulations, Rawlings, groping for straws, conjured up three asinine negatives to incorporate into his report. The three aspects of my lesson that he found fault with were: my lesson plan was written in pencil, there was no medial summary, and some other innocuous negative that I still can't remember no matter how hard I try.

Under normal circumstances, I never would have taken exception to such a great write up, but remembering that Rawlings had requested the formal observation first, really irritated me. Unfortunately, whatever his plan was, it had gone awry due to his underestimation of my teaching abilities. What had possibly been an avenue for him to flex his muscles, had wound up being a failed medium. What he never anticipated was the fact that, although his plan had fallen to pieces, I was not going to let him off the hook that easily. There was going to be another lesson in this "soap opera," and he would learn not to play head-games with Sam Ross!

Throughout this book, I've repeatedly expressed my dislike of assistant principals in particular and all administrators in general. The fact that I now found myself in a new educational environment did not change this attitude one iota. Victor Rawlings, as I would quickly be made aware of, tyrannized the entire seventh grade staff. Female teachers, in particular, related to me how they walked around with knots in their stomachs for fear of coming into contact with him. Rawlings' domineering personality had basically gone unchallenged since his appointment to this position of power at I.S.302. With my eventual arrival, it would only be a matter of time before his feelings of invincibility would come under attack.

During my tenure at I.S.24, I had been through wars with those of far greater stature that a Victor Rawlings and had survived each encounter. I knew that his threat was nothing more than a minor annoyance if handled correctly. The only question was where, and when, our confrontation would take place.

I had learned from my fiasco with Donald that any verbal confrontation had to take place in an isolated locale. Unbeknownst to Victor, he provided me not only with the privacy that was desired, but also the time I needed to prepare him for the "real world" of Sam Ross. How ironic, Rawlings providing me with the necessities to knock him off his high horse. All of this had come to a head due to his insatiable need to prove he was "the man." Yes, the post-observation conference would be the perfect place to welcome Victor Rawlings into my world—a world of dislike and distrust of all administrators, and a place where their comeuppance could and would be a rude awakening!

As I entered Rawlings' office, I slammed down his observation critique on his desk.

"Are you kidding me?" I yelled, undoubtedly pissed off.

Rawlings was already taken aback by the onset of my verbal assault, especially since his review had been so great. I continued. "What is this bullshit?" I asked him. "Are you out of your mind?"

Without giving him a chance to respond to my questions, I explained to Rawlings as graphically as possible what he physically could do with his observation report, as well as his misguided desire to show me who was the boss. Continuing my mini-tirade, Rawlings was given a brief history lesson as to who I was, where I had come from, and who my friends were in this district, as well as the board of education.

Victor sat motionless, and I had no intention of letting up with my verbal barrage. I let him know that he was fooling around with the wrong individual, not only due to my past experience as a chapter chairman, but also because of one undeniable truth: I knew more important people in the district and the board of education than he did. I qualified all of this with the promise that, "I will be the best teacher on your staff, and never bother you as long as you leave me alone!" and I meant every word of this statement.

As I stood up and prepared to leave, I stared at him with a look void of life, and in an almost inaudible low voice said, "If you ever fuck with my head again, you will rue the day that I first walked into this garage!"

Victor Rawlings sat there in a state of utter disbelief. I'm sure no one had ever spoken to him in this manner. Finally regaining his composure, the first words out of his mouth were, "Sam, calm down. I didn't…"

Before he could get another word out, I went off on another rampage, and when I was done, I stormed out of his office.

To say the least, I had put on a great show. Even Mario would have been proud of my tirade since he was the master, and I had wound up being one of his eager pupils. Was I professional? Absolutely not! As always seemed to be my case with administrators, they somehow managed to bring out an aspect of my personality that I didn't like. Never forget that I had spent the better part of two years of my life defending teachers against administrators or other power-hungry fools who, in most instances, weren't deserved of the positions they held. My tirade against Rawlings was also the culmination of ten years of dealing with incompetence of unimaginable proportions, on every bureaucratic level. I would never let any administrator step on me, and Victor Rawlings had just found this out!

My philosophy, "The best defense is a great offense," served me well as far as Vic Rawlings was concerned. My unexpected verbal onslaught put Rawlings on the defensive and eventually earned me his respect. The fact that my teaching ability was of such a high caliber only cemented the respect he eventually would bestow upon me. My eventual recognition of this man's administrative genius led to reciprocity on my part. He truly was a spectacular administrator and assistant principal, and I considered him an exception to my theory. After my explosion in his office, I never again crossed that imaginary line separating teacher from administrator. He deserved the respect accorded his title, not because of the title itself, but because of the dignity and competency he brought to this position.

As the semester progressed and I became more in tune with Vic's habits and thought processes, I realized that, in his case, I had mistakenly rushed to judgement. I was totally wrong with much of my assessment as far as this man was concerned. Yes, he had pulled his power play with me and had lost, but he was not the ogre many staff members made him out to be. They were the spoiled ones who failed to realize that the environment they found themselves teaching in was like heaven compared to the hellholes that many of our colleagues faced on a daily basis.

This annex staff, somewhere along the line, had lost sight of what the possible alternatives could have been if they hadn't been sent to 302. "Let them moan and groan," was my new philosophy. While they were bitching about inconsequential matters, some of my good friends at I.S.24 were fighting for their lives and sanity on a daily basis. Instead of complaining about Rawlings, these ingrates should have thanked G-d every night for giving them the opportunity to teach in this Garden of Eden. Give them two weeks at I.S.24, and they would have kissed Rawlings' tyrannical ass to be able to return. As far as my feeling sorry for them, they could kiss my ass, too!

Numerous experiences as a student, teacher, and chapter chairman had helped hone my non-complementary philosophy and attitude towards administrators. Vic Rawlings was the complete antithesis to these beliefs. I ultimately realized that the reason he was considered tyrannical by numerous members of the faculty was mainly due to their ineptness in the classroom and their inability to perform many of the tasks their job demanded of them. I, who had always been pro-teacher and anti-administration, could never have conceived of a crack in my philosophical armor. How could I possibly change my beliefs, knowing that being pro-labor was ingrained in every blood cell in my body?

If, during my stay at 302, I were given the opportunity to represent and defend a teacher at a grievance hearing, I would have accepted the challenge in a heartbeat. If the administrator in question just so happened to be Victor Rawlings, I still would have done my best to bury him, no matter how much I respected and liked this man. I urge the reader to never forget that I was, am, and always will be pro-union and pro-worker. No matter what my personal feelings were towards Vic Rawlings, that teacher, who is representative of all teachers, would be defended to the best of my ability.

You must have thought, reading the proceeding pages, that I had changed my "Us vs.Them" attitude. No, I hadn't, and I never will! The difference between the old Sam Ross and the new one was the fact that after representing this teacher, I'd invite Vic and his family over for dinner. Hopefully, he could distinguish between Sam Ross his friend and Sam Ross union representative with a job to do. If he couldn't, so be it. I would never betray the right of a teacher, or any individual, to have the best representation possible. I would never circumvent this right. Too many people had sacrificed so much in the fight to secure this privilege. I, in turn, would never disgrace their hard work or memory by not upholding what they had fought so valiantly to attain!

CHAPTER SIXTEEN

Here Today, Who Knows about Tomorrow

Life can be so marvelous when things start going one's way. Here I was, enjoying my job, family life was absolutely great, my health was excellent, except for my ulna nerve difficulties, and my bills were being paid on time. Mentally, I was on an even keel, void of hallucinations, delusions… My mini-breakdown, or whatever you want to call it, had forced me to change my direction in life, and switching schools was one of the best decisions I had ever made.

The fact that I wound up teaching near my house, in a magnificent environment, reinforced my belief in the Lord and all of His goodness. Days turned to weeks and weeks to months, and my happiness escalated with the passage of each day. Before I knew it, March was upon me, and for the first time in what seemed like centuries, I was physically and mentally strong.

In the world of reality, we all know that the expression, "The Lord giveth and the Lord taketh away" is symbolic of the many twists and turns that the course of life holds for each of us. Unfortunately for Sam Ross, the "taketh away" phase would raise its ugly head just as everything seemed to be just short of spectacular. Murphy was now ready to reign supreme!

The drama that was about to unfold commenced with the onset of excruciating pain the likes of which I'd never experienced. With the passage of each day, these attacks grew in frequency, lasted longer, and increased in intensity. At the outset, I conjured up excuses or totally denied what was occurring. I started using hypnosis and even tried the Lamaze method to try to negate the pain that, with each passing week, was becoming more intolerable. Everything had been going so well, but the irrefutable reality of this situation was that something was terribly wrong with my previously operated-on left arm. I knew that my verbal altercation with that inept teacher was the prelude to change, but never did I anticipate such misery.

The ensuing chain of events was almost an instant replay of the medical drama I had participated in during the previous year. It began with a visit to a surgeon who, before sending me for electrical conductivity studies, proceeded to give me an extensive neurological examination. The results of the EMG test indicated something was amiss, and this corroborated Dr. Cole's initial physical examination. I was prescribed pain medication and ordered to rest my arm. Neither complete rest nor a closely monitored limited exercise program, with increased medication levels, helped temper the progressively debilitating pain I was now experiencing. Finally, my surgeon, at a loss for answers, referred me to his boss, who just so happened to be the foremost authority on ulna nerve transposition in the world.

Morton Alexander was an international icon. The man had more degrees on his office walls than I had pictures hanging in my entire apartment. Letters of gratitude hung all along his suite of examining rooms with many signed by famous sports figures and celebrities. My initial visit consisted of Alexander writing down my entire medical history, as well as an extremely painful physical examination. Finally, he put me on different medications and ordered another EMG test, using his own diagnostician who also was a notable in the medical community.

During my follow-up examination some two weeks later, Alexander told me my EMG results had come back like the other one; there was something wrong but nothing extraordinary. Not caring what the test results had implied, I explained that the medications were not helping, and the pain was becoming unbearable. Alexander decided that the only way to alleviate the pain was to immobilize my entire arm. I was placed in a full-length cast, which ran from under my armpit down to the knuckles of my left hand. I would be in this monstrosity for a period of six weeks, and then we would decide if there would be a need for a further course of action. Again, my medications were changed with Vicodins added to a mixture of other painkillers that included Demerol.

Teaching was still spectacular, despite the cumbersome cast and the sling it rested in. By the end of the second week of immobilization, the pain was not only horrific, but my arm was also swelling. With few options available, I called Dr. Alexander for an emergency appointment.

When I arrived, my cast was immediately removed. I have no idea what Alexander's problem was, but to say the least, he was pissed off! In an arrogant tone of voice, he informed me that I had to go see a psychiatrist to make sure the pain I was experiencing wasn't in my head! Guess what? Now I was pissed! I only wished that my pain could somehow infiltrate his arm, and I could tell him to go see a shrink! Besides, even if I was a nut job, how could this explain the noticeable swelling of my left arm? As much as I wanted to blast this moron, I knew I had to keep my mouth shut and play by his rules or he'd drop me as a patient. He was the best and I didn't want to lose his services.

The day of my psychiatric evaluation arrived, and I was livid. After telling this doctor, whom I had never met before, what I thought about this psychiatric bullshit, I went on a 2-3 minute diatribe lambasting Dr. Alexander. After releasing this pent-up aggression, I immediately calmed down and informed this doctor that I would gladly answer any questions he might have. After ten minutes of total compliance on my part, I was informed that I was psychologically normal and that the pain I was enduring was not a figment of my imagination. Wow! What a revelation!

When I stood up to leave his office, I thanked the doctor for his professionalism and apologized for my initial outburst.

He replied, "Sam, I understand the aggressive behavior you displayed earlier. It's due to the pain you're suffering as well as the frustrations you've endured. I can't even imagine what you're going through," he said in a consoling tone.

After a handshake and wishing me the best of luck, I went home and waited to hear from Dr. Alexander's office. The "shrink" had promised me that he would forward a letter to my surgeon by the afternoon. I couldn't wait to hear what Alexander's reaction would be to my psychological evaluation and vindication.

I vividly remember the diminutive son of a bitch standing on a plastic milk crate, using a metal scrub brush to cleanse my soon to be scalpeled arm. He exerted such force as if to let me know that he still didn't believe I was in such excruciating pain, and that I had put one over on his psychiatrist. With each successive stroke, there was increased pain, and finally, blood started to seep through my pores. This bastard was nothing short of a masochist, considering this all should have been done while under anesthesia. I was getting so incensed that I wanted to get up from the opera… The anesthesia had kicked in, and I was out.

"Mr. Ross, Mr. Ross, wake up, Mr. Ross," was all I heard.

It was like someone calling my name in a tunnel. As I opened my eyes, I saw a blurry image that asked, "Mr. Ross, can you move your fingers?" in the most pleasant tone of voice. Still having no idea where I was, I moved my fingers, and it felt like a bolt of lightning had shot through my arm. I remember screaming, that's how intense the pain was. The next thing I felt was a burning sensation in my right hand, and I was gone. A good old Demerol-Vistaril shot into my I.V. had done its job. In the forthcoming days, these shots would be my salvation.

When I finally awoke, I realized that I was back in my hospital room. As I continued to look around, I noticed, and heard, Dr. Alexander speaking with Dianah. "Mrs. Ross," I remember him saying in a somewhat sedate tone, "I'm so sorry that I didn't believe your husband. From what we found in his arm, he should have been on Morphine," he said in a conciliatory manner.

As he started to leave, I remember thinking, *You little arrogant piece of shit! You should be apologizing to me! Not my wife!*

Within minutes of his departure and my return to the living, I tried and finally convinced Dianah that I wanted to get out of the bare-ass hospital garment I was in and put on my own socks, shorts, shirt, etc.

After changing and feeling somewhat like a human being, I asked Dianah to ring for the nurse. When she appeared, I asked her, "Could you be so kind as to lower the bed's side rails so I could get up and go to the day room to smoke a cigarette?" I said in an ultra-pleasant tone.

With a look of amazement, she replied, "Are you crazy? You'll never make it! You'll pass out and fall flat on your face! I can't be responsible for this,"she stated, rattling off one negative response after another.

After bantering back and forth I promised her, "I will sign any form absolving you of any responsibility should I fall."

Finally, she relented and lowered the side rails. She watched as I slowly stood up. Holding on to my I.V. pole with my right hand, and being guided and steadied by Dianah on my left, I managed to get across the hall to the day room. This was truly an amazing feat since I was high on Demerol, Vistaril, Valium, and whatever anesthesia I still had in my system. When I lit my cigarette and inhaled, the nurse looked at me as if I was a certified psycho case.

As I puffed on my poison, Dianah informed me that I had been in the operating room for four and a half-hours, instead of the normal ninety minutes this type of surgery called for. It took two surgeons three additional hours to address the medical disaster that Alexander had believed only existed in my head.

From what Dianah told me, and what I'd later discover by reading the operative report, Alexander and his associate had basically taken my entire arm apart. Their initial incision revealed a tremendous amount of scar tissue and fibrous adhesions which had to be removed. Sensing there was more, they extended the surgical cut until it was over 12 inches in length. They discovered there were more fibrous bands, and these were also trapping my ulna nerve, thus causing the horrific pain that I had been in. After releasing the nerve, Alexander built a tunnel in my arm by bisecting muscles and placing the ulna nerve in them for safekeeping. They then sewed up what they had spliced and diced. The final score was: a huge incision, 38 external and over 100 internal stitches. A half cast, kept in place by two large ace bandages, stretched from my left armpit to my fingers. I guess I showed them I wasn't a head case after all!

With the help of the Almighty, my wife, great nurses, Demerol-Vistaril shots, and my stubborn disposition, I was finally released from the hospital after a six-day stay. I should have recognized it as a bad omen that on the way home my father's car was hit by a truck when its brakes failed. You should have seen the look on the driver's face when I exited the car with this huge half cast, and my arm resting in a bright white sling. My appearance, plus a verbal outburst from Dianah using words that I never heard come out of her mouth, and this guy, no doubt, was ready for at least a 10 mg Valium himself.

Before my operation, I had gone down to the board of education and spoken to the medical director. I advised him that this surgery was a result of my school injury, and he continued my medical leave. I was granted as much time as would be needed to fully recover and resume my career. Considering all possible scenarios, he estimated that I would be on medical leave for a minimum of at least a half a year.

During my convalescence, I received my paycheck every two weeks, without interruption. My in-laws' friendship with the district superintendent helped circumvent the insane procedures of having medical days reinstated at the end of the month and all the nonsense that went along with it. If I had to be part of this insane process, I probably would have wound up in a loony bin.

One afternoon, as now had been the norm for the past two months, I went to pick up my check from the school's payroll secretary. Before I could say a word, I was hit with a verbal barrage that even I couldn't believe. This nice lady, who I had always respected, just flipped out when I asked for my check.

"I know that you know people!" she admonished me. "I know you know people because you were transferred here, and there was no job opening," she adamantly stated.

"You get your checks illegally and if you don't get me transferred to Lincoln High School, which is right by my house, I'm going to turn you in!" she continued in a threatening tone of voice.

The first thought to enter into my mind was *Oh great, someone else threatening me!* I then began to try and assess what happened to a person's mind when they worked in a school. Admittedly, there were some shortcuts taken in securing my checks, but so what? I had been through so much that "they" should have cashed my checks and handed me my money on a silver platter! No matter how they were secured, the undeniable fact was that they belonged to me! As far as creating a position for me, Libby was out of her mind! I.S.302 had an 18-period math program that needed a teacher. The only thing created was the seven periods, which I made into an animal studies class with the approval of Victor Rawlings

Irrespective of all of these logical answers, why was any of this Libby's business? What had the system done to her mind to get her involved in a confrontation with me, one that she had no chance in hell of being victorious? Had she finally gone over the edge, or were we all nuts? Meanwhile, here I was two months post surgery, and my life was in the process of undergoing a monumental meltdown. Again I was enduring intense and at times unbearable pain, and there was no logical reason this should be happening. Four and a half hours of surgery and a tunnel were supposed to have made my arm as good as new! Not only did the surgery appear to have been a failure, but now I had a crazy secretary to contend with.

The cause and effect of this renewed misery was simple: I was venting my frustrations out on anyone I came into contact with. Every vestige of my strength, maturity, and manhood was now being challenged. How could I deal with this devastating pain, which was beginning to envelop and destroy my entire world? Now, to add insult to injury, some miserable, old, chronic, bitching secretary, who I barely knew, was threatening me and my livelihood in order to work at Lincoln High.

By the time I stormed into Vic Rawlings' office, someone with a frontal lobotomy would have known to stay away from me. It had become my steady routine that whenever I picked up my check, I'd visit Vic who, as expressed previously, had become a good friend. Just by the look on my face, Vic knew something serious was going on. When I explained to him what had just occurred, he shook his head in utter disbelief. Through the grapevine, both administrators and faculty members at I.S.302 knew I had some serious backing, and no one was dumb enough to have a world of misery come crashing down on their head by messing with me. Rawlings' had learned this on a personal level, and since I did an excellent job, there was never a need to call in "the troops." Could Libby be so stupid, or burnt out, that she threatened me knowing that I "knew people?"

As I calmed down, I decided that Libby had to be taught a lesson but in no way get hurt in the process. Like others before her, she had picked on the wrong person to play head games with, but I still liked her. I asked Vic to help me out, so Libby could be put back in her proper place, behind a desk in the main office, helping out the principal and doing whatever else was required of her. I explained to Vic that I wanted him to go to Libby, after I left the building, and tell her how bent out of shape I was after her attempt at blackmailing me. He was to show his concern and friendship by letting her know that as soon as I got home, I was going to make a couple of calls to make sure she got her transfer. Unfortunately, it would not be to Lincoln High School as Libby had demanded, but rather to the worst "ghetto school" in Brooklyn.

When Libby's call of apology came, besides feigning surprise, I consoled her by confessing to understand the frustrations she felt. I really could understand her misery considering all that she must have endured during her many years in our school system. I gave her hope that things might eventually work out for her. The end result was, I had a new friend, and Libby did help me out when I was in need of her assistance. I did speak to some people about her "situation," but at that time, all secretarial jobs were filled at Lincoln High School. If an opening should materialize, Libby would not have been forgotten.

So much had happened in the past year. I had been relocated form the "bowels of hell" to the "gates of heaven." Teaching was fun again, as was my enjoyment of family life. Even the unimaginable pain that I endured when my mother, who was my best friend, had passed away that August, had begun to abate somewhat. Other traumatic events had also shed their dark cloaks, and sunlight had been let in. So much misery and sorrow had taken its toll, but I felt the corner towards happiness had been turned.

Then, in what seemed like a microsecond, everything changed. All of my hopes and dreams began to shatter. Happiness in my marriage, job, and so many other aspects of life began to dissipate. I remember thinking how ironic it was that such devastating wounds to my heart had begun the process of healing, but the physical damage to my left arm never had a chance. Only a few months earlier, I knew where I was and where I was going. Now, with the renewed onslaught of indescribable pain, getting through the day was all I could possibly think about. I felt that I was being used as a puppet for someone's entertainment. The harsh reality of this entire situation was the fact that I was not a puppet, and what was happening in my life was definitely not entertaining. Something had to give, and the only option available that made any sense was one that I thought I'd never consider: retirement.

CHAPTER SEVENTEEN

The Party's Over: Six Doctors, One Stenographer,
and Sam Ross, the Center of Attention—My
Retirement Hearing.

March 13, 1981, the day of my retirement hearing, marked the almost two-year anniversary of the day that I had suffered my ulna nerve injury at I.S.24. Words cannot describe the pain I was now subjected to on a daily basis. Switching doctors from "Mr. Egotist" to Dr. Alba, one of the most caring people I have ever known, was the only positive to come out of a deplorable situation. I was now on 2-4 25mg demerols each day along with Valium, Vistaril, and several other medications. Adding to my misery was the fact that I was getting numerous cortisone trigger point injections for a new, debilitating condition called fibromyalgia. Confronted with numerous other maladies, my life was now a living hell.

With Dr. Alba's concurrence, I became an outpatient at a pain clinic for nine months. Various means of pain management were taught and practiced, including hypnosis, biofeedback, acupuncture, and psychiatric intervention. After my initial visit, my shrink and I discussed sports and buying houses. Unlike Dr. Alexander, he easily determined that my pain was real and not in my head. Unfortunately, neither conventional nor unconventional methods of treatment were successful. Dianah, who was such a caring person, was bearing the brunt of my deteriorating health, and our marriage was taking a beating. There were days I was so bombed out of my mind from painkillers that I had no idea what I was doing. With no end to this misery in sight, I decided to put my papers in for disability retirement and hopefully be given a chance to get my life back in order.

My decision to file for retirement was originally a lark. I had been informed by my union, as well as friends at the board of education, Howie amongst them, that the odds of being granted disability retirement were about 1000:1. With nothing to lose, and probably nothing to gain, the day arrived for me to show up at the medical division of the board of education for my retirement hearing. Optimism was not the order of the day.

Upon entering a huge conference room, I encountered six individuals who, I would soon learn, were the doctors who would ultimately determine my fate. Also present was a stenographer who would officially record the proceedings and who most probably would be the only person in the crowd that wouldn't try to screw me. After some minor paper shuffling, I was introduced to the doctors in attendance and familiarized with their individual fields of expertise. I would learn that two of the doctors were neurosurgeons, three were orthopedic surgeons, and the last was a heart specialist, which I found quite bizarre. Adding further credence to the odd nature of this man's presence was the fact that he was the titular head of this board of inquiry.

After a series of background questions, I was taken into an examination area and given an extensive going over. Numerous neuromuscular and electrical tests ensued, thus giving the doctors a better insight into my disability claim. Medical reports from my physicians were also discussed and incorporated into the official record of these proceedings. After 45-60 minutes of being twisted, pricked with sharp objects, and enduring some excruciating pain, this medical mugging was finally over. We then returned to the conference room where I was positive the "fun" would really begin.

After some non-aggressive questioning, the consensus of the five surgeons was to grant my application for disability retirement. Having been involved with New York City's bureaucratic system for over twelve years, I knew that this was way too easy to signify the end of this hearing. During my career, some of the most insignificant forms had to be signed in duplicate, so why would such an important hearing, though void of complications, be over in such a short period of time? That old street smarts mentality of mine kicked in, making me aware that this wasn't the end of the hearing but only the beginning.

There was no doubt in my mind that the cardiologist was going to be the major antagonist in this real life drama. He would invariably be the most obnoxious, uncaring individual I ever encountered in the medical profession. Assuming the role of "bad cop" in this good cop/bad cop charade, this guy went way beyond the normal limits of probity. I wouldn't have been surprised if he and Dr. Morton Alexander had attended the same class entitled, Doctors' Manners and Etiquette while in medical school.

Doctor Carl Tract was approximately 65 years of age, and according to a number of his patients, an excellent cardiologist. Irrespective of this attribute, I was to discover that his role in this proceeding was to confuse and ultimately destroy my credibility. Neither the medical reports from my physicians, nor the post physical evaluation of his colleagues seemed to carry any weight as far as he was concerned. At times I felt that I was being cross-examined by the world's best prosecutor, whose ultimate goal was to have me seated in an electric chair. In my case, instead of the chair, his goal was simple: disability retirement denied!

Tract was a genius! After 15 minutes of questioning, I started to wonder if the CIA or KGB had trained him. The man was like a chameleon, but instead of changing colors, he changed his questioning technique. This man easily switched from being soft spoken and respectful to being harsh and sadistic. As this process wore on, every fiber of my being had to be restrained from unleashing my own verbal explosion, which was what he wanted and which would enhance his case for denial. At this stage of the interrogation, I had to choke on any aggressive response and wait for the exact opportune moment to release my pent-up frustrations. Tract was soon inferring that I was "a liar, manipulator, and basically a malingerer." I couldn't do a damn thing about it. Soon, very soon, my time would come!

Irrespective of the fact that I couldn't hold a book in my left hand due to tremendous pain and uncontrollable shaking, Tract kept up his incessant barrage of questions:

Q: "What if we get you a lab technician who can do your experiments as well as write on the blackboard for you? Would this help you to be able to return to work?" he inquired.

This was pretty bizarre since I was teaching math. I guess Tract felt they'd eventually place me back in the science department since I was now teaching out of license.

A: "Sir, every lab technician in the city has been fired, so there are none available. Besides, the horrific pain I endure on a daily basis and the side effects of the pain medications I take make it impossible to concentrate on anything, no less teach classes of upwards of thirty-five students," I responded.

Nothing I said would get this guy off my back or make a difference in his desire to intimidate me and ultimately castrate my retirement papers.

Tract's maniacal assault continued until I finally decided now was the time to take the offensive, which had always been my M.O. When the opportune moment arose, I inquired, "Could I ask you a personal question, Doctor?" in a harmless tone of voice.

Dr. Tract finally agreed to my request. (Not.)

"Dr. Tract, do you enjoy playing with your grandchildren?" I just assumed he had some.

When he responded in the positive, I stated, "Doctor, I came into this profession with two healthy arms. Now one is basically useless and gives me unimaginable pain, and the other also has the potential of needing surgery in the future. I do not have one healthy arm to lift or play with my own son, so I really don't give a damn about your lab technician! Besides, we both know that the city cannot afford to pay someone twenty thousand dollars to be my personal babysitter!"

True to his colors, Tract just kept on as if I had not said a word. I had no idea what his problem was, but it seemed that he was being driven by some obsession that forced him to go way beyond the scope of this hearing. A neutral observer would have thought that, if I was granted disability retirement, my semi-monthly checks would come out of his bank account..

On he went, badgering, intimidating, and being verbally abusive. If his goal was to get my goat, he had finally succeeded, but unbeknownst to Tract, it was at a point in time that I felt was the opportune moment to unleash a question that would turn this inquisition upside down.

Again, I inquired if I could ask him another question. This time Tract was extremely wary.

"Mr. Ross, this is your retirement hearing, not mine!" he emphatically stated.

Without giving him a chance to continue, I rudely interrupted and stated with authority, "Doctor Tract. Since you control my entire future at this moment, I'm going to ask you the question I had in mind whether you like it or not!"

As Tract was about to protest, without giving him a chance to say one word, I blurted out, "Dr. Tract, do you still get laid with your wife?"

The man turned beet red. The stenographer tried to curb her laughter by placing her hands over her mouth, but still could not mute some alien-type sounds emanating from her being. By the look on his colleagues' faces, they, too, seemed to enjoy the question.

Somewhat regaining his composure, Tract responded. "That's none of your business!" he yelled, utterly pissed off.

Without giving him the opportunity to continue, I verbally jumped all over him, just as he had been doing to me the past hour and a half.

"Doctor, all I know is that I came into this job with two healthy arms. Now, I can't perform the simplest of tasks or enjoy making love to my wife. When I try, the pain is so intense that there is no enjoyment whatsoever! I have no idea what your problem is, but I do know that you can take your lab assistant and this job and shove them both up your ass!" I said, all the while pointing my right index finger at him.

You could have fried an egg on Tract's head. The silence was deafening. For those of you who feel that I didn't use proper etiquette, guess what: tough! The man had shown me no respect, so why should I have to put up with his accusations and demeaning comments. I couldn't care less that he was a doctor! He had no right to degrade me! As I have so often stated, everyone deserves respect, and if he couldn't bestow the courtesy on me, why should I extend civility to him?

I have always believed that there are times when an individual must turn aside what might be construed as socially correct behavior, and this moment was one of those times. A dangerous and formidable adversary was confronting me. I had to use all means available to protect my loved ones, and myself, from this threatening antagonist. I would assume that Tract finally came to this same conclusion when, in a sarcastic tone, he asked, "Is there anything else you would like to ask or say, Mr. Ross?"

"No," I replied, realizing I had gone as far as I could.

"Then this hearing is over!" bellowed Tract.

With that, he slammed down his gavel and stormed out of the conference room. I remember thinking that Banister had that same look when I beat him in the election for chapter chairman.

On a more positive note, either due to the show I had just put on or out of plain decency, every doctor shook my hand and wished me the best. The stenographer walked over, gave me a big hug, and just smiled. She never said a word. I had no idea how this entire event would play out. One thing I was sure of: None of the participants would forget this hearing for a long time.

The ride home consisted of bumper to bumper traffic and my rehashing the two-and-a-half-hour circus that I had been the star attraction of. Mulling over what I could have done differently, my final analysis was: nothing.

Basically, every participant at this hearing had their own role to play, and most did an excellent job. Ultimately, there would be two antagonists, Tract and myself, with everyone else having secondary roles. Could I have assumed a less belligerent stance when being accosted by Dr. Tract? Possibly. Did I go too far in trying to embarrass this distinguished member of the medical profession? Hopefully. Would I do or say anything different if given the chance to have another hearing? Absolutely not!

Being realistic, I was going up against a stacked deck. The odds of my being retired ranged from poor to none. I knew Tract had a job to do just like every other cast member in this fiasco. I could have accepted his desire to get at the truth, but the man went far beyond the scope of civility. With his arrogance, incessant belligerence, and vilification of my character, I had no other avenue open to me except to go for his throat. Tract had gone way over the line of common decency; therefore, whatever I threw in his face, he deserved. The bottom line of this entire process was so simple to decipher. If my retirement papers were denied, I would still be out on medical leave and reapply at a later date.

Two days after my hearing, I began the "Where's my letter from the medical division" vigil. Every day after 2:00, I'd impatiently sit on the steps outside my apartment and wait for the mailman to show up. If he didn't arrive by 3:00, I'd go back inside and pace. Finally, he'd arrive, and as soon as I'd hear my mailbox close, I'd run to it like a lunatic and ultimately be disappointed. This scenario continued day after day until I was a borderline neurotic. I knew that there was no way I'd be granted retirement, especially after my verbal humiliation of Dr. Tract. I just wanted the official letter of rejection, thus enabling me to submit my newly completed monthly disability form and to stop this ceaseless pacing. Hopefully, when I reapplied for another hearing, there would be a new chairman of the retirement board. Anything could happen in a span of 12 months, and if by sheer luck Tract was replaced, I definitely would not shed a tear.

All of my years of interaction with the board of education, both as an educator and as a chapter chairman, should have prepared me for the snail-like pace it would take to process the medical board's recommendation once it had been made. Irrespective of this fact, for at least two weeks, my adrenaline kept me from accepting this truth. Finally, this eventuality clicked in and I stopped my daily vigil of waiting for the mailman and pacing throughout my apartment.

Almost as soon as I was able to resign myself to a month's wait, there was a knock at my front door. The mailman, aware of my situation, handed me a white envelope and said, "Good luck, Sam."

There it was, a white insignificant-looking envelope that could easily have passed for a piece of junk mail had it not had printed on the top left "Medical Division, City of New York, the Board of Education." As I closed my door, I screamed for Dianah to come and witness the long-awaited notification of denial.

When I first noticed the yellow sheet of paper inside, I instinctively knew I was dead! Anything as important as the granting of disability retirement would have been issued on white, legal-sized paper. Yellow to me meant I was S.O.L. (Shit out of luck!)

With Dianah watching, I quickly scanned the letter and noticed: "retroactive to March 13, 1981." With a quick look of disbelief directed at Dianah, I seriously began to absorb the entire contents of this notification. I couldn't believe it! Sam Ross had been granted medical disability retirement.

Later that evening, after having spent hours on the telephone informing so many caring people that I had officially been retired, I was able to reflect on what had been such a joyous, yet hectic, day. Dianah and our son had long since fallen asleep, and I was left to the quiet of the night and my innermost thoughts. It had really been a hard-fought and surprising victory. I had matched wits with a brilliant doctor and through arrogance, some intelligence, or outright stupidity, I had managed to secure what so many had told me was next to impossible: my retirement.

Regardless of all the congratulatory well wishes of family and friends, I was not as happy as those that I had spoken with must have perceived. There was emptiness in my heart that nobody could possibly imagine existed at this moment in time. Yes, I had won, but I had also lost so much. I had fallen in love with teaching again, and it had been torn from my grasp. It had been so great to go to work, enjoy my day, then return home to a loving wife and spectacular son. This, too, had been taken away. The constant smile that had appeared with my transfer to I.S.302 had been sheared off my face, leaving shallow, dark, sunken features. Yes, I had won, but in reality I had achieved nothing more than a hollow victory. One truth, and only one truth, could not be overlooked: My life as I once knew it would never be the same!

If the story of my retirement ended here, as sad as it was, the process would have been over. Unfortunately, when dealing with the New York City Board of Education, it seems nothing is ever over unless you're six feet under.

Approximately one week after receiving my notice of retirement, I was sent a retirement packet from the board of education. It contained numerous papers that had to be filled out and signed. Inclusive in this material were instructions and procedures that had to be followed in order to complete this process.

While sifting through the rest of the packet's contents, I came across a memorandum, which, after perusing, I just shook my head and almost broke down and cried. I could not believe it! In my hand was a declaration from the board of education medical division informing me that for the next five years, I would be required to undergo an annual physical examination to determine if I was still eligible for disability retirement. This examination was to take place at the beginning of the new school year. It was duly noted that the examination would be performed by a doctor on the payroll of the New York City Board of Education Medical Division. All I could think of was, *Will this ever end?*

My first re-evaluation notice arrived in early September 1982. It stated that I was to bring with me all medical reports, x-rays, and other pertinent information regarding my medical status. I was ordered to report to a physician's office located near Brooklyn College, my alma mater. When I looked at the name of the doctor who would perform my examination and determine my disability status, I almost had a coronary. Knowing my luck, as well as my ever-growing cynical nature, can you guess who this physician was? If you guessed Dr. Carl Tract, you're as cynical as I am and 100% correct!

During the eleven years I was capable of teaching, diarrhea would always visit me before the start of the new school year. The one year it hadn't shown up was when I was out on medical leave. Now, for the next five years, I would experience this same physical phenomenon, although for a different reason. Before it was in anticipation of the upcoming school year and all the difficulties of the job. Now it would occur in anticipation of seeing a doctor whom I had embarrassed and demeaned at my retirement hearing. With one stroke of his pen, I could be forced to undergo this entire process all over again.

Although I knew returning to teaching was both physically and mentally impossible, I never doubted for a second that Dr. Carl Tract could make such a recommendation in light of the verbal assassination that I had reaped on him in the presence of his colleagues and a wonderful stenographer. I was totally surprised that he never took such an action. In all fairness, I must give Carl

Tract his due. He was able to separate his dislike of me from the physical and mental misery I had endured since the day I was injured. Tract would never have known how great it would have been for me to hear, "Mr. Ross, after examining all of your medical reports and your doctors' recommendations, I agree with them that you are in good health and, therefore, fit to return to your job at I.S.302."

Under no circumstances could he possibly envision that he would be sending me back to my Garden of Eden!

CHAPTER EIGHTEEN

Where Do We Go from Here?

It's been 23 years since my retirement from the New York City School System. Throughout our great nation, there have been so many changes in both the classroom and in the politics that govern how money is allocated to meet the educational needs of our children. Computers have revolutionized classroom activity, as well as the world our children now find themselves a part of. An entire generation has grown up with a mouse and joystick along with *Sesame Street* and *Mr. Rogers.* Our daily existence moves at such a hectic pace that those individuals with limited, or even average, intelligence find it difficult to keep up with its trials and tribulations.

There have been so many mind-boggling changes, yet some aspects of our society in general, and our schools specifically, have experienced little, if any, change. Violence, drug use, unprotected sex, and lack of respect still exist, although on a more diverse plain. The problems that plagued us in the 60s through the 90s are now part of the new millennium .In a 40-year span, we as a nation have accomplished so much, yet sadly have not exorcised many demons that have existed in our society or the schools that it provides.

As previously alluded to, when many of our problems were entrenched within the boundaries of our inner cities, elected and appointed officials, after throwing crumbs to soothe the "savage beast," patted themselves on their backs for a job well done. Of course they really hadn't done anything. When these problems, especially drug use, with all of its social and physical ramifications, pierced those all-encompassing boundaries and spewed out their damaging effects on Middle America, a tremendous outcry emanated from our populace to fix what had not been competently addressed in the past. Who really cared when those occupants of our inner cities, (i.e. the poor,

213

people of color, those with accents, or newly welcomed or unwelcome immigrants) were affected? They were nothing more than the disenfranchised or second-rate citizens. Now, the proverbial shoe was on the other foot and the silent majority began to scream for help, because they couldn't deal with the realities of a new way of life that now permeated their once impenetrable world.

Social upheavals, like that which took place in a little-known community named Colombine where 12 innocent students were massacred, awakened an American populace to the horrors of school violence. They didn't realize that such violence had existed all along, although not on such a horrific scale. As if emerging from a 40-year coma, legislators, mayors, governors, etc. now demanded action in resolving these innumerable problems, which, in the past, had been swept under the carpet. Now the reality was, how do we fix our social and educational ills so people of all races, ages, etc. could catch up with the "New America" which the technological revolution had produced and which the use of drugs, violence and overall lack of respect were exacting a terrible toll?

If you are looking for Sam Ross to solve all of the problems we face in our schools and society at large, I hate to burst your optimistic bubble. I am not a messiah that has returned from the heavens carrying the answers to the problems we all confront on a daily basis. Realistically, all I can offer are some ideas, which may help lead us in the right direction. The question that must be answered is, are there enough leaders with guts to implement the changes that I will propose?

Please understand that I speak to you as a teacher, which is what I will always be, with hands-on experience that can never be taken away. I also present myself as a parent with one child still enrolled in our public school system. Finally, I speak to you with honesty, hope, and unbridled aspirations, traits which have been lost by too many of our leaders. When all is said and done, you can either accept what I propose or reject my ideas for whatever reasons that guide your rationale. I sincerely hope you realize that the changes I put forth come from the heart and soul of a teacher that toiled in this system and unfortunately suffered a career-ending injury. Of equal, if not greater, importance is the fact that the changes I advocate come from an individual who loves children and realizes that they are our greatest natural resource.

At this point, I'm sure you realize how blunt, crass, and foul-mouthed I can be. I'm sorry that I cannot deviate from who or what I am to suit your taste. Never forget that from Sam Ross, unlike those that speak the "King's English," dress in Armani suits and blatantly lie, you will get the truth, although it might make you sick to your stomach. Yes, you will get the truth, and it will be very difficult to swallow! Guess what? Get out your plates, knives, forks, and whatever else you dine with because here comes "the meal" that represents the entire mess we are in. Your choice is simple: Eat it as it is, or help those who truly want to change what's on the "menu"!

There is an old expression that is as valid today as when it was first conceived: "Money talks and bullshit walks!" What I will propose takes money, enormous sums of money. An inquiry into the past decade shows that our federal, state, and municipal governments have squandered away money on so many failed ventures. If recouped and used wisely, these ill-spent funds would guarantee that nearly every family in this country could live in their own home and have all of the amenities hard work and ambition can eventually attain. Just look at the mega-billions of dollars in foreign aid disbursed by our federal government. What have we gotten in return? In most instances, nothing but hatred for our country and our people! Please, I beg of those with the power to do so, just reroute a portion of these ill-spent funds towards our children's education, and with proper supervision, we as a country will never get a better return on our investment dollar!

I must say this again, and I will continue to do so until the day I die: Our children are our future! The system that educates them is in need of serious repair. Hopefully, someone will listen when we as parents, guardians, or just caring individuals, clamor for the right of our children to get the best education that can possibly be provided. Never forget that not every child will be a doctor, lawyer, engineer, etc. The least we as a society can do is to give our kids the opportunity to try and attain these lofty goals. If they fail, so what! Failure is not incurable! It is just a temporary setback in one's life. With opportunity still available, our children can pick themselves up and try to succeed in some other venue. We must give our young people every chance to be productive citizens.

In order to understand the changes I advocate, I have decided to separate my recommendations into two categories: safety in schools (i.e. the educational environment) and educational practices as they exist in our schools today. Undoubtedly, both go hand in hand, with each having repercussions on the other, but by separating them, the reader and, hopefully, the implementer, will get a better grasp of what I have to offer. Although some of my ideas are in use in numerous areas of this country, standardization on a national level would insure that all of our children receive the quality education they so richly deserve.

I'm positive that a majority of the individuals reading this book realize that I am not that naive to believe that one-eighth of what I propose will ever be implemented. "The powers that be" will never let this happen! Their political agendas call for exorbitant sums of moneys to be spent on numerous programs and projects that will appease their constituents rather than be invested in our war on education. Many are oblivious or voluntarily overlook what is at stake in this war that must be fought now! They know it takes money and guts to participate in this educational revolution that so many in our country clamor for, but knowing this and doing something about it are different animals. It is time for our leaders and power brokers to stand up and fight for a cause that everyone should be able to agree on: the improved education of our children.

The environment, which many of our children encounter each day that they go to the schools we, as a society, have provided for them, is appalling! How can our children learn when they are in constant fear for their safety, both inside and outside these edifices? Our children must have the security they deserve when seeking the education they so desperately need.

The following recommendations are just a few measures that should be implemented in order to counter the dangers that are so prevalent both in and around so many of this nation's schools:

1. Schools must be equipped with metal detectors!

We must keep guns, knives, and other weapons out of the school environment. Undoubtedly, a metal detector cannot possibly deter a sniper, outside the school, from inflicting tremendous carnage on human life. We can and must take every possible measure to keep this devastation from occurring within our educational facilities.

Inherent in this recommendation should be the non-debatable fact that any child caught with a weapon be prosecuted to the fullest extent of the law! It must be mandatory that there exists a national policy of zero tolerance! Failure to have such a law on the books will only insure the continued perpetuation of this epidemic of violence.

2. School uniforms must become the norm!

In the state of Florida where parents were allowed to vote on this proposal, not one district, to my knowledge, voted this proposal down. Data from private, parochial, and pilot schools has shown that with the implementation of a uniform dress code, confrontations between the "haves" and the "have-nots" were substantially lowered, and incidents of violence significantly decreased.

City, state, or federal agencies must subsidize families that cannot afford uniforms. I can't fathom that the most vociferous critic of governmental subsidies cannot recognize the positive implications of standardized attire. Unfortunately, this does not imply that violent or petty altercations in the school will cease. It just insures that such behavior will not stem from what an individual wears to school.

Undoubtedly, some readers are already screaming about too much governmental intervention and that their children are losing their rights under the Constitution. Let's get serious, people! When anyone enters the workplace, in most cases, there is a dress code in effect. If you do not adhere to this policy, the odds are that you will be fired. In no uncertain terms, education is big business, and if the principal, his representatives, or whoever governs this policy states that you are dressing in an improper manner, then you are in violation and should face whatever consequences are deemed appropriate. In plain English, isn't this policy better than having your children getting their asses kicked in so someone can take their jacket, sneakers, etc.? Face it, this happens all of the time in schools where there isn't a dress code in force.

3. External suspensions must be eliminated, except in the most unavoidable situations.

The practice of suspending students for violating the Student Code of Conduct most egregious activities are non-debatable. Excluding such actions, there should be no need whatsoever for any student to face external suspension. This practice is one of the most ridiculous avenues used in so-called behavior modification.

If a student exhibits an unacceptable form of behavior, why should he or she, in many cases, be "rewarded" with a vacation of up to two weeks? If this child's parents or whoever is raising them work, we now have an unsupervised individual that has numerous options available to get into further trouble.

My eldest son was blessed with an extremely high I.Q., as well as an "I hate school" gene. At least three times every year he managed to get himself suspended for 1-2 weeks. No matter what punishment Dianah or I imposed on him, it made no difference. He was on vacation! While on vacation, he received zeros on all of his assignments, tests, and whatever else he missed, thus insuring a failing grade in every subject for that marking period. Using sound logic, he came to the conclusion that since he was already failing everything, why not get suspended again. Always desirous of a vacation, this is exactly what he tried to do.

What I propose is quite simple: internal suspension supervised by a teacher and a security guard. Under this disciplinary action, the youngster now remains in school. He or she stays in the same classroom the entire day, except to go to lunch where fraternization is forbidden. The student is given every assignment and examination that those in the regular classroom setting receive. Their work is then marked and goes towards their grade. Now in a self-contained environment, this youth is no longer a problem to mainstream students, teachers, the school itself, or society in general.

I guarantee the reader that as soon as these offenders realize they will not be sent home if they act out, but rather will find themselves in a contained setting, you will see a tremendous change in their behavior. They will think before they do something that may eventually restrict their freedom of movement for up to two weeks.

Do not doubt it when I state that many of these students will feel like they are incarcerated in a jail cell. Once cognizant of the fact that they can't talk to their friends in the hallway or during lunch, cannot go to their lockers, or partake in other school activities, in most cases, you will see a "new person" when their internal suspension is over.

4. Alternative schools must be available to accommodate those students that cannot function in a normal school environment.

Although there are a number of these type schools throughout our country, there are not enough to remand the numerous students that need this type of educational setting. Once we can get our dysfunctional students out of our mainstream schools, the resultant educational atmosphere will be safer and more conducive to learning.

The youth that will attend these alternative schools will find that they are in classes with fewer students and under the watchful eyes of a greater number of security personnel. They must be able to take the same classes that they would have received in a mainstream school, yet be allowed to work at their own pace and receive the special help they might need. Tutoring must be made available for every subject that is taught with special attention given to reading, which I believe is definitely one of the causes of behavioral problems.

Students that are sent to these special schools must be given the opportunity to return to a mainstream school once they exhibit a change in their behavior and a willingness to learn. These schools should not be considered as prisons and, therefore, used for the purpose of incarceration. They are just alternative avenues of education. If a student does not conform to the behavioral requirements of these institutions and after a year is deemed unresponsive, they must be expelled from the public school system! These schools are for behavior modification and not for incarceration. We have jails and prisons for this purpose!

5. School districts must receive increased funding so they can hire more security personnel and procure the hi-tech equipment needed to fight unacceptable school behavior.

I cannot over-emphasize the importance of properly trained security personnel in our battle to make our schools a safe haven for learning. These individuals must undergo complete background checks to guarantee that we are not subjecting our children to supervision by felons or those of questionable moral character. Simply put, we need the best security people available, and they must be versed in the use of the hi-tech equipment that should be found in every school in this country.

6. There must be improved security on buses, both to and from school.

All students that ride on school buses should not fear for their safety when using this mode of transportation. Security personnel must be assigned to those buses when there have been repeated incidences of unacceptable behavior. The principal of the school, in conjunction with whomever is in charge of transportation at the district level, must have in reserve enough security people so that their quick dispersal can commence on buses that need their immediate intervention. How can we maintain a calm school environment when students depart from buses where mayhem reigns? This must cease!

There are so many other ideas, both obvious and creative, that should be implemented to make the environment of our schools safer for their occupants. What exists now is deplorable and unacceptable! It is time for those in positions of responsibility to take back our schools and make them institutions of learning, rather than breeding grounds for criminal activity, gang indoctrination, or markets for drug distribution.

I ask every parent, politician, or concerned citizen to imagine the unbelievable success our schools could attain if we offered our students and teachers a safe environment. I have no doubt, especially after my own experience, that teachers would be reinvigorated in a less hostile environment, and their desire to be successful would increase significantly. Our children, faced with less threats to their person, would attend school more often and learn at a much quicker pace, thus helping to reduce our dropout and illiteracy rates, which are unacceptably too high.

The other sector of education that must undergo considerable reevaluation consists of numerous outdated educational practices and philosophies that are still considered acceptable by many of today's leaders in the field of education. Areas such as classroom management school curriculum, teacher and administrator accountability, the role of the parent, and numerous other aspects of this system must be addressed. Now is the time to eradicate what is no longer relevant or acceptable. No longer do we have the luxury of waiting until tomorrow to react to the issues that need our immediate attention. As the expression goes, "It's time to either put up or shut up!"

The following pages will detail the changes which I feel are necessary to jumpstart the "Educational Revolution" that I've been referring to. Each proposal is invaluable in its own right. Collectively, they would rival any social change we've experienced in this country's youthful existence. The changes that I recommend would reverberate throughout this nation, and their consequences would be far reaching. All that is needed is cash and the guts to achieve the unthinkable.

1. There must be a daily one-hour reading period throughout the entire public school career of a student!

Simply put, our public schools are graduating an unacceptable percentage of illiterate students! I would estimate, and I believe I am being kind with this number, that 30-40% of those students that graduate from our nation's high schools cannot read on an eighth grade level. This cannot and must not be tolerated!

During this one-hour reading period, our students should be allowed to read anything they want, with the exception of pornographic material. They must be required to read for 50 minutes and use ten minutes to write a few sentences describing what they've read. Only in the lower grades must our students be provided with reading material, since at this age, they need more direction and structure.

Those students that read below grade level must be provided with classroom tutors (i.e. fellow classmates) who will help them with their reading skills. The greatest asset that these helpers will offer will be to ease the pain, suffering, and humiliation that those they tutor have endured due to their reading deficiencies. The teacher's responsibility in this program will be assigning tutors to specific students, inspecting reading materials, and giving individualized attention to the most literately-disadvantaged.

As I discussed earlier in this book, I allowed my students to read what they found of interest to them. I will continue to say it over and over again: The old reading material with the Tom, Dick, Mary, and Jane mentality is an enigma of the past. To make my point as clear as possible, they are dead! We as educators and those that write syllabi cannot be so inflexible in our approach towards improving our students' reading abilities as not to recognize that what was good in the past is just that, the past! Let our kids enjoy reading something that is of interest to them, rather than that required by some antiquated, crusty, old syllabus, which is out of touch with today's realities. If what they choose grabs their attention and gives them the incentive to read, what possible harm can come from this approach?

I fervently believe that if you cannot read, you are doomed to academic and, in many instances, social failure. Sure, there are some exceptions to this statement, but that is the point; they are the exception! I worry about the 99% of those illiterates who cannot fool anyone, as seen by their inability to fill out a job application, open a savings account, or read a simple street sign. How sad and lonely it must be to live in such a limited world. Put these children in my world, and let them learn through my technique, or any technique that has a proven track record. I will match my success rate against the results of other programs that are geared towards improving the reading abilities of our students, yet I am not so egotistical as to think that my method is the only option available. Whatever venue we ultimately choose, it is paramount that we get rid of the obsolete methodology of the past!

Even the most narrow-minded person cannot dispute that reading is a necessity. What many of our reading specialists, coordinators, and creators of reading syllabi have forgotten is that reading should be entertaining and FUN! The formative stages of the reading process should not find our children inundated with grammar, parts of speech, or other technical aspects of the English language. All of this can be incorporated into the process once they've gotten to appreciate the fun of reading itself. Don't kill the process with this nonsense before it has gotten up a head of steam!

My system of one-on-one tutoring is so essential in teaching our students to read. I seriously wonder how many educators and laymen are capable of sensing the relief a "slow reader" will experience when they are helped by one of their "own" in a private setting. I could never understand how any teacher could ask a student to read out loud, no less stand up and perform this task, knowing the shame and embarrassment this child must feel due to their reading limitations. Those teachers that perpetuate this practice should be ashamed of themselves. This is nothing but a form of abuse and a terrible psychological tragedy. I've always wondered which idiot came up with the idea that reading out loud will make you a better reader. If anything, it will make any child crawl deeper into their "illiteracy shell." Irrespective of the reading technique that is ultimately adopted, one-on-one tutoring must be part of this program.

It is time for educators, parents, and anyone associated with teaching our children to read to start using modern and innovative methods. Once our children see that reading can be fun, there will be no stopping their desire to seek this enjoyment. They will be introduced to a new world, a world they unfortunately could not explore due to their illiteracy and the failed practices that helped it flourish.

2. Students that cannot pass a fourth- and eighth-grade reading competency exam must be left back.

It is time for people with guts to go against the failed practices of the past. Besides the implementation of a daily reading class, a non-prejudicial, national, standardized reading exam must be administered at the end of both the fourth and eighth grades. If a student fails this test, he or she must go to summer school where the only objective will be to acquire enough knowledge and skills to pass this required exam. If they fail again, they must be required to repeat the entire process until they are finally successful. The old practice of just passing a child on to the next grade, irrespective of their reading ability, must stop! Not only is it unethical, but it is a great disservice to the student.

What I've found quite disheartening about this entire situation is the fact that those that should share responsibility for this illiteracy fiasco will not accept culpability. As so often is the case, we again come face to face with another "pass the buck" scenario. When poor reading scores are incurred, principals are chastised by district superintendents for not doing their job, which is to make sure their students are getting a quality education. The principal, in turn, comes down hard on his assistant principals for not monitoring the various programs that are supposedly geared towards achieving acceptable test scores. These AP's ultimately take out their frustrations on the teachers, whom they vilify for doing a less-than-adequate job. Once this pecking order of failure has been established, the tentacle of blame ultimately stretches out and lands squarely on the shoulders of those who must also share in the causation of this reading debacle: the parent.

I believe I have heard every excuse why a parent cannot sit down with their child and either teach them to read or, at the least, help them improve their reading skills. The most common excuse is: "I work eight to twelve hours a day, and when I come home I'm tired and have to..."

Please, give me a break! When I hear this "I work" nonsense, I become so infuriated that I could literally strangle its utterer! This response is an insult to other hardworking parents who basically have the same itinerary, yet still manage to teach their children to read. Maybe these individuals just care more than the "excuse maker" and do not conjure up alibis to absolve themselves of their responsibilities. As far as I'm concerned, there are only two plausible excuses for a parent not helping their child to read: their own illiteracy, or the fact that their child has a severe learning disorder.

It is time for everyone to realize that illiteracy pervades every segment of our population. We must also reconcile the fact that this is an age-old problem and not some sort of new phenomenon. Part of the answer to solving this problem, at least from my perspective, is right in front of our noses. Parents must assume part of the responsibility of teaching their children how to read, and teachers must be given the opportunity to use improved methodology to replace the failed and outdated practices of the past.

3. Preschool must be made available to all of our children.

The year preceding a child's entrance into the public or private school system is one of the most critical in their mental and social development. I implore our federal, state, and local governments to grant all of our children a chance to learn the basics of reading, become versed in computer skills, and experience the socialization process during this short window of opportunity.

Those children entering kindergarten who cannot read, who are computer illiterate, or lack socialization skills immediately fall behind their counterparts who are more adept in such capabilities. As they start to learn these processes, they, in many instances, will fall further behind as those already versed in these skills continue their advancement. Unfortunately, some of these youngsters will never catch up with their peers and will always find themselves behind in these critical aspects of development. We, as responsible leaders, parents, and caretakers, must not allow this to happen to our youth. All children must be given the opportunity to go to preschool, in order to learn these acquired skills that will be so important throughout their lives.

4. Every child enrolled in our public school system should be entitled to free breakfast and lunch.

As both a teacher and a parent, I have always found it deplorable that parents must divulge their income and other personal information so their child or children can be eligible for free school meals. Can you possibly imagine the humiliation a child must feel, knowing that all of their classmates are aware of the fact that their family is "poor" since they get free meals? We, as a society, attach stigmas to such programs! Those who are eligible to receive benefits should not be accorded social scorn when they become recipients.

Four years ago, my eldest son was nearly eligible to receive food stamps. I must tell you how proud I was and still am of this wonderful young man who was the biggest pain in the ass imaginable at one time. Yes, my son has a profession and a dangerous one at that. His job can unfortunately claim his life, leaving my daughter-in-law a widow and my grandchildren fatherless. If he hadn't owned a car, he and his family would definitely have been on food stamps. Even today, he receives a WIC allowance, which enables him to get free milk, juice, and a few other items for his three-year-old daughter.

Yes, I'm so proud of my son and all of the other sons and daughters who are his colleagues. You see, my son is a U.S. Marine who can be, and just was, in harm's way. Now, I dare anyone to tell me that there is a stigma attached to my grandchild for getting a free food allotment.

How many of you are aware that nearly one-third of our military personnel are receiving food stamps? There is no stigma attached to the fact that these heroes' families are receiving food subsidies. Why must our school children, some of whom will be part of our military in the future, be embarrassed when they line up for a free meal? If it's good enough for those who defend our freedom and way of life, why isn't it okay for our children who are our future?

It is time for all concerned to realize that hunger is a serious social problem and is not limited to just the poor. Everyone must understand that financial prosperity does not insure a home-cooked breakfast or a well-prepared lunch for the children of working parents. Many parents just cannot find the time in the morning to take care of this responsibility. Why should any of our children have to go through a school day on an empty stomach? What would be so terrible if we gave every school child the opportunity to eat free school breakfast and lunch, irrespective of their family's financial status?

For many years our farmers were paid by the federal government to grow crops that were eventually dumped into our oceans. This action was paramount in attaining an artificial pricing level. Today they are paid subsidies not to grow certain crops. Why can't we stop this deplorable practice and allow crops to be grown for a free breakfast and lunch program that will feed every single child in our public and private schools?

Look at the benefits of such a program:

A. All students, regardless of financial status, color, origin, etc., are now equal. There is no longer a stigma attached to having a full stomach.

B. School crime will drop significantly since students will not be mugged for their lunch money, which, by the way, is an everyday occurrence.

C. Students would now have the opportunity to socialize before the onset of the school day and during their regular lunch hour, thereby diminishing unnecessary verbalization in the classroom.

To allow the program to achieve maximum impact, teachers should also be entitled to free meals. You'd be amazed at the number of teachers who would participate in such a program. You cannot imagine the thrills on my students' faces when I joined them for lunch, which, at that time, I paid for. There was a closeness that never could be attained in the normal classroom setting. It was as if we were a family, and all of the insanity that surrounded us couldn't diminish this special time we shared together. Imagine a free meal and finding out your teacher is also human. Absolutely priceless!

5. Every child of school age must be entitled to free health care.

Although self-explanatory, this issue must be addressed! It is a disgrace that far too many of our students come to school with high fevers and childhood illnesses, some of which are extremely contagious, especially to adults. When asked if they had gone to the doctor, many of my students replied, "My mother has no insurance," or "We have no money." Do you realize that there are parents out there that can't afford to buy Children's Tylenol? This is heinous!

I think every lawmaker should go to a free clinic and see what it's like having to wait five hours before a doctor or a nurse practitioner gets to check out the child who is burning up with a 104-degree temperature. Is it fair that this heavenly creation cannot go to a local physician's office because whoever is raising this child cannot afford health insurance or a set doctor's fee? Why should any of our children be punished for a situation that they didn't create?

This problem, just like hunger, crosses the lines of color, ethnicity, religion, etc. It is a blight on our nation, and all that we stand for, that many of our citizens must resort to homemade cures, potions, and anything that is cheap or free, to remedy family illnesses. How dare we, the wealthiest nation on earth, allow such hardship to befall so many of our people, especially our youth and the elderly. Shame on our leaders for playing politics with our citizens' lives! No one in this great country of ours should have to experience the trauma of having a sick child, or parent, and not having the means to get quality healthcare!

6. Physical education classes must be taken at least two times a week during the entirety of a student's public school career.

I believe it's important for all Americans to open their eyes and realize that we are raising a generation of young people who are the most unfit in this country's history. Our youths' participation in sports and other forms of physical activity are at all-time lows. The days of getting up early and going outside to play with your friends seems destined to be nothing more than a footnote in a history book. The act of writing your name on the floor in chalk so you can have next in a basketball, baseball or touch football game is almost obsolete.

The history footnote might be a stretch, but the rest of what I've stated, unfortunately, is a reality. Modern technology, with all of its attributes, has ushered in the death of many of the physical activities that helped make us a fit people. Physical fitness, in far too many instances, has been replaced by mental occupation in the form of Atari, Sega, Play Station, and other computer games. Yes, computers, the pathway to the new millennium, have eroded a part of our lives and culture that once was so appealing. Now our children get up early in the morning to go online, rather than play outside where they belong. With over one-third of all households in this country having computers, the all-important morning stickball game, punch ball game, or just a catch between friends is being replaced by the joy stick, and the medical results have and will continue to be devastating.

Usually I would appeal to parents to get involved with their children in exercise programs, organized sports, etc. Sadly, we as a society cannot depend on our parents for help on this matter since at least 60% of the adult population in this country is overweight. Thus, it now becomes the job of our public schools to assume another burden that should not be their responsibility.

As so often seems to be the case, now that we have identified a major social issue, we're off to a pathetic start in trying to rectify it. Simple logic demands that we increase the number of physical education classes our students have on a weekly basis. Logic aside, the reality of the situation is the fact that these classes are being cut to the bone. It is time for those in positions of leadership to fight these cutbacks and secure the necessary funds to give our children the physical exercise their bodies' demand. If we do not get our children back into school gymnasiums, the costs that everyone seems to think are so prohibitive to make physical education mandatory will pale in comparison to those that will be due to the medical establishment, as they eventually treat the medical ailments of this physically unfit generation!

7. Drug and sex education classes must be an annual requirement.

Please, I implore every parent, concerned citizen, and lover of children to accept the gravity of what can no longer be denied or excused: Our children are having sex and abusing drugs at the youngest chronological age our society has ever witnessed. Teen pregnancies, sexually transmitted diseases, and rampant drug use are now the norm rather than the exception.

We as a society are almost paralyzed as we watch far too large a percentage of our youth suffering burnout from drug abuse. I wish I could mandate that every adult visualizes an eleven-year-old girl smoking crack. You don't have to be a genius to realize where this child will eventually wind up as the cost of her habit increases. Imagine, eleven years of age and using sex to get high. You better pray every night that it isn't your child! Yet, what are you going to do if it is? And what about that 14-year-old boy, high as a kite, who is now contemplating robbing a 7-11 store? Could you picture him in a shoot-out with the police? Why not? It happened to Willie Grayson, so why not your son or nephew or your neighbor's kid? Just remember that Willie was all of these and more.

Hopefully you're waking up to this real-life drama that is recurring throughout this great country of ours. This is our reality! This is the truth! Don't believe these government surveys that tell you that drug use is down. Down where? The only things that should be down are these surveys—hopefully down the toilet where they belong since they're full of shit!

I'm horrified that I can unequivocally state that at least 70% of the teenagers in my neighborhood are doing drugs. How do I know? They all talk to me about it since I've always been straight with them. Do you realize how staggering this number is? The fact is, I could walk out my door and come back with $10,000 worth of drugs in a heartbeat. Also forget this ghetto stereotype garbage. It's a fool's way of thinking. This crisis is happening in your neighborhood right now, and I don't care where you live! Accept the fact that, if your kids want drugs, they can be obtained in school or where you live.

What is so sad is the reality that obtaining these drugs is as easy as going food shopping.

Whether it's on the street, or in and around our educational facilities, our children are trying, and too many are getting hooked on, a vast array of mind-altering substances. Just in our middle schools alone, our kids are doing crack, crank, trips, rolls, Zanax or zany bars, and so many others besides the ever-popular marijuana. The fact that minimal amounts of heroin are showing up in our junior high schools has to scare the hell out of you when you consider what must be going on in the high schools our children attend.

Wait a second, you don't know what trips and rolls are? Go look them up on your computer! If you don't have one, go to the library. Better yet, why not ask your child or grandchild what these drugs are. You may be surprised that your "innocent baby" knows more about these world-beaters than you ever imagined.

It is time that we, the educators of your children, give our students the realistic drug and sex education classes that will help them make wise choices when confronted with the temptation to participate in the aforementioned activities. Our schools must be allowed to show our children uncensored videos and materials that deal with death from untreated aids, rampant drug use, and the crime associated with this multibillion dollar industry. Bring in guest speakers who will tell our children how their sexual habits helped destroy or severely altered their lives. Bring in the addicts, and let our kids learn firsthand how they would do anything to get a fix. Take them down to the morgue, and let them see up close and personal how they might eventually wind up! It is time to stop treating them like babies when it comes to the cruel realities they may ultimately experience, if they do not change their attitudes in regards to these matters. They are old enough to see firsthand the ramifications of the game of drugs and/or sexual craps that they may be participating in.

The expression, "A picture is worth a thousand words," is a non-debatable issue. I've discovered a smell can be of equal or greater value, especially in our war on drugs. Let our students, your children, inhale the stench of a rotting body from some kid that overdosed. Who cares if they throw up or even faint? Isn't that a better option than dead? You can wash out the taste of vomit from your mouth. You can wake up after you pass out. Let them learn firsthand that they won't be able to do either if they are dead! If by scaring the shit out of one kid, we can save his or her life, we've had a success. We need many successes, but one at a time is at least a beginning.

Drug and sex education classes must be restored if they were, or are, in the process of being dropped due to budgetary cuts. Let's get these programs back up and running so we can disseminate the truth to our kids and, where possible, show it to them. Our children are more aware than you think and at a younger age than you ever thought possible. We must have classes in our schools that are real, truthful, and hard hitting. It is time for parents, guardians, or whoever is in charge of raising them, to accept the fact that it is better for a child to come home from school with an upset stomach from what they saw, than to never come home again!

The reality of modern day America is that too many parents will experience the horror of burying their child. I know you do not want to be one of them! Now is the time to get those who are in positions of political power to respond to our communities' needs. We must make sure that they understand that it is a priority that drug and sex education courses are taught in our schools, and that they are mandatory for a student to be promoted to the next grade. Anything less would and should be considered criminal.

8. O.J.T., or on-the-job training programs, must be an integral part of the high school experience.

It should be mandatory that every high school in this great country of ours has an O.J.T. program in place. This program gives our children a chance to learn and earn! Those students that want to participate in this program should be given the opportunity to have their classes in the morning and work when their school day is over.

So many benefits will be derived from this program. Immediately there will be a sharp drop in teen crime since the youth that might have participated in criminal activity now has money to purchase items that he or she may have wanted but couldn't afford. Of equal importance is the fact that these youngsters will have less idle time on their hands and, therefore, less time to engage in unacceptable social behavior. Just the fact that they can experience, on a part-time basis, what it will be like to participate in the business world, will be extremely instrumental in preparing them for the future when they hopefully will be gainfully employed.

Community businesses will reap tremendous rewards from this program, too! They will be able to tap into a huge labor source and hopefully expand their existing operation. The owners of businesses that hire our youth should be given a tax credit for participating in this program.

Under no circumstances can a student be allowed to "take" the job that belongs to a full-time salaried worker. Severe monetary penalties must be assessed against any business owner who tries to replace full-time employees, and the positions they hold, with students who are participating in the O.J.T. program. A local oversight committee must be established, to investigate charges by employees who feel that they were terminated so their boss could hire students, thus reducing their payroll.

I cannot believe that there is a person who will deny that earning money through legitimate means will only increase the self-esteem of any individual. Can you imagine the sense of pride these young people will experience when they receive and cash their first paychecks? You can just sense their feeling of accomplishment when they see a paycheck made out in their own name. I am positive that, as they prosper in their jobs, our students will also improve their academic performance since, I believe, success leads to further success!

There should be no doubt in anyone's mind that the benefits this program offers our students far outweighs any negative repercussions. I can't imagine any more than a scant few not being in favor of this being a national program. Non-implementation would be scandalous!

9. Community or after-school centers must be reinvented in every school district in this country!

Growing up in the South Bronx and Brooklyn, the youth in our communities had the opportunity to go back to our schools in the early evening, and on Saturdays, to play basketball, Ping-Pong, table hockey, and participate in numerous other activities.

What a great social and physical outlet this was for those of us who had nothing to do except possibly get into trouble. There is great economic prosperity today as compared to when I was growing up, yet many schools that could house these centers are not available to our children. Why? Please do not allow anyone to insult your intellect by complaining that funds are not available for this social asset. There is plenty of money out there, but as usual it's being wasted on other venues.

Many of the recommendations I propose will positively affect so many lives. The opening of community centers is no exception. First there will be the teachers and security personnel who will benefit by supplementing their salaries. As it should be, the children will benefit the most since they will now have something else to do besides "live" on their computers or just hang out. Finally, parents will have some peace of mind knowing that their children are in a safe environment and can easily be contacted.

What is so terrible about a teacher and security guard earning additional moneys? Nothing as far as I can see. I'm sure you won't argue about the attributes of having our kids off the streets and in a safe and secure environment. Our children, at least for these hours, will hopefully be shielded from drugs, gangs, and all of the other potentially disastrous elements that permeate our streets. Never forget that no matter where you live, your streets are not impervious to these social ills.

When my friends and I went to the community center, there was always a police officer on duty. This was the deterrent to keep the gang and criminal element out. Any hint of trouble and backup was there in an instant. A tremendous attribute of these centers was that police officers in the neighborhood had the opportunity to meet and establish a rapport with the "good kids," rather than just interacting with those whose claim to fame was the size of their rap sheet. It was really great for us kids to see a cop smile and realize that he or she could be a friend and still enforce the law. Any police force would gladly assign one or more of its officers to be a part of this program. The benefits are extremely advantageous.

If anyone believes that there aren't enough funds available to designate at least one school in the district a community center, then how about giving some thought to this following reality. Do you know that it annually costs a minimum of $20,000 to $40,000 to incarcerate a youth in a juvenile facility? The cost for this supposedly rehabilitative process is even higher depending on its location. The number of juvenile's now being "housed" is staggering! If the community center program could keep just eight youngsters in the entire district from going down the wrong path, the money saved on their incarceration would be more than enough to pay to keep this center open year round. If you take these numbers and figure out the mathematics on a national scale, every school district in this country could easily afford to open up at least one of these facilities.

This is a program that every parent should fight for. Just knowing that your child has a safe place to go to enjoy themselves is worth its weight in gold. What value would you place on this community center program if it keeps your child from occupying a bed in a juvenile house of detention? It is priceless!

10. Teachers must be paid commensurate with the importance of their job.

The education of our children, whether you like to hear it or not, is big business. In the business world, to get the best workers, you must pay top salaries. For our children to get a first rate education, they must have the best teachers money can buy! We must, through whatever means are available, deter some of this nation's finest young minds from entering the private sector and have them enter the field of education. We must pay all of our teachers, who are charged with educating our nation's greatest asset, our children, salaries commensurate with the great responsibilities this job requires of them.

Idealism and the love of teaching, which I believe was much more prevalent years ago, does not put food on the table or pay the bills that teachers, just like other productive members of our society, receive each and every month. Give our teachers a monetary and benefits package where they can again be idealistic, yet know that they've been realistic as far as providing for their families. Such a package will help attract college students to the field of education since they will feel that they are being fairly compensated for choosing teaching as their profession.

Only in recent years have our leaders and populace realized what those of us in this profession have known from our first week on the job: teaching is not only one of the most difficult and stressful jobs in our society, but also one of the most dangerous. Physical injury can occur in a split second, forever altering the hopes and aspirations of the recipient and his or her family. With this in mind, any financial agreement with our educators must contain an "injury in the line of duty" clause. It must stipulate that any teacher that is injured and forced to retire receive disability payments equal to their last year's salary. Also, any future pay raises, besides cost of living increases, must be added on to their disability allotment.

Over a span of 19 years, I believe I received no more than two or three cost of living increases. Even with an eventual one time $350.00 a month catch-up raise, I am in unimaginable debt due to the prohibitive increase in the prices of the drugs that I must take on a daily basis for the rest of my life. Why should I be financially ruined because I was so unlucky as to have suffered a career-ending injury? Why should my family be financially punished due to the severity of my injury and my inability to work? Hasn't my family been through enough just observing the pain and misery I endure every day? Must they suffer financial humiliation as well?

Wake up, America! Pay your teachers well or you will continue to lose both potential and existing educators to the world of big business which not only offers better financial packages, but an environment less hazardous to one's health.

11. Teachers should be held accountable for their job performance, but so should administrators.

Calm down! Please, read what I have to say before you have an aneurysm.

I implore the reader not to rush to judgement until you carefully absorb what I propose. If after doing this you still want to banish me to hell, go for it!

After countless years of often agonizing thought, I believe I have finally formulated a workable procedure that can resolve the most controversial issue in education today: teacher accountability. If our teachers receive salaries commensurate with the responsibilities of their job and are the beneficiaries of a new and greatly improved benefits package, which includes disability pay raises, then I'm for accountability per se.

I'm willing to bet the farm that you never expected these words to emanate from Sam Ross, especially with my anti-establishment attitude. Before you accuse me of being a sellout, let me first state that it is inevitable that an accountability procedure will ultimately come to pass. Every teacher in this country must accept that accountability is no longer a futuristic concept. It's a reality that must be addressed!

As a former teacher, chapter chairman, and always an advocate of unionism and members' rights, it is with great concern that I raise this issue at all. Unfortunately even a die-hard unionist like myself must accept the fact that this "problem" will not just go away. Although accountability must be addressed, I fervently hope that not a soul thinks that I am blind to the seriousness and dangers inherent in this process.

Despite all of the time spent reading and listening to the advocates and detractors of this type of proceeding, I still have one major reservation that cannot be quelled. I believe that most teachers share my concern on this matter, and it is our lack of trust and other such reservations that make accountability so dangerous. Simply stated, it is, and always will be, my belief that accountability is nothing more than a tool that the "bosses" can use to admonish, penalize, and ultimately fire teachers! Simple logic confirms this fear because, if this was not the case, why would there be a need for accountability at all?

In the chapter dealing with my run for the office of Chapter Chairman of I.S.24, I discussed how power can affect people in various ways. In many instances, power can be defined as a personality altering aphrodisiac, often misused and too often abused. For accountability to work and to counteract possible abuse there must be a built-in system of checks and balances! In essence, there must be a grievance procedure in place for any teacher who is brought up on a charge of incompetence, by either their principal or district superintendent. If this charge is upheld throughout this entire process, that teacher must still maintain the right to file an appeal in a civil court. It goes without saying that any teacher involved in this ordeal must be allowed legal or union representation.

In order to satisfy my requirement of a system of checks and balances, a local "Board of Accountability" must be established to adjudicate the grievance procedure. This board should consist of 12 independent individuals having no affiliation with either side in this dispute. A two-thirds majority vote must be achieved for a final recommendation of sanction, salary reduction, probation, or termination. Failure to achieve this eight-vote majority must result in the charges being deemed null and void, and a full year must elapse before this teacher can be brought before this board again.

If a teacher is terminated due to his/her inability to perform what is required of them, because of age, mental or physical deterioration, and all means of appeal have been exhausted, the teacher, if eligible, must be given a 30-day grace period to file the necessary papers for retirement, thus insuring continuance of medical, dental, and other benefits. It is paramount that this individual, who for so many years was a participant in educating our children, be allowed to retire in a dignified manner, and take advantage of the same programs that were available to those who retired on their own volition.

Any teacher brought before the board accused of engaging in criminal activity must immediately be suspended with full pay and benefits until the case is adjudicated by the criminal justice system. If the accused is eventually found guilty, irrespective of their sentence, they must be terminated, forfeit all wages and benefits, as well as have their license to teach revoked. If at a later date a police investigation, or retrial, finds the teacher innocent of all charges, they must be immediately reinstated, receive back pay, and have the days lost towards seniority and retirement eligibility returned.

Realistically, I can further elaborate on this entire process, but hopefully I've given you an overview of how this procedure will work. I must admit that I purposely left out two crucial components that must constitute part of this process of accountability. I did this to highlight their importance and to let the reader understand that they are critical ingredients towards acceptance of accountability. Omission of either would fail in making this process credible.

A. It is imperative that the individuals that sit on this board of accountability successfully complete a mandatory class that educates them in all aspects of this process. They must learn from professionals, be they lawyers, judges, counselors, etc., whatever is necessary, so they can dispense "justice" in a fair and prudent manner.

I cannot minimize the need for these board members to undergo sensitivity and anger management training. Many of the cases that they will hear will be so gut wrenching that, if left unchecked, their emotional involvement will cloud their decision-making abilities, and the ramifications for those being judged may be compromised and without merit.

B. I cannot overemphasize the importance of administrators also being held accountable for their actions, or lack thereof, just like their counterparts.

Hopefully, I've been able to demonstrate how incompetent some administrators can be. They must not be allowed to slip through the cracks of our educational system! Far too many have accomplished this feat over the years. If you make administrators accountable for their actions or lack thereof, maybe the "Us vs. Them" mentality will finally cease to exist. If these "leaders" are not held to an equal, if not higher, standard than teachers, this entire process will only cause further resentment, and the "Us vs. Them" mentality will continue unabated!

It is time for teachers and administrators to take responsibility for their actions! Exclude no one, and only when this reality is apparent to all concerned will the process of accountability have a chance of being accepted.

12. Teachers must be rotated to other schools every 7-10 years.

Is it equitable that some educators spend a majority, if not their entire and definitely shortened careers, teaching in high crime areas, whereby others enjoy the amenities of teaching in better neighborhoods? Teachers that work in high-crime areas suffer burnout at a disproportionate rate than their counterparts. Is it fair that some must wait nearly 15-20 years before they have enough seniority to transfer to a better school or one that is closer to where they live?

Recognizing the difficulties these individuals face on a daily basis, it goes without saying that they should receive additional dispensation in the form of higher salaries, a reduced work load, increases in both the number of personal and sick days, etc. Reality dictates that these schools must be staffed with extra security personnel and paraprofessionals. It should be mandated that they receive maximum appropriations of supplies and services in order to make the atmosphere more conducive towards teaching and less stressful on the teachers' and students' well-being.

It is a noted fact that far too many district superintendents, in order to impress their superiors, allocate everything imaginable to what I call "model schools." When their bosses show up to see what education is like in the district, they are taken on a tour of these artificially enhanced buildings and are usually quite impressed. This is nothing but educational fraud as far as

I'm concerned! Why not stop this "model school" racism and spread the wealth around!

When I transferred to I.S.302, I assumed, and was later told, that it was just another inner city school. I was just so thrilled to be out of I.S.24 and closer to my house, that I couldn't have cared less. Never in my wildest imagination did I expect to be walking into the "model school" for the entire district. As I expressed earlier, I thought I was in the Garden of Eden. For the first time in years, I thoroughly enjoyed going to work every single day. I cannot over-emphasize the renewed vigor that now permeated every part of my body. Sure, I loved my students at I.S.24, but I had spent over ten years of my life in a virtual war zone. I did not have one bit of guilt as far as my good fortune was concerned. Or did I?

I would be a liar if I didn't tell you how badly I felt for so many of my friends and colleagues that were still stuck at I.S.24. We had all gone through so much during my ten years in attendance. They, too, deserved a chance to experience the happiness, though short-lived, that had finally come my way.

Please, for all concerned, don't make an injury, such as the one that I sustained, a prerequisite towards enabling a teacher to teach in a less dangerous environment. Everyone knows that so many aspects of life are unfair, but working in such a tension-filled atmosphere, for a majority of ones entire career is blatant cruelty. Common decency calls for a system of rotation! Those that opt to remain where they are after this 7-10 year period has elapsed must be handsomely compensated!

13. Our universities must revamp their education programs in order to prepare our future educators to deal effectively with the realities that exist in today's public schools.

When I attended Brooklyn College, it was rated one of the top 20 liberal arts colleges in the country. It's education program was also considered top of the line. Thankfully, student teaching was a core ingredient of this program because without this asset, it would have been a total waste of time! With few exceptions, most of the courses were outdated, insignificant, and did nothing to enhance a future educator's ability to teach, no less survive. The only other course that was a major asset was a six-credit juvenile delinquency and criminology course.

I remember only one teacher having the guts to discuss some of the real situations we, as future teachers, would encounter. This "real" education lasted only one week. How noble! Excluding student teaching, this one-week of reality teaching, and possibly three other classes, my classmates and I endured nothing but educational philosophy and other nonsense. All of these other classes that I had to take never helped me to solve or get out of the many dangerous situations I encountered at I.S.24 or I.S.302. As is still the norm today, they were more of the think tank variety-type course rather than a real world, "this will help you" asset which is what was, and still is, desperately needed. Not only was our system of education failing our public school students, but our institutions of higher learning were also failing those whose job it would be to educate these youngsters. If this weren't so pathetic, it would almost be comical.

Throughout this book I have proposed numerous changes in the field of education. In order for some of these changes to be successful, the agents of implementation (i.e. our future teachers) must also be properly trained. To accomplish this, there must be a total dismantling of the outdated education courses now being offered at our universities. These courses must be gutted and replaced by those of substance and value. The courses that I propose will get to the heart and soul of the problems our future teachers will experience, especially in our junior and senior high schools. They will help the future educator deal with the harsh realities that are so common in our schools and will prepare them to pass through the doors of their first teaching assignment with at least a semblance of competence.

The question that needs to be answered is: Will members of the Board of Regents of colleges throughout our country have the guts, desire, and heart to add just a few of the courses I will recommend to their education programs? For the sake of our future educators and their pupils, I sincerely hope so.

The following are just a few courses that I hope will replace some of the useless and outdated seminars our education majors must take:

Pharmacology 101.1—This class will teach our future educators about all of the different kinds of drugs that are available, and often used, by their future students. They must learn how these drugs are taken, their effects, street names, and why their use is holding our youth hostage.

A narcotics detective, D.E.A. agent, or an individual with firsthand knowledge must teach this course. We cannot afford to use individuals with book knowledge to teach our future educators this type course that demands street smarts and real life experience. We need people who have lived this life, not book worms or computer whiz kids who can look up a million facts, yet have no feel for life on our mean streets.

Those that teach this course must impart to our future educators the telltale signs of drug use, the nuances of dealing, and so many other aspects of this vicious lifestyle. They must explain the relevance of such basics as a runny nose, bloodshot eyes, excessive fatigue, nodding out in class, as well as slurred speech and other easily recognizable symptoms. They must expand their "students'" awareness to such a degree that they automatically become leery when they see a pupil wearing plenty of gold or being inundated with a load of activity near their person.

Our future teachers must have it pounded into their heads that students often buy drugs from other students in and around our schools. They have to be trained to recognize this type of activity. In some instances, this will be quite easy, but it is not enough. They must be taught the language of the beeper, the cell phone, and as many other means of communication as possible, so they can be aware when buys are going down and can inform the proper authorities if this is what they choose to do.

Future teachers must be taught how crack, crank, and speed, to name a few, are made. They must learn how heroin and cocaine are cut and packaged, as well as what goes on in drug labs. They must be taught various lookout systems employed by street dealers, as well as the organizational structure of a drug ring.

Our modern educators must be versed in a world that some have never been a participant in. They might think they know about the world of drugs that many of their students are participating in, but most are extremely ignorant in so many of the pieces that comprise this puzzle. How can a recently appointed teacher speak with their new students and try to give advice on the use and abuse of drugs, when the odds are that they have no idea what the drugs they are talking about even look like?

How can this teacher talk about zany bars when he/she has no idea that they come in different shapes and colors? These youthful educators must be taught to recognize what every drug that's being sold on the streets looks like, as if it was a part of their own body. Only when your students realize that you know what you're talking about, will they at least listen to what you have to say!

B. Gangs.

The new millennium teacher must be taught about the gang culture and all that this phenomenon entails. They must learn about its origins, initiation rites, and organizational structure. It is imperative that they be made aware of the pressures their future students will be under to become members of these groups, as well as what drives many youngsters to join on their own volition.

Gang members should be invited to speak at our colleges in order to give our future educators firsthand knowledge of what life on the streets is like for these individuals. Hopefully, they will gain insight into gang membership and the responsibility membership entails. They must become versed in the significance of colors, tattoos, hand signals, and all other means of identification and communication.

Part of this group's education should entail the social significance of the gang, its history, and its effects on our culture. Our educators must comprehend that, for many of its members, the gang is their extended family and represents a source of protection, love, stability, and trust. Many members felt that these ingredients were lacking in their biological families and reached out to this resource to satisfy these needs. Better yet, how many new teachers will realize that one family may have three generations of members in a gang? There are many 50-year-old gang members!

Part of dealing with the gang problem is understanding its roots and causality. In high schools, where membership is quite significant, how can a new or, at times, experienced teacher deal with this problem if they have no idea what the core ingredients of the problem are? How can anyone attempt to guide a student in a new and socially accepted direction, when they have no idea what they're trying to steer them away from?

As I've stated on so many occasions, the world our students find themselves a part of is vastly different than that of most of their teachers. Before any educator can think of getting involved and possibly changing some aspect of this world, they better know what the ramifications are for themselves and their students. No gang worth its salt will give up one of its members without a fight. In nearly every instance, this fight will be physical in nature. No teacher should unknowingly be allowed to enter this environment without being aware of the dangers that exist. They must understand that by trying to save a gang member, they most likely will be putting their own life in danger!

C. Criminology, juvenile delinquency, and the American justice system.

It is imperative that our education majors be versed in these three areas. I've placed them together since they all relate to the judicial system in America, although each is an entity unto itself. The new generation of teachers must be extremely knowledgeable in regards to the workings of these systems before they ever enter a classroom. How can any teacher explain to a student why they shouldn't steal, sell drugs, run numbers, etc. when the students knows more about the penalties they may face than the teacher does?

I cannot over-emphasize the fact that our students have superior knowledge as to the workings of the judicial system than at least 95% of the teachers that are trying to advise them. These kids can tell you in a heartbeat how long they will spend in "juvi," jail, or prison if they are caught breaking the law. They will know the names of every facility of incarceration in their state, as well as where members of their gang, or friends, are doing time.

As I stated from the get-go, don't be foolish enough to think that you can bullshit your students on matters of such importance. They will "eat you up and spit you out!" The only chance you might have is to learn as much as possible before you ever stand in front of a class of these street-savvy individuals.

The new teacher must never be so naive as to think that if their students want a good grade, they will listen intently to what they have to say. The road is littered with the bodies of those educators that had this misconception. Our colleges must offer their education majors classes of substance that deal with the real world. Knowledge is power, and you'll need every bit of it if you want to make a difference in just one kid's life!

D. Music 2.002

Rap, hip-hop, grunge, heavy metal, rock, country, etc. Every education major aspiring to be a teacher should learn the language of their students. You'll be amazed at the respect you will get if you are able to converse with your students about the music they listen to. The concept is so simple, yet seems so complicated to those that should make this a part of an education major's curriculum.

Five years ago if you would have told me that I would recommend a class inclusive of rap, I would have had you institutionalized! Since then, I've come to realize that rap, just like most forms of music, conveys a message. You may not like the message that is espoused, but if you understand its significance, your job as a teacher will be a hell of a lot easier.

I listen to rap every day when I pick up my daughter from school. Am I its biggest fan? Absolutely not! Yet, at least I recognize its value as far as being able to converse with some of my daughter's friends. They are all amazed that an "old man" like Sam Ross knows about Puff Daddy (i.e. P. Diddy), Eminem, Jay-Z, Snoop Dogg, and so on. It blows their minds that I can make up a rap using words and expressions found in some of the songs they listen to.

This ability to communicate holds true with all types of music. Most students will find it outrageous that their teacher is willing to enter into their world to try to understand what they, and their generation, are thinking about and what messages their music conveys. Listen to today's music! It will give you insight into your students' world and make you more effective when you're standing in front of a class that may consist of upwards of 40 students.

Undoubtedly, some music goes too far in regards to the language used and the messages presented. I truly detest someone advocating "busting a cap" in someone's ass, shooting cops, shooting up, or "smacking the ass of some bitch." No matter how distasteful this garbage is, it's still what many of our kids are listening to. Thankfully, other songs are spectacular, have a great beat, and convey a very positive message. No matter what is being stated, there is a message to be heard, and it can't hurt the new generation of teachers to find out what it is. One fact cannot be denied: The more you know about your students' world, the more effective you will be standing up in front of that classroom.

I'm sure I don't have to remind anyone what the reaction was to rock-n-roll when it first appeared on the scene. Most parents felt it would eventually fade away. The same was true with the Beatles and the "British Invasion." When rap made its public debut, most of the record industry's top echelon thought that it would die out in a year or two. Were they wrong! What all those in the know failed to realize was the fact that this medium presented a message to the youth of America, a message they were receptive to. The big Whigs were wrong, but we as educators cannot afford this luxury. We must listen, understand, and evolve just as this music has.

Colleges must recognize the importance of music as a gateway in trying to reach and understand the modern-day student. A music course representative of all types of music will be a hell of a lot more useful in dealing with today's students than any course that teaches us about Plato's *Republic* or Horace Mann.

It is time that the chairmen of the education departments at our universities get the backing from their school regents and revamp the education programs that exist at our schools of higher learning. Changes must be made so that those who enter the field of education are better prepared to deal with the problems and pressures they will experience. The courses that must be made available must deal with reality and practicality rather than theory and philosophy. The teaching profession is one of the most difficult careers an individual can ascribe to. The least our colleges can do is provide its future members with the necessary tools that will enhance their abilities to reach their students, as well as to survive in such an unpredictable environment.

We as a nation have reached a critical juncture in time, when our leaders, educators, and innovators must work together to modernize the classes that are taught in our public schools and universities. If we do not address these problems, then we must accept the status quo which has failed our youth so miserably these past 40 or so years. It is time to push forward or be remembered as the generation that fell behind the times as far as offering our youth a realistic education. I'm positive that those in positions of responsibility, power, and the ability to make things happen, do not want failure to be a part of their legacy.

EPILOGUE

It's been a long, arduous journey to reach this final portion of a book, which basically details a 12-year period of my life, but in reality also encompasses the lives of so many other individuals. Since its inception, there has been so much personal turmoil in my life, but finally, after seven long years and 11 operations, I can proudly state that my story is now a part of the public record. Even as I put the final touches on this emotional and physically draining autobiography, I now face my 34th operation or procedure in the last 22 years.

As I've stated in the past, I am not looking for your pity, empathy or prayers. I fervently believe that what G-d has in store for me cannot be altered. What I do ask of you is your undivided attention so we can all finish this book on the same page.

Prior to my writing one word, I decided that this book would not contain a single footnote or require a bibliography. It was my belief that if I eliminated such nonsense, I'd be able to establish a bond between real people (i.e. you and me) rather than waste precious time by deluging you with boring statistics that anyone could look up if they so desired. I'm extremely elated that I was able to accomplish this task.

Hopefully, you were riveted to the real-life situations I presented and were able to immerse yourselves in the emotional roller coaster ride that many of my colleagues and I were privy to. I tried, where possible, to inform, rather than preach, when discussing the education system and its realities as they exist in this great country of ours. Admittedly, I wanted this book to be entertaining, but I also wanted it to be a wake-up call as well. Never did I deviate from my goal to bare the truth, which, in today's society, is quite rare to say the least.

As you near the end of this book, I hope you come away with a better understanding of what our children and their teachers face each day they enter education's hallowed halls. Try not to rationalize that what you just finished reading only happens to students and teachers in our inner city schools. The truth is that it is occurring in a vast majority of the schools in this country. When this reality finally hits home, maybe more of us will take responsibility and give those in charge of our children's education as much support and hands-on assistance as possible. Remember, today's children will be tomorrow's "movers and shakers" and hopefully will be the leaders who will keep us as a beacon of hope to so many of this planet's inhabitants.

It is with deep humility, yet unbridled optimism, that I leave you with these parting thoughts. PLEASE, stay involved in your children's lives as much as you possibly can. I know how difficult this can be, but remember, they never asked to be born. With all of my surgeries and illnesses, I've always tried to be there for my children. I am not looking for your approval or seeking a medal when I state that no matter how horrific the pain and injuries, I was, and still am, an integral part of my children's lives.

The summer that I was confined to a wheel chair, I still coached my eldest son and helped him to become a better ball player. Severe pain and injuries stopped me from lifting my daughter from the day she was born, but never deterred me from giving her hugs and kisses when placed in my lap. With all of my physical ailments, as well as the effects of all the narcotics I took to make the pain somewhat bearable, I still went to her dance and gymnastics' classes, and more recently to her softball practices and games. You cannot imagine the pain I experienced sitting in the stands watching her play, nor the happiness we both felt knowing that I was there. It could have been so easy for me to rationalize staying home, but there are times you must show your children you love them through your actions, not just through your words.

Never mistake love for just giving your children a roof over their heads and food on the table. Yes, both are important, but they are not enough. Part of loving your child is fighting them, tooth and nail, to help them become better individuals. I, like so many other parents, am tired of teaching, preaching, eating my guts up worrying, and dealing with so many other responsibilities associated with being a parent. I pray that I'm a good parent, yet like most of you, I've made my share of mistakes.

I previously stated that there is nothing wrong with failure. You only fail if you try, and that's all anyone can ask of a parent. My eldest son once said to me, "Dad, you're the only person in the world I respect." After being taken aback for a couple of seconds, I asked him, "Why?" His response was, "You can handle fifteen problems at the same time, where others can't

handle one." All of this came from my son, who I once told, "I love you with all of my heart, but I don't like you one bit!"

On your best day, you cannot possibly imagine what I went through with this child, teenager, and young man who is now the father of my two grandchildren and a loving husband to a great daughter-in-law. For me to be so hurtful by saying this to him really tore at my soul, but it had to be said! I was not proud of myself for the cruelty I exhibited, but this was not about me. It was about him, and what I said he deserved! With everything said and done, he knew one thing: I loved him because if I didn't, I wouldn't have said a damn thing!

We as adults should have learned somewhere along the line one of life's cruelest realities; once you think nothing worse can befall you, something comes along that makes what was so bad in the past pale in comparison. We forget, or maybe never realized, that this happens to our children, too. Just being there to listen—not hear, but listen—to whatever is happening in their lives is so important. If they are willing to divulge this information to you, especially during their teenage years, absorb every syllable that comes out of their mouths, and later thank G-d for being so lucky and privileged that they confided in you. Never expect anything in return for your guidance and assistance, because if you do, you may be a very disillusioned individual. Maybe, when they have their own families, they will realize they owed you at least a "thank you."

I cannot tell you the number of times I've been called a wonderful father. I also cannot express to you how many times I've felt like the lousiest parent in existence. Eventually, when the smoke clears, what hopefully emerges is the one characteristic that I believe you must have in order to be a good parent: feelings. When you feel your child's hurt, frustrations, and misery, then you are doing a good job. When the crisis they find themselves in is finally over, your child may express their thanks and appreciation. You, in turn, may be so choked up from this simple "thank you" that it will almost make all of the difficult times you've gone through with them worth the misery you experienced. Enjoy that moment while it lasts because in no time at all, it will be back to the normal "insanity" inherent in the job of parenting.

I would be extremely humbled if three actions resulted from the public's reading *My Life in the Trenches*. One would be that parents find the time to thank their child's teachers for the difficult job they are trying so valiantly to succeed in, day in and day out. My next wish would be that parents realize that they should never take their children for granted. The more we take things for granted the greater is the chance that they will be lost forever. No parent can afford to lose his or her child! Finally, I pray that at least some of my recommendations are adopted so that our schools can be safer for our children and they can get the education they so rightly deserve.

As the final curtain descends on this arduous journey, I would like to leave you with this parting thought. I whole-heartedly believe it encapsulates so much of what has been said and what has to be done. Fifteen simple words, linked together to form a sentence of tremendous magnitude. Hopefully, we all have the intelligence and the heart to understand it:

"Never give up on your children, and hopefully they will never give up on you."

G-d Bless.

Printed in the United States
36902LVS00003B/58-60

9 781413 744095